Local Governa
Western Eur

Sage Politics Texts

Series Editor
IAN HOLLIDAY
City University of Hong Kong

SAGE Politics Texts offer authoritative and accessible analyses of core issues in contemporary political science and international relations. Each text combines a comprehensive overview of key debates and concepts with fresh and original insights. By extending across all main areas of the discipline, SAGE Politics Texts constitute a comprehensive body of contemporary analysis. They are ideal for use on advanced courses and in research.

Published titles:

Local Governance in Western Europe

Peter John

SAGE Publications
London • Thousand Oaks • New Delhi

SAGE Publications Ltd
6 Bonhill Street
London EC2A 4PU

SAGE Publications Inc.
2455 Teller Road
Thousand Oaks, California 91320

SAGE Publications India Pvt Ltd
32, M-Block Market
Greater Kailash – I
New Delhi 110 048

British Library Cataloguing in Publication data

A catalogue record for this book is available from the British Library

ISBN 0 7619 5636 0
ISBN 0 7619 5637 9 (pbk)

Library of Congress catalog card number available

Typeset by Keystroke, Jacaranda Lodge, Wolverhampton.
Printed in Great Britain by Athenaeum Press, Gateshead

Summary of Contents

For Mike with love

Contents

List of Figures and Tables

Figures

Tables

Preface

This book arose from a course, Comparative Local Government and Urban Politics, which I taught with Keith Dowding at the London School of Economics between 1997 and 2000. Students on the Public Administration and Public Policy and Regional and Urban Planning masters' degrees could take it as an option. The long title of the course reflected a dialogue between the traditions of urban political science, on the one hand, and comparative local government studies on the other. The study of urban politics originates in the United States of America and focuses on power and policy-making in cities. Scholars take the context of urban politics as the important determinant of decision-making, particularly the exigencies of the economy. They examine individual and group choices within the urban setting, covering topics like the power of local elites, the demands of the business sector and competition between urban centres. As well as carrying out empirical studies, urbanists privilege social science theory, acknowledging debates on pluralism, elitism, Marxism and rational choice theory (for a review, see Judge et al., 1995). In contrast, comparative local government studies is a branch of the study of public administration, mainly concentrating on elected local governments in Western Europe and the English-speaking world. Researchers wish to understand the operation of political institutions, in particular the significance of legal frameworks, the allocation of functions between tiers of government and the impact of the size of local government units. Topics include central–local government relations, systems of local government finance and the role of the courts. Both traditions of study were represented at the LSE: the former in a long-running course called Comparative Local Government, taught by George Jones; the latter in Urban Politics, convened by Patrick Dunleavy. With Jones and Dunleavy away, Keith Dowding and I created the hybrid.

Both urban political science and comparative local government studies have their limitations. The former tends to be ahistorical, taking the USA as the norm and downplaying the importance of traditions and political institutions. Moreover, the term urban politics is a misnomer, suggesting that all local politics is urban in character whilst much politics occurs in rural areas and at spheres above and below the boundaries of the city, such as in communes and regions. But comparative local government studies veers too much in the opposite direction, implying that local politics is about institutions and little else. The approach seems to suck out the lifeblood from the subject by replacing the analysis of power with the description of laws, taxes and procedures. Local government scholars often think that comparison is only about understanding differences and that students should be content with an appraisal of the unique character of political institutions.

Even if institutions were central to the operation of local politics, they are less relevant at the beginning of the twenty-first century. Western European local politicians and bureaucrats have to respond to international economic competition, liaise with a variety of private interests, link to the insitutions of the European Union, reorganize the internal structure of their bureau-cracies and compete with many other local-level organizations. What is interesting about local politics is not just the institutions themselves, but how they operate in the wider context of the restructuring of the economy and react to new loci of power. Governance rather than government best sums up the current state of local politics in Western Europe. To understand the new framework of governing, students need to understand both the traditional institutions of local government as captured by the study of comparative local government and to comprehend the wider structures of power as analysed by urban political scientists. The topics I taught took the best from both sub-disciplines. This book, which draws from the course, seeks to correct both the universalism of urban political science and the particularism of local government studies by setting out a comparative analysis of the transition from government to governance.

The book also draws from my research on comparative local politics that I started in 1987-8 with a one-year research post at Nuffield College, which was for a project on meso government in Europe, directed by Jim Sharpe. Most of all, I extend the ideas that arose in a two-year project I carried out with Alistair Cole between 1994 and 1996, 'Local policy networks and intergovernmental co-ordination in Britain and France', that was part of the UK Economic and Social Research Council's local governance programme (grant number: L311253047). Also I have attended many workshops and conferences organised by the European Consortium of Political Research, the European Affairs Research Association and other bodies, which have been useful in acquiring knowledge from experts across Western Europe.

The book reflects my biases and language skills. The UK is my own stamping ground and the book is also solid on French matters. But I have relied on the secondary literature for the other countries. As a result I can only convey the broad elements of these complex local political systems. The book hopes to overcome the limitations of expertise by being both schematic and theoretical.

Acknowledgements

I thank the master's students who attended the Comparative Local Government and Urban Politics course at the London School of Economics where I was a part-time lecturer between 1997 and 2000. Many chapters of the book started life as lectures, and trying them out helped improve them. I also learnt a lot from the students, as many were from the countries I was trying to describe. I enjoyed informal discussions on the book with Peter Newman, Patrick Le Galès and Mike Goldsmith. I benefited from the many workshops in the UK Economic and Social Research Council programme Local Governance of which I was part. I especially appreciated the guidance and encouragement of Gerry Stoker. I received excellent written comments on the first draft of the book from Patrick Le Galès, Mike Goldsmith, David Wilson, George Jones and the series editor, Ian Holliday. I am very grateful to Lucy Robinson at Sage Publications for her support throughout the project, and for her tolerance of the many extended deadlines. Finally, I finished the book whilst visiting my friend Vicki Spencer in Adelaide. I thank her for her hospitality.

1

From Local Government to Local Governance

CONTENTS

The central ideas of the book

At the beginning of the twenty-first century powerful forces from within and outside nation-states challenge many of the established practices and conventions of local politics. For much of the period since the Second World War, the nature and purpose of public decision-making could be inferred from the bundles of economic compacts, bureaucratic routines, party hierarchies and political traditions that operate mainly at the national level. The practices and institutions of local politics in Western Europe, the subject of this book, largely reflected the consolidation of many national democracies at the end of the nineteenth century. Local organizations, party systems and institutions became embedded in national political, administrative and legal frameworks whilst central or state government bodies managed territorial politics. Even if local politicians and groups pressed first for democratization, with national institutions following rather than leading the establishment of representative democracies, in the end nation-states emerged as the legitimate political organizations. Central governments became the foci for political debate; they sought to resolve conflicts over ideas and resources; and they were the places where political parties and networks of policy-makers found their apex.

Nationalized forms of politics ensured that the public decisions at the sub-national level were institutionalized within local public bureaucracies and political parties, largely because central or state governments created and legitimated local political institutions. Even though national politicians and bureaucrats depended on territorial power bases, local politicians formed close links to and depended on the powerful central government bureaucracies that evolved and spread in most modern nations. This book claims that the subordination of local politics was a feature of an unusual period in European history when a great deal of freedom over public decisions resided with national parties and representative political institutions. At the beginning of the twenty-first century, European states are experiencing the first signs of a more variegated, independent and experimental form of local politics. The way in which local politicians, bureaucrats, interest groups and publics operate is in keeping with the recently emerged internationalized economy and Europeanized polity. These claims are strong, and the empirical chapters examine the many counter arguments and qualifications. Even if the book retreats somewhat from the sweep of these opening pages, it is necessary to state the case unreservedly so that the later detail does not overwhelm the argument. The final chapter of the book draws together the evidence in an even-handed fashion and seeks to understand the nature of these political changes and appraise their expression across Western Europe.

Normative arguments

The argument about transformation is important because of the potential contribution of sub-national forms of politics to democratic life. The underlying ideas in this book reach back to the classic justification of local self-government made by J. S. Mill (1861): local democracy offers citizens the potential to exercise their freedom and to express their local identities in a manner that is different from and complementary to higher tiers of government. The idea is that local political institutions can be closer to citizens than national governments. Locally elected governments offer the benefits of diversity; provide a supply of public goods that reflect the preferences of those who live in local jurisdictions; and can ensure that higher levels of government express a plurality of territorial and functional interests. Not that local government automatically expresses such political values in its practices, though it has the potential to do so. Nor are the consequences of following these values always to be preferred, as many scholars question whether local government can realistically embody such principles as liberty (see Sharpe, 1970 for a review of the debate). Moreover, this book argues that nationalized political systems did not foster the full expression of local democratic practice. One aspect was that the closed institutions of local politics permitted rule by small, elite cabals. These elites used hierarchically organized local political parties and the legitimacy of bureaucracies for their protection and freedom to exercise policy choices. But the current disruption of local politics offers some potential for democratic renewal. The politicians and bureaucrats in charge of local government, as a response to the challenges of institutional fragmentation, internationalization, Europeanization and more populist forms of participation, have the opportunity to re-discover local government's contribution to democracy. The act of re-conceiving local politics in an internationalized and Europeanized context can spur decision-makers to involve the citizen more in public affairs and help administrations respond to the communities they govern. Moreover, the move to a less institutionalized pattern of decision-making could ensure that political elites incorporate a wider range of groups and interests than before. The demands of partnerships and larger policy networks may open up local politics.

The reinvention of local politics has implications for the procedures and justifications of the institutions of representative democracy. In the past, the legitimate forms of political participation created a central role for elected representatives organized into competing groups of political parties; now other forms of political participation, the delegation of political authority to micro agencies and the assertion of power of groups that were marginalized from the political process suggest alternative mechanisms of political decision-making than representation. The challenge for local representatives is to find ways of adapting to the new forms of politics rather than to replicate the patterns of the past. Whilst there are opportunities for sub-national political leaders to reinvent their roles, they can also become marginalized. As elected local government was a key element to the consolidation of democratic rule in many northern European states, it no longer has such an automatic and legitimate role when so many citizens and experts question representative institutions. Local political leaders and bureaucrats cannot claim that they alone can and should make authoritative local decisions. Nor is local government able to respond to the challenges of policy-making as efficiently as it did before.

The comparative approach

The book maps out the transition from local government to governance across Western European states. The idea is that the magnitude of the change may be gauged by charting the differences and similarities between local government systems, since the starting point of the transformation is the distinctiveness of nationally based local governments. The book assesses the claim that the form of the transition from government to governance occurred in highly particular contexts. One such place was Britain in the

1980s, where the Conservative party in power restructured local government, making it respond to the demands of the private sector and replacing
the direct provision of services with quasi-markets. When the focus is on
privatization and limiting the state, governance appears as a feature of the
neo-liberal polity rather than having wider application to democratizing
nations and social-democratic governments. This argument draws on the
idea that the UK or Britain is an exceptional European state, with its North
American influence and non-statist political tradition (Dunleavy, 1989).

There is a weaker and more plausible form of this argument. Northern
European local government systems show more of a tendency toward
governance because locally elected authorities administered large parts of
the welfare state. Reforms of the welfare policies and institutions cause a
series of dramatic changes for local government. New agendas and policies
challenge local professional and bureaucratic monopolies, an argument
which does not seem so applicable to nation-states with more centralized
traditions. This book seeks to counter both the stronger and weaker versions
of the particularist argument by showing that Western European local
political systems have changed in similar ways in response to the economic
and political competition, the Europeanization of public policies, the
explosion of ideas, institutional and management reform and challenges to
representative democracy. Scholars of local politics need to move away
from their preoccupation with fiscal pressures, privatization and welfare
reforms to consider broader forms of local politics and their reformulation.

Guiding the aim to map out the transformation and to apply the comparative method is the idea that there are different forms of institutions
and political practices across Europe, which affect both how effective the
local government systems were, how the emerging local governance system
operates and what normative arguments apply. What aspect of governance
best embodies the unique contribution of the local sphere of action to
democratic life? To explore such themes, the book takes the changing sub-
national political systems of the countries of Western Europe as its focus,
noting the similarities and differences between them and applying the
comparative method to understand how models of local democracy have
evolved.

What is Western Europe?

The nations of Western Europe are a small selection of cases given the large
number of local government systems across the world. It limits discussion
to the economically developed nations. The reason for this choice is that
these countries form a unit for analysis as they are part of a region that is
clearly defined in the south and west by sea borders, even though there is
no accepted view about where Western Europe ends and Central Europe
begins. Western European states share a culture and artistic heritage; they

have similar political ideals and have experienced the parallel development of forms of religion; and many have had similar patterns of economic development. Europe was an entity long before the modern period, having been the source of migration from the East and where various forms of the Indo-European language evolved. At various points in history it has had common government or sources of political authority, such as the Roman Empire, the Catholic Church or the Holy Roman Empire. Now there is the expanding European Union (EU). Even during the heyday of nationalism in the late nineteenth century, the common project of imperial conquest and military alliances linked many European states together as well as made them rivals. Alongside these ethnic and political histories are shared cultural and scientific knowledge that have defined the European space at various points in time and have assisted its economic and political supremacy up to the mid-twentieth century. Not that observers should neglect the diversity both across and within nation-states and the constant migration flows, particularly from East to West, and then to and from the rest of the world. But there is enough of a common history to take the local government systems and their contexts together, especially when monetary union is strengthening the EU.

The coverage of the book

Whilst Western Europe is the context for the book, it is now hard to define what it is in the 1990s and 2000s (see Rose, 1996, chapter 1 for a useful review of the problem). For some comparativists, like Mény and Knapp (1998), the primary focus remains the mainly developed states of pre-1989 democratic Europe, which are of similar size, economic development, length of democratization and extent of the welfare state to maximize the potential inference, as suggested by 'the most similar method' (Przeworski and Teune, 1982). This selection would include France, Italy, West Germany, the United Kingdom, Sweden and, since 1975, Spain. With these cases, researchers can leave as constant many of the crucial determinants of political behaviour and institutional formation to concentrate on the remaining differences. The second version, favoured by this book and some authors (for example, Rhodes et al., 1997), adds some of the smaller states of Western Europe – Belgium, Denmark, Finland, Greece, Ireland, the Netherlands, Norway, Portugal and Switzerland. The selection loses some of the similarity and means that researchers cannot study countries in as much depth as a smaller group. The choice of Western European states has some attractive properties – it neatly divides Western Europe into a number of groups of states with similar features, and facilitates an easy set of comparisons and clear insights into the effectiveness of these systems.

This book, however, recognizes that the collapse of the Communist regimes since 1989 created new democracies that imported models of representative government from the developed world. Their governments, parties and interest groups wished to remake the connections to Western European states that had existed before the 1930s. One of the most important developments was to apply to become members of pan-European organizations, such as the EU and NATO, and soon there was a queue of new countries wishing to become members of both. It is likely that the borders of the EU will extend to Russia and the Ukraine, and that NATO will include almost all European countries except Russia. Since the division into Eastern and Western Europe was artificial in the first place, an artefact of conquest in 1945, the vision of Europe as extending from the Atlantic to the Urals and beyond means that the current practice of European politics has now caught up with its history (Davies, 1997). The incorporation of new democracies into Europe disrupts some of the politics of the old local government systems and the comparisons that have been made. Whilst acknowledging their importance, this book does not examine the local government systems of central Europe. That task awaits the completion of a research project (Hughes et al., 2002).

The elements of Western European local governments

What is government?

The term government refers to the formal procedures and institutions societies have created to express their interests, to resolve disputes and to implement public choices. The idea is that political systems have rules about political behaviour and mechanisms to protect the rights of minorities and to ensure that the supply of public and other goods and services reflects the preferences of citizens. Written constitutions may set in place institutions or they gradually evolve over time as political systems stabilize the mechanisms through which they make decisions. Different electoral systems, legislatures, central bureaucracies, judiciaries and local governments became defining features of Western nation-states. It is not surprising that traditional political institutions became central topics in the early years of the study of politics. Experts emerged on institutions, such as electoral systems and legislatures, who sought to understand the mechanisms of decision-making.

The claim that government is the central aspect of politics is not incompatible with the importance of social values, political movements and the organization of interests. There are two worlds of activity – the political and the social/economic – that interact with each other. Moreover, the key claim of political science during the behavioural revolution of the 1960s was not that social movements and class structures determined the practice of politics, but that the social movements of the late nineteenth century became expressed in structured forms of political behaviour, which became institutionalized over time. Lipset and Rokkan (1967) claimed that the party systems of Western European states had been frozen into place through the operation of electoral systems and the incorporation of the working class into liberal forms of politics. The secret of effective political institutions is not the application of abstract norms to political behaviour, but their ability to incorporate political movements, to stabilize political parties and to accommodate interest groups into the interests of the state. The standard texts of public administration and policy-making stressed the stability of policy-making and the way rules of decision-making privileged certain interest groups. Mass publics supported the main political institutions and approved of the policies these bodies produced. Public administration was largely hierarchical: elected politicians were formally in charge of policy-making and lines of bureaucracies were organized according to principles of command and control.

The role of local government in the political system

This book argues that local governments played a key role in the national pattern of government in Western Europe. Whether elected or nominated, they emerged at different times and in contrasting contexts as formally constituted public authorities with a high degree of control over jurisdictionally defined local areas. They were usually governed by nationally organized parties that ran for office in competitive elections. Local governments emerged and developed at the same time as the central state consolidated patterns of administration and extended the franchise. Political parties came to dominate political representation. Their ideas and bases of support reflected the cleavages at the beginning of the twentieth century, whether socio-economic, religious or ethnic. Territorial politics and the freezing of cleavage structures intertwined and reinforced each other (Rokkan, 1966). With party loyalty came sub-national cleavages and hence patterns of party control and influence over local government.

Most reformers of local government sought to impose a uniform system of local administration across a nation-state. Local authorities have denoted geographic areas for which central governments or parliaments give them powers, functions and finance to carry out public tasks, either solely or in partnership with other organizations. Political parties can compete to run these organizations and formulate public policies, either alone or in coalition arrangements. The idea is that each territory has an equivalent allocation of public tasks; no part of the country is exempt from the provision of public services. Each has equal representation – in theory at least. Every large urban commune in a country like France would have, for example, its own mayor who would be formally no different in election from the leader of the smallest rural unit, though of course every country varied some of the powers it gave to local authorities, giving special powers to metropolitan governments and allowing capital city administrations to tackle strategic issues. In theory all citizens could claim equal protection from the laws and could access public resources pertinent to their needs. The idea is that local particularity had its expression in institutions with clearly defined tasks, with the notion that local representation counted only through established forms of interest articulation, such as the national associations of local government, the lobbying of central government, political alliances with national politicians and bargaining within political parties. The nationalization of territorial politics was reinforced by a gradual de-concentration of public tasks to the field agencies of central government whose function was to administer the services of national government directly and to control locally elected local governments either through the law or by financial sanctions.

The pattern of local government differs. Local governments in northern European states tended to become institutionalized because they delivered the services of the welfare state; in other Western European states, such as France and Italy, central government field services took this responsibility whereas local governments sought to monopolize political representation and to gain access to public resources. Even federal systems, such as Germany, where the powers of the states and local governments are entrenched in Basic Law, the potential for sub-national diversity was constrained by the norms of co-operation within the largely vertical policy networks that characterized the form of federalism that developed (Benz, 1998). In addition to the constitutional protection for local government, the states become like national governments, seeking to regulate their local government systems in line with their traditions.

Whatever the political system, the consequence was similar in the form of government that emerged: local politicians and chief bureaucrats were sanctioned by central state institutions to make the main public decisions in their localities. The price of local subordination to national politics was the substantial autonomy local politicians and senior bureaucrats had in allocating resources and/or in accessing central governments. Western local government systems maintained local autonomy and freedom of decision but within a framework of central lines of command and authority and in a manner that excluded the potential range of participants. Local government systems were relatively stable because of increasing central government budgets, the long lives of central government programmes, relatively stable patterns of voting behaviour that kept local parties in power and the efficiency by which local demands and interests were represented and responded to within the nationalized political systems. Whilst the framework of representation and distribution of power was firmly in place, local governments could respond to local variation and experiment with innovative public policies which were often transferred to higher levels of government.

Defining governance and identifying its causes

Governance is a flexible pattern of public decision-making based on loose networks of individuals. The concept conveys the idea that public decisions rest less within hierarchically organized bureaucracies, but take place more in long-term relationships between key individuals located in a diverse set of organizations located at various territorial levels. Whilst policy networks have been an enduring feature of public administration as observed in studies of decentralization, they have tended to be long term and cosy bureaucratic and professional relationships connecting together central and local agencies as in the UK (for example, Rhodes, 1986, 1988) or complex intra- and interorganizational networks within organizations of the state as articulated in French school of organizational sociology (Crozier and Thoenig, 1975). Governance implies that these networks are more open, complex and potentially unstable than hitherto and that bargaining and the building of trust form more of the story of political life than the standard operating procedures of bureaucracies, the closed nature of party government and the hidden power of local elites. In particular, governance indicates there are stronger and new networks between government and non-government actors (Stoker, 1998).

Governance does not just seek to describe a more networked form of politics, it also refers to the capacity of governing systems to co-ordinate policy and solve public problems in a complex context (Pierre, 2000). No one organization or individual commands enough authority to ensure that certain public choices become authoritative and turn into implemented policies. In the place of hierarchies of power based on traditional political institutions are 'self-organizing, interorganizational networks characterized by interdependence, recourse exchange, rules of the game and significant autonomy from the state' (Rhodes, 1997: 15; emphasis in original). Governance involves non-state solutions to the collective action problem: 'governance can be broadly defined as a concern with governing, achieving collective action in the realm of public affairs, in conditions where it is not possible to recourse to the authority of the state' (Stoker, 2000: 3). Moreover, modern policy-making needs to respond to the perceived failure of many long-running programmes, such the management of welfare and urban policy. Their solution requires a rethink about how the state 'steers' society (Mayntz, 1993).

The causes of governance

There are a number of interlocked changes leading to governance.

The internationalization of economies The globalization or internationalization of economies has led to far-reaching changes in political life and is one of the key underlying factors behind the transition from local government to governance (Andrew and Goldsmith, 1998). The central idea, conveyed in the vast literature (for example, Baylis and Smith, 1997; Holton, 1998), is that many economic organizations, which were previously dependent on the nation-state to monopolize markets, have disassociated themselves from national boundaries and political control. They compete in a global market much more than hitherto. Since the 1970s multinational companies have become more powerful, capital markets have internationalized, the rate of information transfer has increased, cultures interact globally and political choices alter. The term globalization suggests that competition in world markets and the rapid speed of economic transactions affect almost all aspects of economic organization and political regulation. Businesses pick and choose locations according to the global calculation of advantage; in response, political leaders of whatever party label follow policies to please the market. The term internationalization (Hirst and Thompson, 1999) implies that there has been a more gradual shift to an international market and the choices remain open to national politicians to follow independent policies. Whatever the preferred term, researchers are sensitive to the complexity of the phenomenon and how it affects politics. For example, Garrett (1998) shows how social welfare parties and labour institutions are capable of implementing preferred policies in the context of the global economy. One clear consequence of the international market at the local level is the increased competition between cities and between different groups of cities, such as world cities (Sassen, 1991). The implication is that localities need to tailor their policies to those that help them beat their global competitors. Baldersheim (2000), for example, shows that Scandinavian municipalities adopt competition minded policies to varying degrees.

Yet Clarke and Gaile (1998) find that city decision-makers do not lose their capacity to produce policies designed to improve social welfare in global economic markets. They can still formulate imaginative social policies and have much freedom to act. Globalization does not mean that elites carry on as before, but that local leaders build alliances with businesses; think of new local solutions to policy problems, behave like entrepreneurs, abandon long held political shibboleths and link to higher-level organizations to acquire resources. As a consequence of global pressures, many writers refer to a 'new localism' (Goetz and Clarke, 1993), which is the inclination of local leaders to re-activate policy-making in response to global forces. By re-emphasizing responses that are particular to a place, local leaders can help their economies compete.

Competition does not mean that localities have to behave or be the same as each other. As Teune argues, 'Territory matters, even after . . . the near encapsulation of the entire world into a single trading system' (1995: 14). Cities in Western Europe have long traditions of social-democratic rule and civic cultures that equip them with resources to respond to the competition and maintain democratic control over public policy-making (Castells, 1994). Elites in continental Europe have a long-term commitment to the vitality of their core urban areas (McKay, 1996). At the same time as localities re-position themselves, state politicians and bureaucrats also rethink their strategies. They are still powerful actors, but they do not have such a monopoly of power as they did in the modern age: they have to build alliances, think creatively and generate governing capacity in a similar way to city and local governments. Local governments can take up some of the space left by the retreat of the state from direct economic management, planning and welfare, and negotiate with non-governmental and supra-national actors. As Le Galès and Harding argue (1998), globalization creates opportunities and constraints for local political leaders and their coalitions. The new localism is not universal, as some local economies decline whilst others regenerate. The result of the transfer from local government to local governance, in the context of a global economy, is the greater unpredictably and contingency of political life. As Sellers (2001) finds in his comparison of cities in France, Germany and the United State of America, city policy outputs and outcomes vary as much within countries as between them. The implication of globalization for the study of comparative local politics is that the old divisions across Western Europe do not resemble the straightforward classifications of the past.

Greater demand for the private sector to be involved in public decisions The involvement of business gives a new direction to public decision-making and can circumvent the traditional mechanisms of representative democracy. The participation of private companies in local politics is nothing new, as thirty years of critical urban research can attest (for example, Castells, 1977, 1978; Saunders, 1980). However, the interests of both business and local politicians have changed in both degree and quality. In an era of greater economic competition, businesses find they need to secure the competitiveness of their environment, which is affected by issues on the political agenda, such as the efficiency of transport links and the quality of the labour force. They need to engage with policy-makers to operate effectively in a more cut-throat and changeable national and international market. Local municipal leaders in the 1980s became more interested in dealing with private business because they realized that economic development policies that just relied on state investment and local planning often did not work and that the active involvement of private sector leaders in politics can unlock the economic development potential of cities (Parkinson et al., 1992).

Europeanization of public policies The states of the EU are unique. They have ceded some of their sovereignty to a supranational body. They are bound by the decisions of the EU, which has a law-making capability. Even though nations are the key decision-makers, Europe-wide policies initiated by the European Commission and the European Parliament affect all citizens, organizations and political institutions. European legislation and funding regimes impact upon local governments. As many have commented (for example, Goldsmith, 1993; John, 1994b), Europeanization occurs because local authorities and other organizations become aware of the importance of EU policies and funding opportunities. They seek to influence EU decision-makers to the advantage of their areas; and they try to ensure the receipt of collective benefits. Europeanization involves searching for European information, participating in European-wide policy and information networks, lobbying, setting up an office in Brussels and adjusting policies at the local level. These activities reinforce the trend to governance because they foster new or stronger partnerships across local organizations. In time, stronger vertical networks emerge, followed by the rapid transfer of solutions to public problems between the supranational and the local levels.

New policy challenges   As indicated by Mayntz (1993), the context within which local government makes policy has changed dramatically, partly because of the internationalized economy, but also due to social and physical changes, such as high levels of migration, the degrading of the environment and the ageing of the population, which directly affect local public bodies as regulators and providers of welfare services. Andrew and Goldsmith argue that the changeable contexts place 'a premium on governments (both local and national) to be flexible, innovative, and adaptive, to 'reinvent' themselves, or to move away from (local) government towards (local) governance' (1998: 105). Policy challenges also increase the complexity of the decision-making networks because holistic solutions require many sorts of agencies to be involved, both across the functions of public regulation and the various levels of government. The complexity of the problems and the growing criticisms citizens have of central governments create an incentive to find solutions to public problems. Moreover, central state bureaucrats and politicians take more of an interest in local policy problems than they did before, such as the standards of education, the co-ordination of public and private transport and the level of primary health care. Public sector professionals are no longer as able to contain issues within closed policy-making communities. Central policy-makers focus on the delivery of services and seek to respond to consumer pressures. New policies emerge because of the greater awareness and activity of interest groups and mass publics; they also derive from economic competition. For example, education has become more of an economic issue because of the need to train workers for new industries. Also, the willingness of municipalities to consider new policies derives from their investment in international networks of decision-makers (Baldersheim, 2000). Ironically, policy challenges create tensions within the state. Just as the state disengages from traditional policy concerns, such as regional planning, it reinvents new areas of intervention. Rather than the new politics being about the retreat of the central state, it reinvents its role, just like its local counterpart. It becomes weaker in some respects, such as over national planning, but strengthens its capacity to intervene in the micro-economy through, for example, creating central organizations that compete with the existing organizations of local government.

Shifts in political participation   Local politics, in part, builds up from citizens' views, voting behaviour and the activities of interest groups and political parties. Citizens in many Western democracies have become more dissatisfied with the outputs of government since the 1970s. They are also more cynical about politicians, less willing to vote in local elections, more willing to take part in unconventional forms of political behaviour, more active in associations and interest groups and less interested in traditional political parties (Norris, 1999). The bedrock that underlay local political systems has shifted. Policies no longer have such a high level of legitimacy, parties cannot rely so much on a corpus of supporters to vote them into office and new interest groups challenge local administrations. Local politicians and bureaucrats face declining effectiveness and legitimacy if they continue with tried and tested methods of determining local policies. They need to find alternative ways of governing, such as building links with new interest groups and involving citizens outside the representative process.

The move to the post-bureaucratic state   Many of the changes that drive the move from government to governance, such as transnational economy from the international, are external to local state organizations. More internal to local government is the revolution in public management that has spread across Europe. What is called managerialism (Pollitt, 1993) or the New Public Management (NPM) (Hood, 1995) is a contradictory set of ideas about how best to organize the administration of public services, which transfers across the world in diverse ways. NPM has a number of varying elements. The first is the reassertion of hierarchical procedures – what some authors (Pollitt, 1993) describe as neo-Taylorism – which advocates the clear measurement of the outputs of government, the creation of a split between the setting of objectives and the means to achieving them and techniques to improve performance. Hand in hand with the apparent centralization of management, but essential for the implementation of more precise policy objectives, is the decentralization of functions and administration to micro agencies or decentralized units within public organizations whose objectives are clearly stated, measured and enforced by higher levels of government or regulators. The consequence is the breakdown of older notions of hierarchy and the introduction of less visible lines of control. Other aspects of NPM are a series of administrative mechanisms designed to improve efficiency: the quasi-markets that make micro agencies compete for resources, new budgeting systems, the contracting out of services to the private sector and management organizations, performance related pay and new techniques for financing public services. These ideas partly transfer from country to country, but are also propelled by policy challenges, economic competition and fiscal pressures. NPM complements the other changes occurring to local government. The break-up of organizations puts a greater premium on informal internal networks that may complement those operating between organizations. Similarly, the creation of micro agencies further multiplies the number of interorganizational networks.

The contracting out of services can involve private interests in local policy-making. Most of all, the greater complexity of policy-making in a fragmented institutional context, the restructuring of decision-making systems, the loss of direct control by policy-makers over the implementation of their policies means that the internal life of organizations becomes more unstable at the same time as their external environment becomes more uncertain.

The local context

No state can escape these pressures for change. Their intensity, however, varies according to place and context. Given that governance involves the replacement of uniformity by variation, it would be puzzling if it was always driven by the same set of processes. The private sector may be involved in public decisions to a greater or lesser extent, depending on the strength of the local economy, the political colour of local business organizations and the willingness of central and local governments to set up public–private partnerships. Internationalization has varying impacts. Some countries, such as Britain, are highly sensitive to changes in the international economy, whereas others, such as Germany, have stronger nationally owned economic bases. Similarly, localities are exposed to the global economy in different ways depending on the extent they trade outside the nation-state and the type of commercial activities that predominate elsewhere. A locality that makes manufactured goods for export will be affected more than an agricultural centre with a local market. Similarly places with new industries, such as telecommunications, may be poised to benefit. Localities may be differentially exposed to migration and the diffusion of international cultures, for example. Localities vary in the extent to which they are affected by EU policies and initiatives. States differ in the way they respond to new policy challenges because of the permeability of their bureaucracies, the degree of media and public pressure and the extent to which the political executive can push through major changes in policy. Levels of participation, such as turnout in elections and the role of voluntary organizations, vary across Western Europe. The impact of NPM differs according to the willingness of bureaucracies to respond to these ideas and to fiscal pressures. Later chapters examine the extent to which these trends deviate and assess their implications for the emergence of local governance, whilst not accepting the argument that they differ so much that local governance becomes just a blanket term covering causes and trends which are so different that categorizing them as one makes no sense.

Governance and an ideal type

Given these pressures for change, it is possible to map out the end-state of governance as an ideal type. A benchmark for the identification of the phenomenon in different countries makes it possible to conclude that there has been a move from local government to local governance rather than just adaptations of local government systems. There are four elements to the change, each with two parts, which are manifestations of the causes identified above.

(A) INSTITUTIONAL REFORM
1   *Institutional multiplication* is about the creation of new levels of elected sub-national government and special-purpose local, regional and central agencies. Governance implies institutional proliferation and a blurring of the clarity between the public and the private sectors as state and sub-state decision-makers seek to respond more effectively to public problems (Stoker, 1998).
2   *Institutional restructuring* is a result of the adoption of NPM ideas and/or the move to decentralize power of the central state. It involves privatization, contracting out, the creation of micro delivery agencies and the introduction of new budgeting systems.

(B) NEW NETWORKS
3   *Stronger horizontal networks.* With the greater institutional complexity at the local level and the stronger presence of the private sector, new policy networks can form to create links that build trust and increase governing capacity. Some localities may form strong, long-term coalitions between the public and the private sectors, what North American analysts call regimes (see Stone, 1989 and Chapter 3).
4   *New cross-national networks.* The implication of the reform of the nation-state in the face of globalization and the growth in the power of the EU, is that local authorities have stronger cross-national links to access resources and to influence policy.

(C) NEW POLICY INITIATIVES
5   *Local innovation and capacity building.* As regimes form, bureaucracies fragment and new actors enter the decision-making process. Decision-makers require solutions to the public problems that arise from the greater competition for public and private resources between local areas. There is more opportunity for local innovation in sectors where the state has retreated or does not take so much of an interest as before, such as local and regional planning. The Europeanization of public policies allows for the easy transfer of ideas from one country to another and across levels of government.
6   *Revived central initiatives.* It may be thought that the retreat of the state means that it becomes a less important actor in local politics. The decentralization of power, however, does not necessarily follow. Whilst the state may not be able to pursue the same strategies as it did between the 1950s and the 1970s, it can develop other measures to achieve its ends. One area is the micro management of the economy, especially

supply-side initiatives, such as improving the efficiency of labour markets. These policies may involve highly targeted and centralizing instruments, such as special funding programmes or new layers of bureaucracy. The state reinvents its role in some policy sectors rather than retreats; it becomes an actor and more prominent partner in the networks. State restructuring affects the balance of power (Pickvance and Preteceille, 1991), but not in obvious ways.

(D) RESPONSES TO DILEMMAS OF CO-ORDINATION AND ACCOUNTABILITY

7   *The search for new mechanisms of control and accountability.* A and B imply more complexity of policy-making, which means it is harder for elected representatives to control public decisions and for interest groups and publics to hold office holders to account. Broader networks diffuse the lines of command and control so that it is not so easy to know who makes decisions. Local government, for all its defects, made it easy for the citizen to identify who the decision-makers were. The lack of clarity of governance puts a strain on the democratic system which cannot rubber stamp and legitimate policies so straightforwardly as before. To counter the failings of representative democracy, leaders of political institutions seek new ways of involving citizens and legitimating public policies. Citizens may become more active and express their discontent in novel ways, which in turn stimulates politicians to consider the effectiveness of the mechanisms of democratic accountability.

8   *More prominent forms of executive leadership.* The complexity of public policy, the fragmentation of institutions and the growth of decision-making networks precipitate a crisis of political leadership. On the one hand, pressures to decentralize and to include new actors and groups become manifest; on the other hand, elites and masses demand leaders who can pull the shifting framework of local decision-making together, act as entrepreneurs in the highly competitive environment and be the people whom the public can identify as responsible for decisions affecting local areas. Paradoxically, just as the institutionalized pattern of decision-making falls apart, the office of leadership strengthens to fill the vacuum. The move to governance implies reforms of the executive structure to enhance the independence and authority of political leaders. Even systems with strong leaders adopt reforms that redefine the conditions of office and relieve some of its burdens.

These four categories link in a sequence. Institutional reform may come about from a variety of factors, such as the demand for privatization. Networks follow from institutional reforms. Solutions to public problems are needed, partly because of the new institutional environment as well as from the changed economy. New patterns of leadership and participation help manage complex networks and assist the implementation of policy. These elements to governance link together and reinforce each other. Whilst none of the features in themselves constitute a new form of governing, when taken together they interact to shift local political systems away from the institutionalized pattern of the past.

To make the form of transition more readily identifiable, Table 1.1 show the four dimensions of change from local government to local governance. When contrasted is this way, each system of governing has its reinforcing logic.

TABLE 1.1   *Local government and governance contrasted*

	Government	Governance
1 Number of institutions	Few	Many
2 Bureaucratic structure	Hierarchical Consolidated	Decentred Fragmented
3 Horizontal networks	Closed	Extensive
4 International networks	Minimal	Extensive
5 Democratic linkage	Representative	Representative + new experiments
6 Policies	Routinized	Innovative Learning
7 Central government	Direct control	Decentralizes + micro intervention
8 Leadership	Collegial/clientelist	Mayoral/charismatic

The categories are broad brush and have different expressions in each place. Some countries already have strong leaders, so the change cannot be from collegial to mayoral forms of government. But the argument implies that even strong mayoral leadership changes in response to similar pressures and contexts. Moreover, the figure is a guide to understand change rather than a blueprint. The other reason to be cautious is that local governance does not replace the institutions of local government because much of the institutional framework of local government remains: similar laws and sources of revenue, competitive political parties and the power of senior bureaucrats. Moreover, the institutions remain embedded in existing local political cultures. The difference is that these institutions have been reformed, interact with a large number of organizations and have to respond to new problems. Local governance changes how traditional institutions work because they operate in a more protean environment.

Alternative scenarios

The extent to which new practices and organizations supersede the old ones remains to be ascertained. That is the task of the rest of the book.

Theoretically, all Western European local government systems could be recast anew. If that were the case, the emergence of local governance would lead to the convergence of local political practice across Europe. Instead of institutionalized forms of local politics, locked into nationalized patterns of administration and regulation and reinforced by persistent local political cultures, there would be a multiplicity of networks and informal patterns of government that do not depend on organizational routines and traditions and adapt existing patterns of regulation to solve local public problems. Such a form of local governance is probably not a realistic form of politics. In part, political life is routinized and processed by existing institutional routines and regulative frameworks that continue over time. National policy-makers are locked in by history, what some writers on national politics call 'path dependence' (Coleman and Grant, 1998; Goldstone, 1998; Pierson 2000), something that has its counterpart at the local level (Woodlief, 1998). The division of powers within a state continues to influence policy-making as do standard operating procedures and political cultures. The most plausible scenario is that locally elected politicians and bureaucrats remain as the key local decision-makers, but they adapt to the framework of governing. The trends toward local governance could make so little difference to the existing patterns of local government, that the new approach would be misplaced. But it is more likely that economic pressures and reform ideas disrupt local government systems and make them adapt in similar ways across Western Europe even though they retain much of their distinctiveness. A weaker account of the evolution of local government to local governance would recognize that families of local government systems are distinct, but would suggest they present a less striking contrast than before. Thus much remains for later chapters to assess and discuss.

Complementary perspectives

There are other ways to understand recent changes to local politics and policy-making than within the framework of government to governance. These perspectives seek to add more theory to the explanation of institutional change; they link the account to models of human action and the operation of modern economies and societies; and they use a wider literature than in the internationalization, policy transfer and public management readings this chapter discusses. As many urban and local researchers use these perspectives in their accounts of the politics of cities and regions they will seek to find them in a book of this kind. So it is important to consider and evaluate the contribution of regulation theory, the new political culture and rational choice theory to the changes to local politics. This book argues that researchers do not need the added clutter and problems of these perspectives to understand the transition. The treatment of governance as a dependent variable influenced by a range of exogenous factors that differ from place to place has the virtue of simplicity. None the less, all three perspectives appear in parts of the discussion of the following chapters, suggesting that they offer insights and additional explanatory power if not an all-encompassing framework.

Fordism to post-Fordism

Similar terms to government and governance are Fordism and post-Fordism, which are concepts in regulation theory (see Aglietta, 1979; Amin, 1994; Boyer, 1990). Fordism is the appropriate form of political regulation for the period of mass production and consumption in market economies in the twentieth century. The predominant form of enterprise is large factories specialized through the division of labour, uniform products and large undifferentiated markets. The political form that regulates Fordism replicates its organizational and legal framework. After a crisis, the post-Fordist economy replaces the Fordist one. Smaller more specialized and high-technology enterprises become more important; markets become more specialized; line hierarchies are no longer so appropriate; and labour markets become more flexible. As with Fordism, the state both regulates and constitutes the change by managing the costs of transition, providing direct support and changing its organization form and legal framework to manage the economy more effectively.

Researchers apply regulation theory to local politics (Hoggett, 1987; Painter, 1991; Stoker, 1990; Stoker and Mossberger, 1995). Fordist regulation involves large line bureaucracies in local government organizations and uniform ways to regulate the private sphere, such as rigid planning guidelines. The bureaucratic structure of local authorities fragments in the post-Fordist era because of management reforms and the contracting out of services. The procedures for the regulation of the private sphere become more flexible. In part, state structures reflect changes that have been happening in the economy; they also regulate it by adapting social policies to assist the more flexible and specialized markets. Such a transition resembles the move from local government to governance and appears to give it a theoretical basis. So why not adopt regulation theory as an overarching framework for the study of comparative local governance? There are two objections. The first is that academics from contrasting perspectives contest its theoretical foundations and supporting evidence. Nothing about it is certain. Did Fordism ever exist? Does Fordism need regulation? Was there a crisis? Is there such a thing as post-Fordism? These questions are just a few that critics pose. There are even more problems applying the theory to local government (see Painter, 1995 for a critical review). In contrast, the terms local government and local governance carry little intellectual baggage and are useful descriptions of states of governing. Researchers can analyse local politics without the risks of adopting regulation theory. The second reason not to use regulation theory is that it refers mainly to the reforms of northern local government systems of Western Europe, with their large bureaucracies, rather than to reforms applied in the south. It is possible to consider the reforms of the central state and decentralization experiments as post-Fordist, such as in France (Clark, 1997), but such an approach deviates from the core interest in the regulatory role and shape of the state. Instead, the term local governance is better able to capture similar and different changes across a variety of political systems.

The new political culture

Clark and his associates use the term the new political culture to describe the rapid changes in local politics across the world (for example, Clark and Rempel, 1997; Clark and Hoffman-Martinot, 1998). This term refers to the breakdown of class politics, the reaction against hierarchies, the decline of parties and the rejection of the classic division of left and right in politics. Researchers attach the term post-materialism to the rise of new social issues. Clark and Inglehart (1998) present much data, some from the Fiscal Austerity and Urban Innovation (FAUI) programme of surveys of attitudes of mayors, bureaucrats and councillors across the world, to show changes in the views of citizens and elites. They also report case studies of local political change. They argue that these profound social changes have had an impact on the attitudes and behaviour of elites, particularly the political leaders who no longer advocate traditional social democratic policies. The new political culture has redirected local policy outputs toward populist measures concerned to reduce taxes and advance liberal policies on new issues such as the environment.

There are similarities between the old/new political culture and the government/governance dichotomies. The stress on the changes in political participation is one link. The presence of critical citizens as a cause of the crisis of old bureaucratic and representational structures is another. Further common features are the emergence of new interest groups and the decline of clientelism. A further connection is the observation that there are new forms of public policy. Clark shows how political leaders grapple with public issues. Both governance and the new political culture approaches stress the moderation of traditional social democratic goals and the emergence of market-led policies. Indeed, it would be surprising if a cross-national account of change in local politics did not come up with some aspects of the move to local governance, even if the main focus of FAUI is culture rather than institutions.

The reason for not adopting the new political culture as a framework for this book is because it focuses on sociological rather than institutional change. The governance perspective takes institutional processes and how they reform as its foci. Such a decision does not deny the importance of the changes Clark and his associates highlight, but political scientists and public policy scholars prefer to examine the reformulation of institutions and public programmes before the social context, rather than the other way round. The other reason to be cautious about the new political culture is because there may not be as great a shift in political attitudes and behaviour as the advocates suggest. These changes are seismically slow. Moreover, political sociologists debate about the extent of the decline of class politics and its effects on the political process, with some authors detecting trendless fluctuation whilst others insisting on the erosion of class politics (see the debate in Heath et al., 1991). The jury is, in effect, still out. Whilst the perspective of the new political culture is useful as context for the changes, the change from government to governance does not need extra sociological theory and evidence to map local political change.

Rational choice theory

Rational choice theory applies to any political context, and comparative local politics is no exception. The parsimony of the assumption of self-interest and the rigour of formal models of relationships create hypotheses that are capable of being falsified. Rational choice theory can offer explanations of changes in local politics, offering hypotheses ready for testing in local politics, such as the competition of local governments for populations and resources (for example John et al., 1995; Tiebout, 1956), the behaviour of sub-national coalitions (Downs, 1998), collective action problems in metropolises (for example Dowding et al., 1999) and budgeting choices (Biggs and Dunleavy, 1995). Its main contribution to comparative local governance is the conception of public goods and their impact on the division of powers in the modern state as captured in the literature on fiscal federalism (King, 1984; Oates, 1972). The argument is that public goods may be allocated to different levels of government to promote efficiency. Some goods apply at the central level, but the consumers may increase their utility if decisions about the administration of a public good are located at the state or local level. The implication of such arguments and their application in a wider literature (see Bailey, 1999: 1, 18–24) is that there should be a clear constitutional division of powers that allows boundaries to be drawn that reflect consumer preferences. But a quick examination of the highly varied distribution of public functions to levels of government across Western Europe shows that fiscal federalism does not represent the state of play (see Table 2.2). Traditions, political struggles and the effects of reform movements seem to explain the distribution of powers across governments rather than a theory of public goods.

However, rational choice accounts of public goods do not disappear with such a peremptory dismissal. When examined closely, the functions of government are highly complex. Some are local public goods whilst others are private ones (Dowding and John, 1990). There are spillovers of effects between tiers of government. Some apparently national-level goods have the potential for local choice, and local public goods need national regulation (Inman and Rubinefield, 1997: 94–95). The pattern of provision of public goods in Western Europe need not contradict the nature of public goods as their relationship to territory and the provision of private goods are complex.

Public choice classifications illuminate aspects of the transition from government to governance. Much of the existing complexity of public goods was hidden by uniform forms of local government that did not directly seek to maximize the preferences of the residents who live within jurisdictions. If inclined to administrative reform at all, governments preferred to simplify the provision of public goods and reorganize service delivery in large organizations. But rapid economic change, fiscal austerity, recent advances in knowledge about how to co-ordinate decentralized delivery systems and more sophisticated demands from consumers mean that the organization of public services need to be designed flexibly. Bennett (1989) argues that flexible decentralization requires a greater role for the smallest administrative units and measures to reap economies of scale as well larger units capable of reaping the benefits of specialization. The variation in population sizes required to maximize consumer preferences means that flexible aggregation to different sizes of group is the only means of maintaining an adaptable but stable financial and administrative structure (1989: 7). These requirements lead to a demand for administrative reform that creates decentralized but flexible forms of administration. Public choice arguments not only complement those of governance, they set out the causal mechanisms that are missing in the descriptive account. They show why less institutionalized and more fragmented structures appear in different guises at the same time and indicate why networks are needed to co-ordinate actions between the levels of government. In short, public choice ideas may offer explanations not found in other approaches.

Organization of the book

This chapter lays the ground for the discussion and the use of evidence in the rest of the book. It sets out the context and outlines the purpose and underlying logic of sub-national politics. Local politics was integrated into the hegemonic project of the nation-state and its legitimating mantle of representative democracy. This chapter places the research into local political systems in Western Europe in a wider context than is usually the case. The reason why scholars need to examine both similarities as well as differences between local government systems is because cross-national forces and new ideas have restructured government systems and re-directed the course of local politics. Current local government and politics are better described by the term 'local governance' rather than as an extension of established patterns of decentralized government. The periods of reform of local government in the 1960s and of fiscal austerity in the 1970s altered the structure of opportunities, but did not fundamentally change local government systems. Events and reforms since the early 1980s have shifted the character of local politics so that old concepts and sets of research problems do not apply so neatly as before. The institutional patterns, the mechanisms for making local decisions, the types of local actor, the problems to be addressed and the role of the centre have shifted so much that scholars and practitioners need a new vocabulary to describe what has happened. Although the terms representation, hierarchical bureaucracies, mechanisms of central control and the autonomy of local elites best describe local government, the emergence of networks, regimes, multiple tiers of government, rapid policy change and innovation increasingly characterize local politics. Even though institutions do not vanish, institutionalized forms of local politics have given way to more flexible and networked patterns of public decision-making.

The following chapters assess how, in their different ways, the local political systems of Western Europe have been transformed. The book does not hide how different are the countries as the changing context of local politics shapes the operation of governance. The continual variation in local institutions takes place with greater similarities in decision-making and policy outputs. The book cannot cover all of the changes. The subsequent chapters examine the central elements of the transition and draw on experience from the different places. Chapter 3 is about local regimes. It discusses the local context, highlights the importance of the private sector in the governance of localities and examines the emergence of coalitions that can learn to solve public problems. If it can be demonstrated that public–private coalitions govern many West European localities, then one of the central elements of the new system of governing is in place. Chapter 4 assesses the contribution of the EU to the governance of the locality. As with Chapter 3, the focus is on networks, but these are more international and vertical than local and horizontal. Chapter 5 examines the trend of privatizing public services and creating new structures of organizations, often under the influence of ideas about management reform. These changes are internal to local government and affect the way it operates, complementing the greater dependence on horizontal and vertical networks which Chapters 3 and 4 map out. The subsequent chapter examines the institutional responses to the greater complexity of governing, in particular the way in which sub-national governments seek greater co-ordination of policies. It appraises the fashion for creating new institutional layers at the regional level, which have emerged in most Western European countries since the 1970s, suggesting that they show the differentiation of modern states. Chapter 7 explores the responses of local decision-makers to recent challenges of public policy, assessing the changing role of political leadership and the reform of executive structures, appraising the fashion for creating directly elected mayors. Chapter 8 examines the implications of governance for local democracy and assesses the likelihood of renewal, focusing on the success and possible transfer of democratic experiments.

This chapter brings the debate back to the normative issues, and assesses whether local government systems are capable of responding to the lack of clarity implied by governance. Can local governments re-invent themselves in the face of increasing cynicism on the part of the public? Chapter 9 assesses the changes as a whole and attempts to perform the final comparison, before giving a verdict on the central claims of the book. However, before examining governance, Chapter 2 explores local government to set out the baseline for the change and to give some details about the systems under review.

2

Local Government Systems in Western Europe

The preceding chapter outlined the main argument; this one elaborates the character of the old system of government so as to give some context to the reader and to act as a baseline for understanding the thematic changes that appear later on in the book. The first section of this chapter reviews the main classifications that scholars have applied to Western European local government systems. Of particular importance is the scheme developed by Page and Goldsmith (1987), which divides local government systems in Europe into those in the north and south. It is important to understand this framework clearly and to appreciate its limitations because the book claims that the move from government to governance has disrupted this pattern and supplemented it with a more variegated and multi-speed system of decision-making. Finally, in the form of a few summary statistics, the chapter briefly summarizes the basic elements of each of the sub-national systems the book considers.

The comparative study of local government systems

The comparative study of local government systems focused on formal institutions. The main idea was to understand the principles that inform the territorial distribution of power within the modern state with reference to the decentralization of functions and finance to democratically elected local governments. Anglo-American writers dominated the subject, with their interest in the British system of local government and the principles behind federalism (for example, Fesler, 1965; Maas, 1959). Later scholars examined the developed democracies of Western Europe and elsewhere (Bowman and Hampton, 1983; Humes, 1991; Humes and Martin, 1961, 1969; Leemans, 1970; Norton, 1993). In terms of the study of Western European local politics, researchers generally take decentralized northern European democracies as the norm and then seek to incorporate the experiences of other nation-states, such as those in the south of Europe.

The Page and Goldsmith framework

The most straightforward starting point is Page and Goldsmith's division of Western European local government systems into two groups (Page, 1991; Page and Goldsmith, 1987). There are other more complicated sets of divisions that researchers make, but Page and Goldsmith's scheme has the virtue of simplicity. Moreover, it clearly focuses on the different roles local government plays in liberal representative systems even where the state appears to be centralized. Their classification of local government systems takes the pattern of central–local government relationships as the key phenomenon to be explained. The framework acknowledges the subordination of local politics in generally 'unitary' states, and the team examined Sweden, Norway, Denmark, Britain, France, Italy and Spain, which were not federal or quasi-federal when Page and Goldsmith wrote their books.

The central idea is that there is a relationship between the number and type of the functions allocated to sub-national government, the legal discretion open to local policy-makers and the access of local politicians to the central state. By functions they mean the responsibilities that central states assign to lower levels of government (see Table 2.1). The authors recognize there are many nuances to the provision of services and the allocation of functions may not do justice to the extent levels of government share responsibilities for public services. Nevertheless, up until the mid-1980s at least, lower levels of elected local government in some countries generally controlled services like housing, health and education, whereas in others they did not, though the picture today is rather more complex (see Table 2.1). Discretion refers to the legal and administrative freedom locally elected authorities have in deciding how to administer services and to allocate resources. Page and Goldsmith include central government circulars and sources of professional advice as part of the constraints on discretion as well as legal rules, administrative powers of control and sources of local revenue. Access refers to the extent of contacts between central and local actors. The idea is that when local decision-makers have a low level of discretion, they maintain good contacts in central ministries and with central government politicians to obtain central resources and favourable decisions. In terms of outcomes, lobbying the centre or making local decisions may amount to the same thing, such as building a bridge or a road, but the process and form of politics are different.

Page and Goldsmith claim the framework is a useful way of classifying central–local government systems because they explore the association between low discretion, weak functional allocation and high access in some countries and the reverse of these attributes in others. They avoid the narrow legalism that has characterized the study of comparative local politics, with its focus on the law and the structure of local government. They realize that legal powers do not necessarily create power relationships, but they do not believe that networks always circumvent institutional and legal constraints as there is a subtle relationship between the formal and informal aspects of politics. They claim the framework is not descriptive, but 'suggests some of the forms that any explanation of such differences may take' (Page and Goldsmith, 1987: 9). The authors cautiously specify the causal mechanisms. They suggest the inverse relationship between access and discretion may result from the tendency of actors within bureaucratic systems to exploit areas of uncertainty by blackmail. The argument implies that access and discretion are both affected by another characteristic as some countries have large, dysfunctional, rule-bound bureaucracies. Another reason they give is that extensive functional allocation makes central government bodies more interested in local government because of the importance of local services. This factor suggests that access is more important than in systems where local government controls a large amount of public services because local actors use their national contacts to avoid central government control.

Page and Goldsmith's scheme captures much of the variation in the character of local government systems across Western Europe. They find that some countries have high levels of discretion and a wide set of functions whilst others have the opposite. In the former category are nations with welfare states. These expanded in the post-war years, where local government was given the responsibility for administering welfare services, with finances and the legal discretion to do the job effectively. These states generally occupy the northern part – Britain, Denmark, Sweden and Norway are the cases Page and Goldsmith select. The relationship is the opposite in the south of Europe. Local politicians are powerful at the central government level, but they represent local communes that have little legal discretion and few responsibilities. The countries Page and Goldsmith pick – France, Italy and, in part, Spain – demonstrate this fact neatly. The simplicity of their scheme is that it is based on four sets of antinomies – parts of Western Europe, functions, discretion and access, as Figure 2.1 represents.

	Functions	Discretion	Access
North	High	High	Low
South	Low	Low	High

FIGURE 2.1 *Functional allocation, discretion and access in the local government systems of Western Europe*

The legacy of the past

The appeal of the framework is its location in the historical development of Western European states that institutionalized territorial identity and power in different ways. The approach is consistent with principles behind the exercise of state power. In northern countries the state expanded to respond to the demands for equality. Such preferences became expressed in the institutions of the welfare state. Provided equality could be protected by central laws and local government finance systems sought to compensate for the different spending needs across territories, national elites thought it appropriate for local government to administer public services. In this sense, Britain, northern Germany and the Scandinavian states had a similar pattern of development. In contrast, the centralized French political system was based on universal principles that had emerged before the development of the welfare state. The reforms of Napoleon created a uniform administration across France, divided territory accordingly and appointed officials, the prefects, to administer it. Napoleon's conquest of Italy, Belgium and Spain allowed the French to introduce the administrative code and system of prefects, and these countries were happy to follow the lead of France once the formal dominance ended. France carried on being influential in all matters administrative and political throughout the nineteenth and twentieth centuries, and countries such as Spain, Greece, Portugal and Italy were happy to imitate the system. When the welfare state developed in the twentieth century, these functions fell to the central state which extended its tentacles through the de-concentration of functions to the territorial organizations of central ministries. Local communes remained small and without many functions of government, but their leaders were politically powerful, often holding formal positions at the national level, whether within political parties, the national legislature and/or in the central government. Whilst the formal reach of the central state was strong, local interests mediated the way it operated in practice as mayors used their contacts in central bureaucracies to get things done and to access resources.

As well as stressing the continuing importance of the state traditions in northern and southern Europe, Page and Goldsmith also highlight the importance of religion – the Protestant north and the Catholic south – that influenced the political culture of the two sets of countries and affected whether the secular state administered the education service directly or decentralized it to local government institutions (Archer, 1979). Different patterns of urbanization occurred so that small rural communes could continue to be viable as local government units. Moreover, the tradition of patron and client relationships and personal contacts typical of rural societies extended longer into the twentieth century than elsewhere. With urbanization came social-democratic parties that held office for long periods in some northern states. They imbued policies and institutional structures, such as systems of central finance for local government, with the values of equality and equity. Partly in a utilitarian spirit, connected to the need for the efficient and fair administration of public services, northern states showed a greater willingness to experiment in the reform of local government boundaries, whereas the communal boundaries of France and Italy remained sacrosanct as they embodied the identities of local communities. Whilst the whole of Europe had primary units of local government, whether called the commune or parish, they only became inviolable in some countries, such as France, Italy and Belgium, whereas elsewhere they have been marginalized or swept away by reforms aimed at improving the efficiency of services.

The two patterns embody different choices states made in their histories about how to decentralize. As Maas (1959) discusses, power may be divided in many ways, such as by process, by function or by constituency, and may be exclusively allocated to a tier of government or administration or shared. Governments seek to provide a mix that reflects their values. The pattern of decentralization in each country in the nineteenth and twentieth centuries embodied developing state traditions, with local institutions incorporating different ideas about the weight of the state in a democracy, such as the myth of the weak state in Britain as opposed to the legitimacy attached to strong central intervention in some Western European states (Dyson, 1980). Whereas many areas of Europe had similar patterns of decentralization up until the sixteenth century, with local communes and a fused church and state, the Reformation in the north and the Counter-Reformation split Europe into two groups. The secularized and professionalized administration of the north contrasted with the more authoritarian form of rule in the south, whether it was the emergent Catholic states, the Napoleonic forms of rule or the more openly nationalist regimes of the twentieth century (Bennett, 1989, 1993). Once the state solidified into its modern forms, the pattern of decentralization in each country reflected the expression of that modernity, such as government by an delegated system of public law or by administrative authority of the central state. As Smith (1985) concludes, the form of decentralization reflects political choices and interests. National elites and other actors sought to manage political conflict by decentralising activities to elected or to non-elected bodies, and the management of territorial politics takes different forms depending on the balance of power between centre and locality.

The academic body of knowledge

As well as being historically grounded, Goldsmith and Page's work is based on a solid body of research, either comparisons of two or more countries or single-nation studies. Page (1991) builds on the work of a generation of researchers into the prefectoral and clientelist systems of France and Italy where the main finding of research has been the importance of local politics, such as the work of Tarrow on grass-roots politicians (1977), Fried's (1963) book on the Italian prefects and studies of French intergovernmental relations by Worms (1966), Mény (1983) and Grémion (1976). Page and Goldsmith place these continental findings against some of the key aspects of the British system of central–local relations, notably the thesis of the separated or dual polity as set out by Bulpitt (1983), the idea that, during much of the twentieth century, British statecraft separated decisions between central and local government, in particular distinguishing between the 'high politics' of managing external relations and economic management and the 'low politics' of delivering public services. Rather than seeing Britain as an exception to the northern pattern, these authors categorize Britain with other welfare states. Page (1991) draws on the work of Hintze (1975), who argues that Britain and other northern European countries, such as Sweden, did not develop centralized bureaucracies in the eighteen and nineteenth centuries but relied on local elites to carry out national policies. The absence of a strong feudal tradition meant that independent locally elected self-government developed. The result of the similarity of Britain with other northern welfare states is that the conflicts between central and local government were caused by the same factors: the tendency for the centre to be interested in the spending and performance of local governments, partly because of their impact on the total of public expenditure, and the growing attention central government paid to the standards of public services. Page and Goldsmith do not depict static systems, but indicate the stresses and tensions within the two models of central–local government relations.

The normative dimension

The final advantage of the Page and Goldsmith approach is that it offers two accounts of the role of local politics in a representative democracy. Goldsmith (1996), whilst acknowledging the considerable variation in theory and practice of the countries within the two groups, advances this theme. Northern democracies developed the theory of local self-government based on the independence of locality to decide matters of importance. Extending Goldsmith's argument, local government becomes like a political system in miniature, with local interests, parties, manifestos and policies, if in a position of subordination to national legislatures and bureaucracies. The justification of local government is similar to that of central government save that the former is not formally sovereign. As some writers have commentated (Sharpe, 1970), the tension between the existence of the elements of representative government but without full legal autonomy creates a fundamental ambiguity for local self-government. There are conflicts and tensions in central–local government relations, even in countries that have a constitutional protection for local government. When the defects of representative systems are added to the uncertain political status, it could be argued that the values of local representative democracies cannot sustain themselves indefinitely.

Whilst there are similarities across Western Europe, Goldsmith argues that different principles – those of territorial representation and political localism – govern the politics of the southern group of nations. The function of local politics is to represent the interests of the locality to the central level of government. The commune embodies the local community and is only responsible for matters that are genuinely local. In a clientelistic system, politics is personal, which aids representation. As with the northern countries, this form of rule excludes many, like those who are not in the mayor's personal network. Moreover, clientelism encourages political and personal corruption. It could be argued that, as with local self-government, the values that underpin the system legitimate the benefits that personalized government brings, but they are a source of illegitimacy in the long run. The forces that create instability, urbanization and rapid economic change can also expose the negative features of such practices and undermine clientelistic political systems.

Some criticisms of Page and Goldsmith

Page and Goldsmith's comparative framework of local government is a good baseline from which to judge the evolution from government to governance. However, it is important to acknowledge the limitations of their work. The first is that they present a narrow selection of cases within Western Europe – they leave out Belgium, the Netherlands, Germany, Ireland, Portugal and Greece, Switzerland, Austria and Luxembourg. But the inclusion of some of these countries causes few difficulties, and it may be possible to treat Portugal and Greece as further variants on the southern model. Other cases cause more difficulty. Belgium is a southern state in some of its administrative structures but is northern in geographical location. Ireland is a northern state without a tradition of local self-government where local authorities become lobbyists, as in the southern European model. The Netherlands is northern in the way it allocates functions to local government, but retains a Napoleonic state form with relationship between the centre and the provinces. Page and Goldsmith leave out the federal countries of Germany, Austria and Switzerland because they contain several levels of government, though they could be included if each state is regarded as a different local government system. The Page and Goldsmith approach is limited to unitary states. But the unitary state has never existed in its pure form, even in the United Kingdom. Moreover, constitutional change and the emergence of state and regional governments creates a continuum of federal and quasi-federal arrangements across Europe.

The second line of criticism is that there are several types of local government system in Western Europe not just two. Page and Goldsmith have oversimplified the groupings. Influenced by Leemans (1970), most accounts identify three or four (Bennett, 1993; Hesse and Sharpe, 1991; Humes, 1991; Newman and Thornley, 1996; Norton, 1991). The authors separately classify Anglo-American local government systems of Ireland and the UK. Norton (1991) considers them to be closer to the US, Canada and Australia rather than to other Northern European states. The Anglo systems – what Leemans calls dual systems – are an early forbear of Bulpitt's dual polity. Local government enjoys local autonomy, but is the creature of statute, and has little protection from re-organization and centralization, and by implication cannot resist privatization and marketization. Local government has a weak constitutional status and is characterized as government by committee. The second classification resembles one of Page and Goldsmith's categories – the Napoleonic or fused systems or Franco group – which was France before the 1982 and 1986 reforms, and Belgium, Spain, Portugal, Italy and Greece where central government is represented by a prefect who heads a tier of administration, the department, but with the mayor of the commune who is the direct connection between central government and local communities. Many texts (Bennett, 1993; Hesse and Sharpe, 1991) classify Germany and parts of central Europe as a special form of fused local government system. There is also a northern or middle European variant which includes much of Germany, the Netherlands and Austria, which were also influenced by Napoleon's reforms of administration and the creation of local government and efficient forms of central administration. These systems are fused because they have a local government system and de-concentrated state administrations. Reflecting the development of legal forms of political rule, these systems of decentralization are guided by strict procedural rules and local autonomy is protected in the constitution. Scandinavian or split hierarchy systems have a hierarchy of government departments and a parallel one of prefects and local governments. The main difference between split hierarchy and fused systems is the absence of the commune in the former. Some authors prefer to treat the Nordic systems as one group with a great deal of similarity in the development of the role of local government (Albæk et al., 1991).

Defending Page and Goldsmith

In defence of Page and Goldsmith, these classifications of Western European systems are nuances rather than fundamental differences. The pure Napoleonic systems remain intact as a group, and there are many similarities between the German and Scandinavian systems as both have developed local governments with a broad set of functions. The main difficulty is the issue of exceptional character of British local politics, a re-occurring theme of the literature (for example, Blair, 1991), which implies that Britain has a more centralist and subordinate character to its local politics than elsewhere, something that appears to be borne out by the long programme of centralization of the Conservative governments of the 1980s and 1990s (John, 1994a), followed by the Labour governments in power since 1997, and the resistance of these governments to some of the trends in Western European governance, such as the move to more functions for elected local government and the democratization of levels of administration.

Whilst the differences between the UK and the rest of Western Europe should not be ignored, in particular the concentration of power in London and the constitutional legitimacy of centralized and strong executive power, the assumption of exceptionalism should be examined cautiously because every country can seem different from the others if looked at in great detail. Some of the assertions about constitutional autonomy need to be examined carefully, such as the extent to which central government has been able to control finance in the UK, as such controls exist in Denmark for example. Many Napoleonic countries, such as France, have constitutional protection for local government, but this does not prevent central government ministries making crucial decisions that affect local choices. Nor should blanket provisions, such as a general competence, encourage observers to think local authorities enjoy a strong independence. There is little difference in what local authorities can do from day to day under the doctrine of *ultra vires* in the UK and countries with powers of general competence, because local governments need to exercise their powers in relationship to those that govern central government controlled functions (Grant, 1992: 20).

Observers need to be cautious about the ascription of Britain as a dual state – or any state as dual – as this proposition has been stated in the theoretical literature (Bulpitt, 1983; Saunders, 1980), but has not been tested. Far from being a separated polity, the UK has always had a high degree of contact between central and local government in professional and policy-making communities (Dunleavy, 1981; Rhodes, 1986). Central government took initiatives through its field offices and politicians in powerful local parties, such as in Birmingham and in London, had an influence on national politics. Once researchers examine central–local policy systems in detail and according to policy sector, there is less difference in political relationships than the allocation of functions to tiers of government would suggest. The exceptional character of local politics in Britain only lasted during the 1980s, the period of radical initiatives to control local government (Gyford, 1985). Central policies like rate capping, abolition of the London authority, the Greater London Council in 1986, and the centrally run organizations with power to control special areas, the urban development corporations, were succeeded by a more moderate set of central reforms for local government in the 1990s. Many observers believe that the 1980s did not mark much centralization (John, 1994a; Travers, 1990). Moreover, many of the initiatives, such as management reform, contracting out and the imposition of partnerships, were part of the move toward local governance that was imitated later in the rest of Europe. In short, if the UK is added, with some qualifications, to the Northern European group, then the map of Western Europe matches Page and Goldsmith's and is the benchmark from which to judge the shift from government to governance, even if most researchers would like to weaken their claim about the differences in political relationships across Europe.

The third line of criticism is that there is not such a great contrast between the northern and southern system as there was in the 1990s. The southern countries have modernized or created welfare states, created tiers of local government, given them new legal powers, reduced the powers of the prefects, whilst local governments in the north have been fragmented by new management reforms and the transfer of functions to special purpose bodies whilst the power of the central states has increased. However, while this book argues that the overall structure and distribution of power between public and private and between centre and locality has altered in comparable directions, many of the distinctions that Page and Goldsmith highlight remain, with some lessening as an effect of the democratization of the departments in France and the creation of regions in Italy, France and Spain. The final section of the chapter reviews the main aspects of each system to illustrate the differences and similarities between the countries.

The contrast between northern and southern local government systems

The structure of local government

Crucial to the definition of local government is that it is a democratically elected authority that exercises political choices within denoted boundaries, though of course local governments co-operate across boundaries and ally in quasi-federal bodies, such as urban communities. As much is open to the discretion of central government and arises from historical accidents, there is a great variation in the size and number of these units across Western Europe and how they are organized in tiers of sub-national government. In the classic literature on decentralization (see Smith, 1985 for a summary), the size and number of sub-national units reflect a trade-off between efficiency on the one and community on the other, though there is much discussion as to whether the size of the local government unit has any effect on efficiency and community identity.

Table 2.1 shows the number of primary units in the countries this book considers and gives some summary statistics about northern and southern local government systems. The table assumes that Belgium, France, Greece, Italy, Portugal and Spain are in the southern group whereas Denmark,

TABLE 2.1 *Western European sub-national governmental structures*

	North/ South	No. of tiers	No. of authorities[a]	Average pop. of lowest tier (rounded)	Rank order of average population
Belgium	S	5	601	11,000	6
Denmark	N	2	289	18,000	4
Finland	N	2	455	11,206	5
France	S	3	36880	1491	14
Italy	S	3	8215	7182	9
Germany	S	3	16514	7900	8
Greece	S	2	5878	1803	15
Ireland	N	1 or 2	114	36,100	2
Netherlands	N	2	584	2723	11
Norway	N	2	458	9000	7
Portugal	S	2	4526	2342	12
Spain	S	3	8149	4997	10
Sweden	N	2	333	33,000	3
Switzerland		3	3021	2352	13
UK	N	2[b]	472	137,000	1
Northern average		2	386.42	35,289.8	
(Standard deviation)			(154.24)	(46,514.4)	
Northern average minus UK			—	18,338.17	
				(135.09)	
Southern average		3	10,708.17	4802.5	
(Standard deviation)			(13,125.81)	(3745)	
Southern average minus France			5473.8	—	
			(3141.5)	—	

The northern countries are Denmark, Finland, Ireland, the Netherlands, Norway, Sweden and UK; the southern are Belgium, France, Italy, Greece, Portugal and Spain.

[a] Includes all tiers.
[b] UK has two tiers in Scotland and Wales, two tiers in some parts of non-metropolitan England, one tier in metropolitan areas, two tiers in London and two tiers in Northern Ireland.

Source: Council of Europe, *Structure and Operation of Local and Regional Democracy*, country reports

Finland, Ireland, the Netherlands, Norway, Sweden and the UK belong to the north. Germany and Switzerland are excluded from the calculations because they are hybrid systems containing states or cantons which have both sets of traditions and structures. The north of Europe tends to have few levels of government, smaller numbers of local authorities and larger average size of local authority, and these differences are quite large if the averages of each group are considered. However, as indicated by the large standard deviations, some of the massive differences are explained by one country that has a large number of authorities – France – and another country, the UK, that has much larger authorities than the rest. When these countries are taken out, the difference between the north and south remains, but is not so great as before. The reduction in the standard deviation suggests the new average better reflects the spread of authorities across Western Europe.

The functions of local government

Sub-national governments are political institutions that run public functions that are given to them by law. They may also acquire others by powers of general competence or initiative, and share functions with other levels of government, either formally or informally. Table 2.2 shows the distribution

TABLE 2.2 *Selected functions by tier of government in Western Europe*

	Education (Prim., Sec)	Housing	Health/ Hospitals	Welfare	Refuse^a	Leisure	Fire
Belgium	PM	RM	PM	MP	M	RMP	M
Denmark	C	CM	C	CM	M	SCM	M
Finland	M	M	M	SM	M	M	SRM
France	N(DM)	M	S	MD	M	SDM	M
Greece	N	N	N	NM	M	NM	N
Germany	SM	SM	C	SM	M	SM	M
Ireland	N	CB	N	N	CM	M	CM
Italy	P	PM	R	RPM	PM	RPM	M
Netherlands	M	PM	PM	M	M	PM	M
Norway	CM	M	C	M	M	M	M
Portugal	N	N	N	N	NM	NM	NM
Spain	PM	M	SRM	RM	PM	NRPM	NRM
Sweden	M	M	C	M	M	MC	M
Switzerland	CAM	M	CAM	M	M	CAM	CA
UK	(CM)	M	N	NC	CM	CM	CM

Key: C = county; M = municipal; N = national; S = state; R = regions; P = provincial; D = department; CA = canton; ( ) indicates local control but highly constrained.

^a Both collection and disposal

Sources: Coopers Lybrand Deloite (1990), *Appendix D, International Experience* (Joseph Rowntree Foundation), Council of Europe, *Structure and Operation of Local and Regional Democracy*, country reports, OECD; OECD (1997) *Managing Across Levels of Government* – http://www.oecd.org/puma/malg/malg97/overview.pdf

of a selected number of functions across Western Europe, showing a broad similarity across the countries, with a few exceptions of countries where local government does not provide many services. Local government tends to provide the public goods, such as parks, but varies to the extent it provides private goods or welfare services. In general, as predicted in the comparative local politics literature, local government in the northern systems tends to provide the welfare services whereas regional or central governments provide them in the south. However, while this distinction would have been very clear twenty years ago, the transfer of functions to sub-national authorities lessens the contrast.

The relative importance of local government in the state

Next are some statistics on the size of the sub-national sector, broken down into levels of government to indicate the strength of the locally elected public sector in relation to the central state. Financial statistics are notoriously unreliable as they contain numerous assumptions. Here, Table 2.3 presents the numbers of public employees, which gives some indication of the importance of the local public sector, though the type of services local government is engaged in are labour-intensive and the table excludes services financed by the local authority but are public because of contracting. Here we find a much stronger contrast between the levels of government than in the other countries, with a major difference between the north and south. Perhaps the most telling set of figures is the rank ordering of size of the local government sector which shows that every northern country's local public sector employment is bigger than any southern country's.

Conclusion

This chapter describes the background to the local government systems that the book discusses in later chapters. The idea is to give some indication of the variety of sub-national government systems that exist in Western Europe in terms of the functions they administer and their roles within their wider political systems. The chapter introduces some of the main ways in which scholars have classified local government systems according to their powers, histories, functions and roles of the central state. Of key importance is the framework elaborated by Page and Goldsmith.

The central argument of the chapter is that the contrast between northern and southern government systems remains as a key distinction which describes the distribution of power, the impact of local politics, the form of representation and the capacity of local government to administer services. Whilst Page and Goldsmith framework is something of an oversimplification of complex systems that vary within each country as well as across

TABLE 2.3 *Share of public employment by level of government, northern group (percentages in 1994)*

	North/ South	Level of government	%	Rank order of local size
Belgium	S	Central	33.2	
		Regions and Communities	39.9	
		Local and Provincial	26.8	8
Denmark	N	Central	27.1	
		Local	70.8	3
Finland	N	Central	25.0	
		Local	75.0	1
France	S	Central[a]	74.4	
		Sub-national	18.4	9
Germany		Federal	11.9	
		Länder	51.0	
		Local	37.1	6
Greece	S	Central[b]	85.3	
		Local	14.7	10
Ireland	N	Central	87.3	14
		Local	12.7	
Italy	S	Central	63.0	
		Regional	23.0	
		Local	14.0	11 =
Netherlands	N	Central & other	72.4	
		Local & provinces	27.6	7
Norway	N	Central	26.0	
		Local	74.0	2
Portugal	S	Central	86.0	
		Local	14.0	11 =
Spain	S	Central	47.1	
		Regional	31.4	
		Local	14.0	11 =
Sweden	N	Central	17.3	
		Local[c]	52.9	5
Switzerland		Federal	32.5	
		Cantonal	39.0	
		Local	28.4	
UK	N	Central	47.7	
		Local	52.3	4
Northern local average			52.18	
Standard deviation			(24.18)	
Southern sub-national average			32.38	
Standard deviation			(21.0)	

[a] Includes health.
[b] Excludes public establishments and public enterprises.
[c] Includes the autonomous communes.

Source: OECD, *Managing Across Levels of Government* (1997)
http://www.oecd.org/puma/malg/malg97/overview.pdf

them, it reveals the broad elements of difference. As the tables show and the discussion at the end of the last section highlights, the reforms of both southern and northern local government systems since the 1980s – breaking up some traditional local government activities in the north and strengthening local governments and adding new tiers of sub-national government in the south – have only softened the differences rather than indicated a convergence.

The continuing contrasts between local government systems across Western Europe have implications for the transitions from local government to local governance. They reinforce the idea that institutional transformation is only one part of the story, but that governance is about the development of differing relationships and activities at the local level which traditional institutions attempt to negotiate. The fact that traditional local government activities remain in place shows that each system of local governance will develop in different and similar ways across Western Europe. Later chapters chart how these systems have evolved along the six main dimensions. We begin with the most important of all – the growing importance of the private sector and the emergence of local regimes.

3

Local Regimes in Western Europe

Governance is about the move toward a more informal form of politics. As a shift away from relatively restricted and formalized patterns of public decision-making, governance derives from the diverse sets of relationships across the many organizations occupying the local space. Chapter 1 discusses how this practice of governing derives from the multiplication of agencies and from the greater role the private sector plays in local politics. The shift from formal patterns of policy-making means that decision-makers build new or stronger relationships with each other to solve the central problems of public policy. European local political scientists have turned to the study of local politics in the United States to understand and research the changes. US scholars often call the informal pattern of governing localities an urban regime. As well as having a local focus, the study of regimes addresses one of the key aspects of governance – the fusion between public authority and the market in a highly competitive market economy. Further, the discussion of regimes engages with the normative debate about the most appropriate form of political leadership and governing arrangements for contemporary localities (see Elkin, 1987: 1–17). Not that regimes automatically produce a better form of governing, but a consideration of how the co-operative arrangements for ruling localities inhibit creative policy-making can help scholars to imagine ways to enhance democratic practice and to focus on the creative aspects of local governance.

Defining regimes

A regime describes the long-term informal networks that govern US cities (Stone, 1989). To find out who governs it is not enough to identify the political leaders and the prominent public sector organizations because these people and bodies do not operate on their own, particularly as local administrations have less formal power than state and federal governments. Researchers need to look beyond the formally constituted organizations because the potential for creative policy-making lies in the behaviour of the members of the local elites who operate in long-term relationships with each other.

Stone defines a regime as 'the informal arrangements that surround and complement the workings of governmental authority' (1989: 3). Members of a regime have access to institutional resources; they are the most powerful people who come together to solve public problems; and they have more power together than if they tried to govern alone. A regime is a non-governmental co-ordinating mechanism that makes up for the weakness of political authority. The main gap is inadequate political control over the economy which is always fragile and subject to change. A local regime is 'the informal arrangements by which public bodies and private interests function together in order to be able to make and carry out governing decisions' (Stone, 1989: 6).

Stone argues that regimes assist the management of conflicts and foster adaptive responses to social changes. Whilst the private interests refer to trade union officials, party managers and officers from the voluntary sector, Stone argues that the main group is the business leadership because of the importance of private investment in the local economy. Businesses control important resources which means they do not need to intervene in politics directly, but can rely on others to do their bidding. Stone argues that businesses deploys their resources, which are mainly financial, as 'selective incentives' to encourage the difficult process of co-operation. The task of building a regime is difficult because co-operation imposes costs on the participants as well as benefits, and the regime limits freedom of action. Regimes emerge and transmit themselves over a long period of time. They need to adapt in the face of constant pressure from their economic, social and political environments.

Regimes are not only about economic development politics. They extend beyond the traditional 'growth machine' (Logan and Molotch, 1987), which describes the boosterist economic development policies fostered by local property owners and their political allies. Regimes make policy about education, transportation, welfare and over many other public issues. There are also different types of regime that vary according to the 'array of organizations and collectivities available for federation, personal leadership skill and particular policy stance' (Stone, 1989: 238).

Stone places his work in debates about the influence of market economies on politics. In local areas, as elsewhere in developed societies, there is a division of labour between businesses that make decisions about private resources, such as private investment, and the politicians who control the state. Whilst both groups can act alone, each needs the co-operation of the other to get major things done. Politicians seek to affect the economy, but cannot have much effect through normal policy instruments; on the other hand, business leaders cannot directly control political decisions, such as over land use. Businesses compromise some of their objectives to obtain co-operation, but politicians trade in theirs as well. The result is a form of governance that is creative, but where the outputs are skewed toward the interests and preferences of the private sector.

The skewing of public policies is the central focus of Elkin's (1987) work. In his view the bias of local politics is complete since the power of the market systematically shifts political institutions away from following the public interest. Elkin argues that businesses exercise their power through the dependence of localities on the bond market rather than through selective incentives. US municipal authorities need a favourable rating; if they do not get it, bankruptcy or severe fiscal constraint is a possibility. Local leaders favour a path of economic growth that is in the interests of businesses. Policy-makers regard the locality as a pattern of land use. Narrow 'growth coalitions' between politicians and property developers re-arrange the use of local land and citizens do not get much of a chance to influence policies. Developers make a profit and politicians distribute some of the benefits of growth to their electoral allies. In this part of the analysis, the regime appears like the coalition of the growth machine literature, where politicians and developers manage the land supply to maintain the local area's prosperity and foster its expansion. In addition to favourable land use policies, businesses seek low municipal taxes and budgets.

Stone is more optimistic than Elkin. Whereas Elkin regards the exercise of power by business as wholly negative, Stone believes that business leaders, politicians and other elites in the locality can achieve much together. Businesses act to produce socially advantageous outcomes and exercise power to do things, as well as power over others to achieve objectives that benefit themselves only. In his study of Atlanta, Stone shows how the governing coalition pushed through radical policies in response to the rapid social changes facing the city. Atlanta differed from other North American cities because its policies reflected the capacity of the governing regime to innovate. The moderation in race relations arose from the accommodation and forward-looking policies of the regime that incorporated the black middle class. The regime gathered momentum and gained a life of its own; it acquired a learning capacity and social intelligence that allowed policy-makers to solve problems and to prevent conflict. Whilst Atlanta produced pro-business policies, such as high transfers of land from domestic to business use, the city also introduced ameliorative social measures, such as a large programme to build social housing. Stone's work is not a restatement of pluralism, as he recognizes the systematic power of the private sector, but he does not accept the elitist view that co-operation between the public and private sectors only has negative consequences.

Regimes in Western Europe?

The case for Western Europe regimes

In what way are the accounts of coalitions in Atlanta, Dallas and other US cities pertinent to the study of Western European local governance? The main relevance is that regimes describe a set of conditions that are similar to those that drive the move from government to governance; moreover, regime theory provides a set of concepts to analyse the changes, delineates possible causal relationships and suggests the means to evaluate governance. Students of local politics are able to identify the exercise of political power in Europe's main cities, to understand how regimes can produce creative policies to deal with the rapid changes in Western European politics, societies and economies. They can find out if the form of governing replicates the skewing of public policies toward the preferences of the private realm. European local politics becomes more like that in the US, more oriented to responding to the market rather than to addressing economic injustices as in the social-democratic tradition.

Whilst the public involvement of the private sector in Western Europe does not even approach its dominant role in Northern America, comparative regime theorists claim that business has become more important. The regime idea is a good description of an emerging form of governance and gives an indication about what may happen in the future. The private sector was dominant in the nineteenth and early twentieth centuries and its leaders were prominent members of local political elites. But business retreated from direct involvement with local politics in the mid-part of the twentieth century. Local business leaders moved out to the suburbs and had less day-to-day contact with the social-democratic parties that often run urbanised localities (Harding, 1994c). The strength of the state in Britain and France ensured that public sector elites dominated local policy-making on land use, public transport and local development, whether they were from local elected agencies or the de-concentrated bureaus of central government ministries. In addition, the state consolidated its power through its control over public finances, whether it was the direct supervision of local expenditure in countries, such as France, or through controls over capital projects as in the UK, which meant it was hard for local politicians to finance public–private projects and to bring business representatives into policy-making. The local private sector built relationships with national decision-makers as it was these people who counted over decisions on planning and public investment. Moreover, the development of national equity markets and banking organizations gradually centralized most businesses; large companies took over many local private sector concerns. Even if businesses retained their headquarters in their original cities, they directed their attention to national and international markets as well as to central government decision-makers. Moreover, the culture of much local government in Europe, with its focus on delivering services in the north or in accessing central government resources in the south, did not encourage close relationships with the private sector. The classic literature on local political power and central–local government relations did not discuss business participation (for example, Tarrow, 1977).

The conventional approach restated

But the portrait of business withdrawal from local politics, the social welfare preferences of the local elite and the ubiquity of political centralization control is much too simple an account. Certain local businesses continued to be interested in local politics, such as construction companies eager to win contracts. These businesses sought to persuade local politicians of the virtues of new building materials and housing construction projects (Dunleavy, 1981). Many members of local elites believed more in virtues of private sector-led economic development and formed a close relationship to the private sector, such as the growth coalition in Swindon, UK (Bassett and Harloe, 1990). French chambers of commerce have extensive power because of their access to local taxation; moreover, they are part of the local state and directly run some services. Private sector capital partly financed public housing in France (Castells and Godard, 1974; Coing, 1977). Public–private partnerships originated in the 1920s and have been common in France since the 1950s (Lorrain, 1991). Lorrain draws attention to the large number of local private sector operators in France which partly derives from the mixed form of provision of services (Lorrain, 1987). Lorrain's description of the communal private sector, which comprises private sector operators and quasi-private sector organizations, with its complex linkages, is reminiscent of a regime. A survey of the contacts of mayors, council members, departmental heads and party leaders in 55 middle-sized cities in the US, Sweden and the Netherlands found that the countries were similar: businesses and other groups exert as much pressure in all the countries, although the leaders in Western Europe do not reciprocate as much as in the US (Eldersveld et al., 1995: 161). Finally, Le Galès' (2000) survey of the evidence from many West European countries shows that businesses do have an interest in local politics even if they are usually fragmented and have varying levels of motivation.

However, the involvement of the private sector in delivering services and the interest of firms in particular sectors did not disrupt the basic institutional framework of governing and did not amount to a regime in the North American sense of the term. The implication of the regime idea is that the public–private coalition constitutes the governance of the locality. Whilst the private sector is embedded in networks of pre-existing relationships, the current set of relationships are much broader. These conditions mean that it is in the interest of business to set up a long-term coalition with the public sector.

The new economic environment

As Chapter 1 indicates, a series of transnational economic changes have made local economies more vulnerable to competition. Public decisions have an impact on the economic competitiveness of the locality and the fate of enterprises that do business there. Businesses take an interest in economic development policies, such as measures to attract inward investment (both private and public) and investment in public and private transport. Moreover, they become concerned about social policies, such as those that affect the education level of the workforce and thus the efficiency of local labour markets. They develop an interest in measures that improve the image of the local area to outside investment, particularly those that reduce crime and improve the appearance of the locality, such as its public housing and the cleanliness of its streets. As important is the contribution of higher education institutions to the prosperity of the locality and for particular businesses. Even good recreation facilities, such as high quality arts provision, are important for the image and help businesses attract clients. As businesses become more interested in the whole range of policies produced by local public agencies, they realize they need to affect the political as well as their economic environment. At the same time, local bureaucrats and politicians realize the importance of co-operation of business to the health of their local economies. They create policies to help local competitiveness so that the locality has a good reputation amongst businesses, to prevent exit and to encourage inward investment. Central governments and the EU increasingly require the private sector to participate in and to contribute to public funded projects, such as those aimed to promote economic regeneration. Local bureaucrats and politicians cultivate relationships with local businesses so that leverage is forthcoming. As the public–private partnership culture developed during the end of the 1980s and early 1990s, sponsors became more adept at spotting the hastily assembled group of partners from the long-term and fruitful exchanges with business from which bids for funding could spring.

The changed role of central government

As well as introducing rules attached to the award of funding, central government policies have changed dramatically. States have removed their direct controls over industrial locations, both in state dominated political systems, such as France, and in countries with more locally determined planning decisions, such as the UK. The power of the central planners was powerfully captured in Savitch's account of the role of the prefect of Paris in reorganizing the location of industry (Savitch, 1988). Under pressure to respond to economic competition and the requirements of the EU, the central planning agency, the Délégation à l'Aménagement du Territorie Régionale (DATAR), relaxed controls on the expansion of metropolitan

Paris. The decentralization reforms of the 1980s also liberalized some central controls over the detail of local planning decisions. Other Western European countries have experienced similar changes. Newman and Thornley's (1996) outline of the international and European influences on national planning systems indicates an element of convergence, even when acknowledging extensive national variations. The retreat of the welfare state and the move to right of the Swedish political system led to a greater decentralization of functions to local government, which encouraged policy-makers to reform the planning system. The Netherlands has witnessed the introduction of partnerships, privatization and US-style local management (Levine and Van Weesep, 1988). More generally, the decentralization of government functions and the emergence of regions, often with their own planning powers, have reorganized the planning systems in most Western European states. Common provisions have emerged, even though national differences remain prominent (Newman and Thornley, 1996). It is easier for entrepreneurial political leaders to build growth coalitions to attract capital because there are fewer constraints on public–private initiatives. The state tends to let private ventures be and to allow local political leaders to lobby for public and private sector resources. The entrepreneurial city has emerged, where local elites seek to compete with those in other centres for public resources, populations and investment (Harding et al., 1994).

The revival of the city

Several writers locate the emergence of regimes in the history of the Western European city (for example, Bagnasco and Le Galès, 1997; Le Galès and Harding, 1998). The starting point is Tilly and Blockmans' (1994) analysis of the retreat of cities at the beginning of the modern era. Whereas cities were at the heart of the Western European economy and formed important governments in themselves, they were defeated by the superior power of nation-states. Under challenge from economic forces, Europeanization and internal restructuring, the state retreats and the city re-establishes its central role in the economy and polity. Advocates of cities point to their revival and mobilization as economic entities after their reverse. Of central importance is the activism of city elites rather than the leaders of local government or larger entities, such as regions. As cities regenerate their economies, so they mobilize their political communities to their place in the sun. Activist political leaders bond with the private sector to form coalitions that can compete with those in other localities. Sometimes large elites in local centres ally with their regions to lobby the centre (Hoffman-Martinot, 1996). The private sector takes more of an interest in local politics because of the political benefits and the gains. The rest of the local system takes more of a backseat as the big power holders fight it out. As local economies become more similar in terms of their relative advantage, the competition increases (Harvey, 1989). Le Galès and Harding (1998) bring in regulation theory for added spice to the argument, though it is not clear why post-Fordism implies a specific city form of governance.

Even with extensive political and economic competition, Western European localities are never going to be like their North American counterparts. Chapter 1 mentions Castells and other writers' argument that Western European cities have a large stock of social and political capital, in particular social-democratic traditions and parties that address non-market issues and respond to the challenges to social cohesion. Moreover, local parties seek to provide a stream of benefits to their supporters in the form of favourable policies. With their need to address social policy issues, Western European cities see-saw between responding to economic and social demands.

The academic disputation

The regime research programme and its critics

Many local political scientists have embraced the regime argument, either in theory (for example, DiGaetano, 1998; Harding, 1994a, 1994c; Kantor et al., 1997; Levine, 1994; Stoker, 1995; Stoker and Mossberger, 1994) or for empirical studies (for example DiGaetano, 1997; DiGaetano and Klemanski, 1993, 1999; Dowding, 2000; Dowding et al., 1999; Harding, 1997; John and Cole, 1998; Stewart, 1996; Ward, 1997). Their work amounts to an ongoing research programme that takes evidence from some of the leading cities of Europe. Nevertheless, there is a dispute about the nature of regimes and how they apply to the Western European context, with even sympathetic authors expressing caution (for example, Harding, 1997; Le Galès, 1995). The main criticism is that the strength of the central state makes the regime label a misnomer. Central or federal states control vast stocks of financial and legal resources; they are the dominant source of legitimacy; and they can affect the ways in which cities make policy. It does not make sense to refer to autonomous regimes. The types of public–private coalition that emerge reflect the funding schemes and policies central and local public bureaucracies follow at any particular time. In this version the public and private partnerships that formed in the 1990s reflected the fashions of local, central and Western European policy-makers who sought new forms of public–private partnership and arranged funding regimes to bring the private sector into public development projects. In turn national and international businesses have little interest in the parochialism of local politics bar an incentive to arrange favourable planning outcomes. Even these are more accessible from central government bureaucracies than from local politicians. As Peck and Tickell (1995) detail in their colourful accounts of Manchester, only some businesses have an interest in forming growth coalitions. Those businesses that stand to gain directly from large-scale public sector investment in, for example, infrastructure projects, have a direct incentive to participate in local policy-making.

In Western European countries, most business and business representative organizations tend to react to rather than shape local issues. Officials tend to be the leading actors in French public–private associations. In general, French chambers of commerce take a direct role over the areas where they had direct control through ownership, such as airports. French chambers can be conservative (Le Galès, 1993). Harding (1997) comments on the separation of the politics of consumption and production in Western European cities because few businesses seek to affect public service decisions. Harding considers that the central government finance of local government in Western European cities means there is little financial incentive to attract business to local areas because of the equalization of local tax burdens, a point emphasized by Newman and Thornley (1996). The other difficulty for regime analysis is that Western European cities differ from their counterparts in the USA. The stock of community values in Europe derives from long evolution of cities as economic, social and political entities; the strong sense of community and civic culture affects the role of the elites and their sense of duty to wider public objectives. Moreover, social-democratic parties have governed many cities and have transformed political institutions to reflect both the development of working class ideologies and a belief in the public intervention in social affairs.

The reformulation of regime theory

Many scholars working with the regime framework do not challenge the notion that local politics is dominated by state actors and that Western European cities are different from their North American counterparts. Writers such as Keating (1995a) and Newman (1995) incorporate the main decision-makers from the public sector into Western European regimes. Dowding (2000: 11) argues that the 'model must allow for few time-specific features and a broader array of possible economic structures'. Stoker and Mossberger (1994) re-conceive regimes in their comparative review. They do not assume that businesses must be the key members of regimes; instead they consider regimes to have a large number of participants of different types. They focus on the way in which informal networks across organizations foster creativity in policy-making. Many of the key features of regimes vary according to their aims, the motivations of the participants, the sense of common purpose, the quality of the coalition and the relationship with the wider local policy environment. US coalitions are only one type of regime, taking on an instrumental character and concerned with economic growth. Other sorts of long-term alliance have differences in the basic elements, such as traditionally based organic regimes that aim to maintain the status quo whilst symbolic regimes that are more ideological in purpose and expressive in their motivations tend to use strategic symbols and include as many local elites as possible. These regimes appear in different places. There are US-style regimes in cities such as Birmingham, but symbolic regimes occur in other local centres, like in Glasgow, with its high profile campaign to improve its image. Coalitions play an important part in determining policy, but they operate in different ways.

With this broad-ranging analysis, Stoker and Mossberger seek to 'cleanse' regime theory of its ethnocentric preoccupations and to apply a set of criteria that enables scholars to identify different sorts of governance. Thus re-figured, the regime encompasses the varieties of local political system in Europe, recognizes the importance of ideas, ideologies, symbols and movements and acknowledges that policy outcomes do not always reflect the preferences and interests of businesses. Stoker and Mossberger describe a form of local politics that is richer and more diverse than the interest-based politics of US cities. They place regimes in different institutional contexts and forms of political practice. Certain kinds of regime emerge when local elites in countries like France and Spain have good access to the central state, whereas countries such as the United Kingdom have other sorts of regimes when local political elites do not have such good contacts.

The implication of this approach is that regimes may be found in many Western European localities. The task of researchers is to identify them – which is what the many studies attempt to do. For example, Dowding et al. (1999) provide an eight-point characterization of regimes designed to cover all cases, arguing that not all need be present for a regime to exist but that the larger the subset, the more a governing coalition constitutes a regime. They then apply the idea to six London boroughs during the 1990s, arguing that three of the cases are different types whilst the other three constitute failed regimes. Henry and ParamioSalcines (1999) use the notion of symbolic regimes to evaluate the role of sport in policy-making in Sheffield. They try to show that the regime approach provides an appropriate framework to analyse the mobilisation of interests behind the development of a symbolic project, an image for Sheffield as a city of sport. DiGaetano and Klemanski (1993) attach the regime idea to Bristol and Birmingham through analysing the development of partnership arrangements. Ward (1997) calls regimes the partnership arrangements in specific projects in Leeds, Birmingham and Manchester. Newman (1994) deploys regime theory to examine the sub-metro politics of development projects in the UK (King's Cross and Greenwich) and France (La Plaine St Denis and Seine Rive Gauche).

Criticisms of regime studies

The ascription of the regime label to Western European cities presents a number of problems. The first is that some of the cities that researchers discuss do not have stable coalitions. For example, DiGaetano and

Klemanski's (1993) account of Bristol raises issues of interpretation. As Bassett (1996) notes, the history of the city shows many divisions and splits in the Labour leadership, mainly between the hard left and more moderate elements. At best there was a fractured regime, though there has been a move toward a more consensual approach in recent years and the greater involvement of business.

The main problem with these typologies is that they extend the definition of regimes to cover almost any informal arrangement for governing. As there are some relationships between the main organizations and interests in every local area, therefore almost everywhere has a regime. When defined so inclusively, the task of the theorist is to show there are variations between different sorts of cities, such as between the organic, instrumental and symbolic regimes in Stoker and Mossberger's account. Such an approach, however, loses much of the analytical power of regime theory. By lessening the argument based on the exchange between the state and the market, the regime idea becomes vague and descriptive. The elaboration of typologies sometimes side-steps one of the key claims of Stone's original work: business and local politicians form a coalition that learns to produce policies for the locality, even if they are skewed toward the interests of businesses. Western European researchers do not discuss the use of side payments by business to get its own way in politics and they are content to study partnerships, especially in economic development, which may have a limited life span and are often focused on one project. Some writers apply the concept of regimes to the local boroughs within a locality and compare them (for example, Dowding et al., 1999). Yet Stone wrote about a coalition that gradually emerged and adapted over a forty-year period. It encompassed the whole city with its complex political factions, ethnic divisions, multifarious interest groups and competing land use projects. The regime affects many policies, such as education, recreation, arts, public housing and the protection of the environment.

John and Cole (1998) argue that that concept should be applied more parsimoniously in comparative local studies. They argue that researchers should read the original texts more closely. If they did so, they would find an account of regimes that applies mainly to big city politics, which mainly comprises the long-term coalitions between the political and business leaderships, even if other groups are subsumed, and gradually develop a capacity to solve public problems. Even in the North American context, the conditions for the formation of regimes are not ubiquitous. As Stone acknowledges, regimes are hard to create and can easily be unstable, implying that there are many large cities that do not have regimes. Stone's discussion of the history of Atlanta shows there are five sets of conditions that help form regimes. They are not necessary or sufficient conditions, but increase the probability of a regime-like politics emerging in a city.

The first is that there should be a local dimension to business interests. Ideally, businesses should be owned by local people or there must be a large degree of discretion open to local managers of national and international firms. The business actors in Atlanta, as identified by Stone (1989: 25), are members of the local business community who are able to articulate an interest of the city. The condition is important because if business is not local or locally orientated, then there is less chance of an exchange-based relationship between the public and private sectors emerging. There would be little inclination for business to provide selective incentives to win over the political actors.

The second condition is that businesses need to be relatively integrated (Stone, 1989: 165–173) and that those who represent businesses speak for the interests of the private sector. Defections from the coalitions would undermine even a long-standing regime, and business participation in politics should not be just based on land developers or those who are dependent on public spending decisions. Relative integration need not imply that the whole of business is involved with politics since businesses differ in their willingness to contribute to public goods. Nor does the condition imply that business is unified on every public issue as business is composed of many interests.

The third condition is that regimes are likely to form and to stay in place in large metropolitan areas. Although regimes depend on localism, they are not fostered by parochialism. Elites need to have high standing and have a large amount of resources to have the capacity to co-operate in the long term. Elite capacity is about vision and the ability to enforce co-operation. In the United States regimes are found in the big cities, such as Dallas and Atlanta, rather than in small places. Fast growing cities do not foster the spirit of co-operation (Stone, 1989: 185). In Eldersveld et al.'s (1995: 178) study, larger cities have more contact between the elite and interest groups than small cities (though this was not true for the Netherlands). However, not all metropolises have regimes. Large sprawling urban areas may not have sufficient collective identity to bring public and private elites together. Similarly, some small cities may have dynamic local elites that resembles a regime. Also regimes may form in dynamic regions or large county areas. As with business integration, the condition is probabilistic – larger cities have more of a chance of having regimes.

Fourth, a tradition of pragmatism and trust in local politics helps a regime to work and to last, which may be part of the political culture, perhaps formed over many generations. Past histories of co-operation between elites and between organizations assist the formation of regimes since they are built on pre-existing feelings of trust. A stock of goodwill helps regimes survive the inevitable conflicts of local politics. More generally, trust begets trust. The higher the initial level of trust, the more likely that a creative and innovative regime will emerge. It is important to be careful with this condition because pragmatism and trust may both define and cause a regime, which would be a circular argument. Pragmatism here should mean something that is part of the political culture and values of the political institutions rather than the values of the members of the governing coalition. It should exist prior to the existence of the regime.

Finally, regimes emerge in places that are slightly different from the average. The uniqueness of a locality can foster the politics of exceptionalism and a sense of difference from other centres. If a locality is slightly ahead or behind in its level of economic development compared to the others, there are extra incentives for the public and private sectors to co-operate to stay ahead or to catch up. It is possible that in atypical prosperous or deprived cities co-operation takes the form of an assurance game because the potential benefits of co-operation are high and risks of non-co-operation are low whereas in typical places, co-operation takes the form of a prisoner's dilemma because these benefits are not so high. This point is not highlighted in the regime politics literature, but is indicated by the localities these writers select. Atlanta and Dallas are prosperous cities that aggressively wish to stay ahead. Atlanta's business and political elites, through their coalitions and in adapting to the resurgent black electoral politics, were more advanced than their rivals in other Southern centres, as illustrated by Stone's (1989: x) remark that 'Atlanta is not a typical city'.

If there are special factors that lead to the emergence of regimes, the number of cases in a country may be small. Regimes are an exceptional rather than a general form of governance. They appear in the urban centres that meet some of the five conditions set out above. Given that regimes are, to an extent, voluntary phenomena, requiring political will, they may not appear even when these conditions are present. If this analysis is correct, there is less of a problem in applying a theory from the USA than comparative critics expect. Regimes are rare in any nation-state, not just in state dominated systems. The conditions allow the comparative researcher to focus on the leading cities. In terms of the move from government to governance, the local political system as a whole becomes less institutionalized, with closer relationships with the private sector and greater fragmentation of local service delivery. In large cities this form of politics takes a regime-like character through the work of strong public–private coalitions that emerge particularly in cities that have a strong private sector and meet some of the five conditions outlined above.

Regimes and governance

Regimes are at the pinnacle of the process of governance; they are an extension of the processes of networking, trust-building and problem-solving. Cities with regimes embody these facets of political behaviour more than other places. They are a subset of governance occurring where the relationship between the political and economic elites is the dominant form of politics to which other interest groups accommodate. Trust and the ability to solve public problems are much greater for regimes than for the rest of local governance; but the greater involvement of the private sector also leads to skewed policies that do not reflect the preferences of public bureaucracies. The concept of regimes allows the researcher to pick out a special case of governance and highlights the capacity of elites to solve public problems. Moreover, regimes are in the vanguard of the new politics. They emerge in some cities, then spread to others in the course of political change across local political systems. The more limited form of regime analysis acknowledges that regimes in Western Europe are a recent phenomenon and that up until the 1980s business had retreated from local politics.

The UK

Some of the research on regimes follows or is analogous to the argument here. John and Cole (1998) examine the emergence of a regime in Leeds in the UK, and apply the five conditions. Leeds is a northern English city, with a population of about 800,000, with a highly prosperous economy initially based on manufacturing and latterly the service sector, particularly financial products. Until recently many businesses were locally owned. The city has a clear identity and culture, distinct from other urban centres, even from its neighbour Bradford. There has been a long tradition of public–private co-operation, which came from prominent local business people who had a sense of social responsibility and public spirited beliefs. Public and private elites co-operated over many projects in the 1960s and 1970s. Even in times of political conflict in the 1980s, there was good informal co-operation between the political and business leaderships over matters such as the transport strategy and releasing land for development near the city centre. By the 1990s, when public–private coalitions were the fashion, Leeds was easily able to put together a partnership, *The Leeds Initiative*. Leeds jumped ahead of its economic rivals, such as Bradford and Sheffield, and competed for business investment with Manchester and Birmingham, the larger English cities. John and Cole argue that pre-existing good relationships and informal coalitions between business and politics in Leeds helped attract inward investment and maintained the city's competitive advantage, particularly in the era of municipal radicalism of the 1980s when the city's leadership retained its reputation for pragmatism. In the 1990s the regime became more prominent as the concern was to keep the city's economy ahead of its rivals that adopted similar policies to Leeds. Not all experts on Leeds accept John and Cole's analysis. Haughton and Williams (1996) argues that Leeds shows the dominance of corporate culture and fashion rather than a coalition between the public and private sectors.

Whilst the regime in Leeds was exceptional, similar patterns appear in other cities. Birmingham is probably the next candidate for a regime, with its pro-growth policies of the 1980s, extensive public–private partnerships and reputation for pragmatism. Comparative researchers DiGaetano and Klemanaski (1993) are on solid ground in identifying a regime in contrast to their account of Bristol. They note the prominence of certain individuals who pioneered economic development and coalition politics. Slightly more ambiguous is Manchester, which was a 'hard left' council in the 1980s and eschewed good relationships with the business sector. Like many local councils at the end of that decade, Manchester lost its desire to make radical local policies. Such a flowering of municipal radical politics had become discredited and largely outlawed by neo-liberal and centralising Conservative governments that used legal and financial controls to impose their ideological vision. At the same time as councils started to realize the benefits of working with local private interests to develop their cities, central government either required or encouraged public–private partnerships to be part of funding projects. The city's early public–private partnerships did not amount to a regime, but Harding (1997) argues that a broader and sustainable set of partnerships emerged on bigger projects, such as the city's bid for the 2000 Olympic Games. The people involved were the 'Manchester Mafia' (Cochrane et al., 1996), who backed major projects in the city. The emergence of a fluid network of actors is similar to the type of relationships in a regime, though Harding argues these elites lack the gravitas of their counterparts in the United States. Harding provides a similar analysis of Edinburgh in Scotland, where there is an informal coalition of key public and private sector actors that makes things happen in the city. Other cities in England and Scotland do not show such a regime-like quality, such as Southampton (Cole and John, 2001).

Rasmussen (2000) carries out a more comprehensive test of the John and Cole model. He selected ten British cities, found out whether regimes exist in them and used the Boolean method to discover whether combinations of factors predict regime success. The Boolean approach is a form of qualitative data analysis for a small number of cases which permits the researcher to identify combinations of factors that predict a dependent variable (Ragin, 1985). He collected data on the five 'John and Cole' variables and identified two regime cities – Leeds and Birmingham. He finds that that a tradition of pragmatism and a large city context are necessary but not sufficient conditions for the formation of a regime. Surprisingly, the degree of integration of the business community and city uniqueness are not important. Rasmussen elaborates a stages model of regime formation, which highlights the importance of political leadership and the role of the public sector in the early period of regime formation in the UK; then there is a 'pluralistic' expansion of regimes to include more members of the private sector. Rasmussen conjectures that some cities, like Manchester and Sheffield, if they re-gain their traditions of pragmatism, have the right combination of factors to form regimes. He suggests that his method needs further research and testing, especially with comparative data.

France

In France, John and Cole (1998) take Lille as an example of a local regime. In contrast to Leeds, this city of one million inhabitants had experienced rapid economic decline. It has also been a more traditional socialist city, without a tradition of a good relationship between the public and private sectors, and has a highly divided political elite located in its often warring eighty-five communes. Yet, when driven by the economic crisis, its leader, Pierre Mauroy, created and sustained a coalition between the private and public sectors to form Euralille, a massive city centre redevelopment project attached to the new terminus for the cross-channel tunnel and other projects across the metropolitan area. Although some businesses remained implacably opposed to the socialist politicians, a spirit of co-operation emerged which has a regime-like quality. Not that old-style networks have become less important; the new mayor, Martine Aubry, is plugged into the national political elite. However, these networks need to operate in relationship with new ones between the public and private sectors.

Some analysts have been content to apply the regime idea to the entrepreneurial type of politics that emerged in France of the 1980s. After the Socialist government gave communes freedoms and lost interest in centralized planning (Levine, 1994), mayors took great pride in becoming heads of development coalitions. Whilst the emergence of entrepreneurial mayors in the 1980s cannot be doubted (Garraud, 1989), it is not clear that regimes emerged because the coalitions were not long-lasting. Many collapsed in the face of the municipal corruption scandals of the late 1980s. In the city of Rennes, for example, the public–private coalition was short-lived. By the late 1990s the locality experienced conflicts between the businesses and the local political leadership (Cole and John, 2001). Négrier (1999), in his survey of changes to French local politics, doubts the strength of local public–private alliances.

Germany

Many German cities have developed formidable local coalitions because of the relative freedom they have in the formulation of policies. Hamburg's leaders have re-thought the way they govern: they have ceased to focus solely on the prosperity of the port and seek to create a media industry. The city created a large public–private business corporation. The massive chamber of commerce, with 80,000 members, shifted policy dramatically (Harding, 1997). The result was a success, especially in comparison with other German cities. Another example was the rapid development of Frankfurt (Kunzmann and Lang, 1994), where the city administration created policies to compete with other financial centres, involving extensive co-operation between the public and private sectors, though it probably does not classify as a regime because of the driving role of the parties and the role of the Land government. Another example is Berlin and Brandenburg (Kleger et al., 1995). Kleger et al. argue that the existing two organic regimes transformed into an instrumental one under the pressure of global economic pressures. Coalition building occurred in planning for the new airport and between the state governments of Berlin and Brandenburg. Informal coalitions operated at the level of the development area rather than the boundaries of the *Länder* and the private sector drove the decision-making process. Kleger et al. identify the main members of the regime as the two state governments and the private sector. Other political actors were involved to a lesser degree, such as the political parties, though with varying levels of enthusiasm. However, substantial opposition threatens to undermine the adapting regime.

Strom (1996) also considers Berlin to be a candidate for a local regime. She places Berlin in a context of the move away from formalized politics to one where most cities have encouraged public–private partnerships. Nevertheless, the relationship between the state and the market operates in a different way in Germany because of fiscal equalization and the existence of political parties with ideological programmes that affect central and local policy-making. In addition, West Berlin had constrained economic development and a weak business sector because of economic planning and its geographical isolation. In the reconstruction period, leaders sought investment to remake Berlin as a world city. Like Manchester and other Western European cities, the entry into a competition to host the Olympic Games 2000 played a role in bringing together public and private elites. A better indication of a regime-type politics was the planning for the Potsdamer Platz, with its large vacant sites in the centre of the new metropolis. Strom remarks that the state and its bureaucrats played a crucial role in all decisions, and in no sense had they abdicated policy to the private sector. Strom emphasizes the special character of Berlin, which suggests that regimes have emerged in exceptional places, such as redeveloping capital cities, newly developing port cities and financial centres. Indeed, most capital cities of central Europe benefit from economic expansion, as they enjoyed property booms, and the consequent development of public–private coalitions (Newman and Thornley, 1996: 14–15).

Further examples of regimes

Changing coalition politics have characterized the development of other northern European states. Certain large cities in the Netherlands have seen the emergence of public–private coalitions. Rotterdam's local elites have embraced the entrepreneurial approach since the late 1970s when the city needed to attract footloose 'sunrise' industries even though the marketing activities were lead by the municipal authority (Harding, 1994b; McCarthy, 1998). The city's leaders fostered massive development projects, such as the Waterstad and the Koop van Zuid schemes. Using the John and Cole (1998) framework, McCarthy identifies Rotterdam as a case for a local regime with its history of pragmatism, trust between the elites, large metropolitan context and sense of difference from other cities in the country. McCarthy shows how the city leaders have linked closely to the private sector in a series of public–private partnerships. McCarthy writes that 'the city elites have operated in a way that is perhaps more characteristic of US cities, a factor that supports the emergence of urban regimes in this context' (1998: 342). Linking with the creative capacity of regimes, McCarthy notes the elites emphasized that a programme of social renewal was integral to the city's renewal, though other commentators argue that the city has tended to neglect the welfare of socially excluded inhabitants (Hajer, 1993).

The rise of local regimes has implications for the study of Western European local politics. There is no reason for the strict north–south pattern to emerge, as what is important is the capacity of local elites to form coalitions. The variation in the presence and form of regimes across Europe takes other forms than the classic division of local government systems. Harding and Le Galès suggest various patterns. In Italy the mobilization of local elites for economic development has not really occurred as metropolitan government is highly fragmented. The medium-sized cities of Bergamo in Lombardy, the cities of Emilia–Romagna and those in the Venice region have grown without the help of municipal leaderships. Likewise in Milan, the political parties drove local policies and business sought to influence them (Newman and Thornley, 1996: 90). But local businesses have been active in cities like Bologna and Milan because of the reforms of local chambers of commerce (Perulli, 1999).

Cities in the classic northern nations, such as Copenhagen and cities in Sweden, show the effect of the dominance of the welfare state and the longevity of the social-democrats in power. Countries with strong social welfare traditions maintain their bureaucratic and hierarchical forms of local politics. On the other hand, local leaderships in cities in France, Germany, Spain, England and Scotland, such as Montpelier, Hamburg, Barcelona, Manchester and Edinburgh, have transformed their city politics and fit the regime model well. One of the reasons for the difference in the coalitions is the state tradition. The pattern of transformation does not fit the north–south divide as entrepreneurial cities appear in the Mediterranean countries as elsewhere. Portuguese cities have sought to develop institutional capacity through building coalitions (Da Rosa Pires, 1994). Through a revolution of the planning system and rapid urbanization, the private sector has become more significant (de Seixas, 1999). Several cities in Spain have formed large-scale public–private partnerships to promote their image as boosters (Martinez, 1994). Areilza (1998) assesses Bilbao as a case of an emerging regime, using the John and Cole criteria. She finds that Bilbao is a large city, with high unemployment and an important private sector, though business is fragmented and withdrawn from local politics. Nevertheless, the city's government has fostered a pro-growth coalition. Likewise in Barcelona, the mid-1980s saw the emergence of a growth coalition, at first orientated around the projects for the Olympic Games (Garcia, 1991). More generally, Leontidou (1995) contrasts the local economic growth and policy successes in Spain in the 1990s with the weak progress of Greek cities. McGuick (1994) finds that the planning regime in

Dublin has gradually moved more in the interests of capital in line with the growth machine model.

Comparative research

The most comprehensive and sustained research on public–private coalitions in Western Europe has been conducted by Harding (1994c, 1996, 1997, 1999). Harding's work draws on the change in coalition politics in the UK of the early 1990s (Harding, 1994a). Whilst noting the differences between the UK and the USA because of the power of the UK state and the low incentives to create local growth coalitions because of the strict rules of English local government finance, Harding suggests that a form of growth coalition emerged in British cities. Rather than confine the analysis to the UK, Harding argues that Western European cities have seen the emergence of informal public–private partnerships based around production issues in response to economic competition. Harding seeks to re-fashion the moribund research on community power in UK cities by shifting the discussion away from power *over* – when a section of the elite accesses resources and makes policy choices in its own interest – toward power *to* – the ability of the elites to co-operate for the common good. This distinction is central to Stone's analysis and it adapts well to the Western European context of strong nation-states where local elites are starting to assert their power. Harding's research links to the work of other Western European local scholars, sometimes called neo-localists (for example Bagnasco and Le Galès, 1997; Le Galès, 1998a), who argue that cities are the new loci of power in the Western European polity whose fate is linked to the revival of local and regional economies.

Harding and his colleagues apply these ideas to cities in Europe. The research started with a comparative study financed by Directorate-General XVI. They carried out a study called 'Urbanization and the functions of cities in the European Community' (Parkinson et al., 1992). The group of researchers examined the possibility of economic renewal in Birmingham, Brussels, Amsterdam and Rotterdam (the old core); Frankfurt, Lyons, Milan and Montpelier in the new core; and Dublin and Seville on the periphery. They developed their ideas in the subsequent academic volume (Harding et al., 1994), arguing that cities are growing in importance and seeking to compete with each other. Decision-makers, the local elites, have responded to a common set of problems and constraints that push them to adopt the policies of the competitive city.

The focus on the politics of cities appears more strongly in Harding's project on coalition formation and urban redevelopment, funded by the UK Economic and Social Research Council, as part of its local governance initiative. Harding examined Manchester, Edinburgh, Copenhagen, Hamburg and Amsterdam (Harding, 1995, 1997). He concludes that these cities have been driven by a common logic even if tempered by national and local differences. Public and private sector elites became more concerned about the economy, worried about the fate of locally owned businesses, sought to promote policies to attract inward investment and fostered employment creation policies. Stronger public–private coalitions emerged at the time of the single European market initiative though they had their origins many years before. Harding stresses how the five cities formed informal networks to solve problems that seem to work best in the absence of formal institutions. Even chambers of commerce were not the best means for the private sector to express its interest and looser networks of business actors tended to be involved. Harding describes how the private and public sectors in cities have been able to co-operate and create imaginative policies.

Harding holds back from regarding Western European coalitions as the same as those in North America. The large public sector in these cities precludes a strong role for private enterprises. Municipal councils own much of the land in many cities, as in Amsterdam where 70 per cent of land is owned by the local authority. The development of social policies since the 1980s has been accompanied by fiscal centralization (Terhorst, 1999). As important are the national public agencies that have a major role in economic production in most Western European countries. National governments have promoted spatially specific local economic development programmes. The caution in Harding's work derives from a sceptical turn amongst Western European academics who believe that the trends toward entrepreneurialism are short-term and largely rhetorical (Peck and Tickell, 1994). Other authors are more scathing. Haughton and While (1999), taking the example of Leeds, regard the partnerships as nothing other than municipally inspired ideas that have little to do with the private sector. Such a view sits neatly with arguments that regime theory is a US import whose application distorts an understanding of Western European local politics. Analysts, such as Harding, need not be so cautious in setting out the research agenda as the existing findings are supportive of regime theory independent of national contexts. Whilst national institutions and policies and local conditions structure local regimes, there is no escaping the changed governance of Western European cities.

Conclusion

The US literature on local regimes helps scholars identify one of the central pillars of local governance: the emerging long-term public–private coalitions that are central to public decision-making in many Western European localities. The informal pattern of co-operation between the public and private sectors has always been important in local politics though it never gained much attention by academic researchers. The claim of this chapter is that economic competition and institutional reform have revitalized business–political relationships so that public–private partnerships have become an essential element of governance. Rather than US regimes emerging throughout local government systems, North American theory and research alerts us that the relationship between the public and private sector may constitute a strong link that affects most of local public policies in large cities. In the special context of large cities that seek to stay ahead or catch up in the economic race, the regime generates capacity to solve public problems. It fosters policies that assist economic development and seeks to balance competition with policies to promote social cohesion. Not that regimes are a nirvana of co-operation as local politics retains its factional character. Fights between the many public agencies are common and businesses retain their systematic power to shape public outcomes in their own interests. Most of all, the regime idea does not capture the ideological character of political conflict in Western European cities, with their histories of socialism, right-wing movements and the emerging agenda of green politics. Yet, even with these limitations, the regime idea uncovers much about the politics of localities that has hitherto been forgotten and points to the future.

This chapter shows that regimes are a central feature of local governance and they contain many of the key features of the new politics. They extend certain aspects of governance, such as the capacity to act and to plan in the long term. Their emergence across Western Europe breaks down some of the rigidity of the north–south pattern. But regimes do not define local governance – they are a sub-set of the wider political system. They are important and prominent features of the new politics, but researchers need to pay as much attention to the more prosaic politics of the European Union, regions and public management to see the whole picture.

4

The Europeanization of Sub-national Governance

The international dimension to local politics

The move from government to governance implies that local and international public affairs are more connected and interdependent than they were before. In the past, strong independent and sovereign states contained and regulated local political behaviour; now local political actors engage more with their counterparts elsewhere in Western Europe and seek to influence the decisions of supranational organizations. The influence of international organizations and ideas is one of the factors propelling the transition away from traditional local government. Chapter 3 sets out a similar argument for the economic sphere where the internationalization of the economy creates localities that are more in competition with each other. Whilst operating in parallel, the changes outlined in this chapter are more directly political and take different forms according to country and locality; moreover, they can either reinforce or counteract the economic forces at work across Europe.

Before the 1980s, the international dimension to local politics appeared to be the dullest aspect of local government and passed unnoticed even by local politics experts. There were two main activities. The first was the individual links between local governments, such as small towns in different countries; the twinning arrangements. The image is of locally elected leaders and their allies setting off for enjoyable, but largely meaningless trips to each other's municipalities as an addition to the calendar of municipal ceremonies. The second aspect of cross-national local politics was the activities of the international local government associations, such the Council for European Municipalities and Regions (CEMR). Each local government association has an international arm. For example, the Local Government International Bureau organizes European representation for English local authorities. Again the image is of international visits by senior local government politicians where resolutions of mutual congratulation dominate the agenda of meetings. The international appeared to be unimportant when compared to such matters as local government finance and the provision of services, and served only as an incentive for politicians to be involved in public affairs. These activities were probably much more meaningful than this caricature suggests. The transmission of ideas and practices often takes unexpected routes where chance and contingency play as much of a role as powerful political movements and ideologies (John, 1998a). Moreover, the more visible networks of today may have had their origins in more informal and less pressured times.

Nevertheless, the picture changes in the 1970s, affected by two important causes of the move from government to governance. The first is the familiar driver of economic competition between sub-national areas. The previous chapter shows how economic change and the perception of it shape the internal politics of local authorities and lead to the formation of local public–private coalitions. Yet there are long-term implications for international activities as the outward image of the city or region and its ability to access public and private resources become part of the competitive game. Working within the literature on federalism, Duchacek (1990) follows up these insights. He argues that that states engaged in diplomacy by setting up information offices in the capitals of nations to encourage trade and co-ordinate their delegations. Duchacek argues that these forms of parastatal diplomacy are far more significant than they might at first sight appear. Whereas their primary purpose was to act as trade delegations, they helped sub-national governments cross the traditional national barriers of political decision-making, an effect Duchacek calls the perforation of sovereignty. In a similar fashion Hocking (1993) claims that the breakdown of the dominance of the national elite over policy-making in Canada and the USA over trade and environmental matters occurred because of 'multi-layered diplomacy'. Both these writers iterate a familiar theme in the literature: local political decision-makers, when following their short-term economic interests, can re-invent their political roles. By engaging with transnational decision-makers, localities contribute to a political world that is more complex, changeable and interdependent than before. There is a complementary set of demands between the international level and those in the locality. International ideas and prerequisites drive local politics and local ideas move upwards to the international sphere. Guay (2000) investigates the growing involvement of local government in global politics. He reports a study of how legislation in Massachusetts interlinked with domestic and international politics.

The European Union

The second influence is different from the first, though it is complementary. The creation of the European Community, latterly called the European Union (EU), has affected sub-national politics. The EU appears to affect only relationships between nation-states in matters of policy that they cede to supranational institutions. But the creation of a policy-making body, with legal powers to override the decisions of nation-states, has profound implications for local politics. The development of a European polity has been slow, affecting only six states at first and was mainly confined to a few sectors, such as agriculture. Moreover, supranational bodies have relatively few responsibilities compared with those of nation-states. The EU, however, creates a different basis for the exercise of political power and authority. Formerly the apex of political systems was the nation-state, whose leaders could authoritatively resolve most political decisions; now many decisions lie elsewhere, in the institutional mechanisms of the EU which has responsibilities in specified policy sectors. Whilst nation-states still bargain over the final decision in the Council of Ministers, the European Parliament has powers in the co-decision procedure, the European Court of Justice resolves disputes and the Commission proposes legislation and is responsible for the implementation of EU decisions. Though the powers of these institutions are circumscribed by nation-states, which set the agenda and seek to control personnel within the Commission, the framework within which national power is exercised is different to that of international treaties. Nation-states have to negotiate with EU actors and they must follow the rules of voting in the Council of Ministers which makes policy choices and their implementation different from what they would have been had they been negotiated in other international bodies, such as the World Trade Organization. However, it is hard to map out the direction of change as many of these constitutional and institutional reforms are recent. There is a jostling of position between supranational and national institutions and the resulting balance of power will take some time to emerge.

The European Union and the role of sub-national government

The interaction between national and supranational power in the EU makes the role of sub-national governments particularly hard to divine. In formal political and legal relationships, the EU makes no observable difference to the role of local government in nation-states. Most European legislation is still in the form of directives, which pass through the European law-making process, but have to be implemented by nation-states in each of their law-making procedures, whether the UK parliaments or through the institutions of the German federal system. From the perspective of sub-national authorities, especially those in unitary or union states, such as France or the UK, there is no difference between responding to European activities and national legislation. European laws have the imprint of the national and/or state legislature. Public authorities may look to the courts to enforce a law. If local authorities are unhappy with a piece of legislation, their first point of contact is with their central government that has the power to make a new decision – albeit with the agreement of its European partners and EU institutions.

But if the European aspect of domestic politics is hidden from view, the balance of power has major substantive effects on the content and the operation of policies. EU policies often have different objectives from national ones as they have been argued for by Europe-wide institutions and groups; moreover, they have arisen from the deliberations of EU bodies. Implementation is by no means straightforward. Though European legislation is mainly implemented by national laws, an increasing amount is directly applicable into national law. Moreover, as has been shown by the *Fratelli* case in 1989, citizens may now appeal to their local courts to require the enforcement of directives by an 'emanation of the state', such as a local authority. Central or federal government does not enforce the law in these cases; local government and the local courts do. Sub-national authorities must search for European judgments to find the new laws they should follow. Local law officers find the numbers of judgments that affect local authorities daunting; but from the internationalization perspective, the effects are far-reaching in that the mechanisms for enforcement highlight the importance of local and regional governments and their direct relationships to the EU.

The mechanisms sub-national authorities use to influence European policies are different from those they deploy at the national level. Lobby groups, such as local authorities, cannot use tried and tested routes into the national legislature once a directive has passed into law as the typical response of the executive is to say that its hands are tied by European legislation. The classic example in the UK was when the local government associations sought to influence the provisions of the Environment Protection Act 1990 as it passed through the national legislature. The associations discovered to their shock that about 90 per cent of the bill implemented European directives. If a public authority wishes to influence European public policy, it needs to influence the national government at an early stage in the decision-making process, long before a directive reaches a decision. Lobbyists need to shape the thinking of the Commission directorates-general which have the task of proposing European legislation or using contacts in the European Parliament to influence the course of events. Commentators on the European policy process remark on the long process of agenda setting, which can make European policy hard to influence, but rewards expertise and networks within Brussels (Mazey and Richardson, 1993). The Europeanization of policy-making means that the range of influences upon local policy-making has expanded. Those who seek to affect European policy link with a much wider set of actors than before. They need to gather information and to make contacts in Brussels.

Constitutional reform

Europeanization changes the relationship between central and sub-national government. Rather than being bipolar, central–local relations become just one of the dyads between the three levels of government. The already dense networks that join levels of government within nation-states become even more complex as a result of Europeanization. The resulting pattern of decision-makiong is what some researchers call triadic governance (Ansell et al., 1997; Hull and Rhodes, 1977; John, 1996a; Mawson and Gibney, 1985; Rhodes et al., 1996). The increase in the number of possible relationships allows for more strategic interaction. Governance becomes more complex and the outcomes of political negotiations are hard to predict. Complexity defines the practice of governance in contrast to the more formalized relationships within nationalized intergovernmental communities.

Optimistic writers argue that the expansion of the responsibilities and powers of the EU could decentralize power and authority to local and regional governments (for example, Bogdanor, 1991). But European public policies can lead to centralization as central governments take more powers into their hands to implement directives, such as over red meat inspection and environmental regulation in the UK (John, 1996a). The loss of functions from central government to European institutions could lead central or federal bureaucrats and politicians to draw up functions from the sub-national level. Moreover, many of the alliances between the Commission and local and regional authorities, such as a partnership during a battle with a member state, may be short-term and instrumental. Once these reasons for these coalitions pass away, European-level actors may ally with other sorts of organization and may not need strong coalitions with local and regional public bodies. Triadic governance implies that European legislation creates new opportunities for all the actors involved, which may lead to different outcomes, some centralising and some decentralising, and depend on the bargaining strategies each deploys.

The extent to which the relationship between sub-national politics and the EU has affected intergovernmental relations and the practice of local policy-making is an empirical matter. The central part of this chapter summarizes the evidence to determine the extent of Europeanization and its character. But the argument also depends on wider theoretical and empirical issues (Hooghe, 1995b), which the chapter can discuss only briefly. There are two approaches. In the intergovernmentalist or realist position, the EU is a compact between nation-states and the way to understand policy-making is to comprehend bargaining between them (Hoffman, 1966; Moravscik, 1993, 1999). The power of nation-states to set the agenda extends to the decisions of European institutions that provide ideas and information to support the compact. In this view, local and regional authorities are part of the nation-states of Western Europe and do not have much impact on policy other than to advise. Their influence mainly occurs during the implementation of policies that nation-states anyway dominate. In the alternative view, what has been called neofunctionalism, European integration creates a new political system (Haas, 1958, 1964), which confers substantial autonomy on European political institutions to engage in entrepreneurial activities and creates links between European institutions and lobby groups, particularly between the Commission and sub-national authorities. Recent analysis of the EU as a political system revises and extends these neo-functionalist propositions (Hix, 1999).

The development of the EU

The historical context

One of the reasons sub-national government did not find the EU important was because the first thirty years of European integration concentrated on a few policy areas that were mainly the responsibilities of national or federal governments. It was not surprising that Hull and Rhodes (1977) conclude that European legislation has little impact on policy-making. The main areas of regulation were of minor importance, such as local authorities' role as an inspector and over trading standards, which were not key activities of local and regional governments. Although there was an active period in the 1960s, by the mid-1970s the European Community did not initiate many policies even though much research and planning were afoot.

The Commission renewed its energy in the 1980s. A strengthened coalition of member states, led by Germany and France, pioneered legislation in new fields, such as environmental policy. This period of activism culminated in the Single European Act 1986, which allowed majority voting in the Council of Ministers on certain issues. The European Community approved 282 measures to implement the single market, which were implemented by the end of 1992. The single market aimed to remove physical, technical and fiscal barriers to the European economy. Many of these measures affected local and regional governments, such as changes to planning regimes, vocational and professional training, local transport, the environment, trading standards, health and safety and consumer protection (Hart and Roberts, 1995). If the requirements to contract out public services are added to this list, no area of local and regional government escaped

European regulation (Baine et al., 1992; Bongers, 1992). With the growing amount of legislation, local authorities need to keep watch on European policy developments and it makes sense for them to seek to influence policy in these areas. Because of the activism of the Commission, policy becomes far more open to influence from actors other than nation-states. Policies from the Commission were often accompanied by pots of money in Community Initiatives, designed to interest local public and private authorities in the European project, to implement policies and to take the agenda forward.

The EU cannot impose a hierarchical relationship between it and the public and private bodies that implement its policies. Though the EU makes authoritative decisions over specified functions, in practice the Commission is weak and cannot impose its policies. Its bureaucracy is small (about 13,000 people, not that much bigger than a large local authority (for example, Leeds City Council employs 8,000 people); it cannot supervise the implementation of the directives that have different nuances in the fifteen member states. Whilst the Commission can bring infringement proceedings against states that refuse to implement EU decisions, it is usually reluctant to proceed in this fashion and prefers to gain a consensus. But working directly with public organizations in member states is crucial. Regional and local authorities often do not participate in the decision to introduce a policy, but they are faced with the task of implementing it. The Commission believes that collaboration with local and regional authorities is an effective way of incorporating the practical experience and expertise of levels below national governments into European policy-making. The strategy works to the political advantage of the Commission which seeks to extend the legitimacy of European-wide policies. By taking into account the views of elected governments that are not the direct emanations of nation-states, the Commission hopes to advance the European project and bypass national governments.

European funding

The main aspect of the EU that preoccupies local and regional governments is the disbursement of funds. Any public authority becomes alert if it can access pots of money, and for many this incentive is the main reason for engaging with European affairs. As well as regulating social and economic activities, the EU is a distributive body – it receives finance from national states through its share of Value Added Tax and then it sets out the distributive criteria for giving it back to them. It applies a formula and creates rules of eligibility and/or decisions made over their merits, though the latter are often delegated to national governments. Territorial units – whether nation-states, regions or municipalities – are particularly interested in distributive politics because small changes in the eligibility rules or a favourable lobby of the proximate Commission official can have large implications for a particular area with no overall extra cost to the programme – a zero sum game. The benefits can easily outweigh the costs, particularly if only a few local authorities engage in lobbying. Regional lobbying encourages 'rent seeking', whereby interest groups seek to create a monopoly of access to decision-makers and thereby benefit from public funds. These benefits can be 'competed away' if every public authority engages in lobbying, in which case the benefits do not exceed the costs, making it not so productive to engage in these activities. There may be a cyclical pattern whereby interest groups engage and then disengage from lobbying, which is not far from what has happened with the sub-national representation to the EU since the 1980s.

In the early years of the EU the main funds were for agricultural and social policy matters. Local authorities are particularly interested in the European Social Fund (ESF) because it can finance training programmes, which many seek to run. Unlike other programmes that restrict the applications for funds to designated areas, all public and private bodies may apply for ESF funds, which has attracted interest from local governments in more prosperous regions that are not normally eligible for regional funds. Local governments in rural areas have also applied to the Agricultural Guidance Fund. The territorial dimension appears in aspects of agricultural policy; however, it was not until the creation of the European Regional Development Fund (ERDF) in 1975 that the EU began a concerted programme of funding with regional objectives and set up a directorate-general, DG XVI. Progress was at first slow, as the ERDF was mainly a mechanism to redistribute budget surpluses and deficits across the EU, and until 1984 about 94 per cent of the total was allocated according to national quotas. National governments used it to support their regional policies.

The regional policy agenda rapidly changed with the adoption of the Single Market initiative in 1986 (Hooghe, 1996a, 1996b). The Commission predicted that the single market would increase growth of the European economy, but that the benefits would be concentrated in the inner core – Germany, East France, North Italy and South-East England (Cecchini et al., 1988). In the act and in subsequent European policy statements, the Commission embarked on a policy to enhance 'economic and social cohesion', which was especially important as it appeared that some parts of Europe – Spain, Portugal and Greece – would be adversely affected by economic integration. The co-operation of these member states was needed to get the single market reforms through, so the larger countries bought them off in a large side payment (Hooghe, 1996b: 97). Spain vetoed the European Community budget in 1988, and agreed to support it only when decision-makers agreed to expand the structural funds massively (Morata and Muñoz, 1996: 195). As a consequence, in what was called the Delors package, the EU doubled the regional policy expenditure, the structural funds, between 1987 to 1993.

As important for sub-national governments were the reforms of the funds which accompanied the massive increases. The Commission periodically proposes reviews of the rules allocating the structural funds. In the reform of 1984 it sought to improve co-ordination and the definition of the tasks of the ERDF. It wished to concentrate the funds, to adopt a programme approach and to require that policies are genuinely additional to national expenditure. The main reform was in 1988, when the EU both decentralized the administration of the funds to nation-states and refined the principles that guide their administration, which included partnership with the public and private authorities, such as local and regional authorities. The regulation required close co-operation in the partnership, reflecting the Commission's concern that there should be full involvement of public authorities in the administration, preparation, financing and evaluation of the funds. The emphasis on the governance of the funds was a change in approach. The reformers rejected the old top-down ideas of the 1970s and 1980s, with their emphasis on physical regeneration projects. Instead, the Commission encouraged more flexible and dynamic forms of policies targeted toward economic renewal. Though national governments have the responsibility for making the final decisions on the allocation and monitoring of the funds, they are in a partnership with sub-national and other bodies that deliver the projects, a practice that could, in theory, contribute to a more open form of local politics. Whether these arrangements mean nothing more than the paper they are written on will be discussed later in the chapter. In addition, the Commission tried to reduce bargaining between nation-states by introducing more technical criteria to govern the allocation of the funds. The effect was not to eliminate bargaining as the rules were often breached, but it gave sub-national authorities the opportunity to make arguments about the eligibility rules in their lobbying exercises. In the late 1990s the structural funds continued to grow in real terms and as a proportion of the EU budget. They increased to 157bn Ecu in 1995 prices for the 1994–9 period, rising from 17.5 per cent of the budget in 1998 to 36 per cent in 1999. The EU created the cohesion fund in the Maastricht Treaty of 1992 (TEU), which benefited small countries such as Portugal and Greece. In 1999 the Commission reviewed the structural funds for the period 2000–2006. In the reform the EU simplified the funds' objectives to three and targeted them more to central Europe.

Writing on Europeanization tends to be obsessed with the ERDF, partly because of the vast size of the budget. But other funds are as important because they allow for more entrepreneurial behaviour on the part of sub-national authorities even though the sums of money are not as large as the ERDF. Community Initiatives are measures proposed by the Commission to help resolve problems of special EU interest, and they took up about 9 per cent of the structural funds. In 1989, at the same time as agreeing the expansion of the ERDF, the EU decided to allocate 3.8bn Ecu to Community Initiatives. These are also pilot projects that take up about 1 per cent of the structural funds budget. Initiatives are proposed by the Commission and then have to be approved by the Council of Ministers. But the European Parliament has successfully proposed some, such as KONVER, to help areas affected by the rundown of the defence industry. Once the initiatives have been decided, the Commission has the discretion to allocate the individual projects, effectively by-passing nation-states. But applicants need to find at least 50 per cent of the funds from other sources than the EU if they are to be successful – what is called the match funds. For many public sector projects, central government is the only realistic provider, which gives it the capacity to decide the projects.

Subsidiarity and representation

The EU also affects the constitutional position of sub-national government, though not as dramatically as some advocates of decentralization suppose. Before the Maastricht Treaty sub-national government had no legal existence other than as an interest operating under the legal authority of member states. Local authorities and regions were just like any other European interest group. The exception was the requirement for partnership, as acknowledged in the structural funds regulations from 1988. Though this legal definition translates into political practice, it is a long way from the kind of recognition that exists for the other political bodies below the level of the EU, the member states. It appears that the doctrine of subsidiarity offers a constitutional recognition for sub-national government. Subsidiarity is a principle of EU governance that states a public activity should be regulated by the appropriate territorial level of government. Member states agreed a definition at the Treaty on European Union, and refined it at subsequent council meetings. It seems that the doctrine gives a right to sub-national authorities to administer European functions and implies a reasonable degree of autonomy with some legal force. But the definitions in the protocol at the Edinburgh summit and in the European Commission's clarification show that subsidiarity means that national regulation is the norm and European regulation needs explicit justification. There is no mention of the roles of regional and local authorities.

A more promising development for local and regional governments has been the creation of institutions that formalize representation and deliberate on EU policy matters. In 1988 the Commission created the Consultative Council of Regional and Local Authorities, which had a right to be consulted on regional policy. It had 42 members who were nominated by the Assembly of European Regions, the International Union of Local Authorities and the Council of Communes and Regions of Europe. After much lobbying at the Maastricht intergovernmental conference, particularly by the German *Länder*, the EU agreed to set up the Committee of the Regions, a body that has the right to be consulted. It replaces the consultative council and is composed of representatives from local and regional authorities across Europe. Whilst the Committee of the Regions gives local and regional authorities a toe-hold into the European policy process and has symbolic value, it is not an institution of the EU and has no role to limit or amend

European legislation and budgets. The chapter discusses later whether it has managed to forge an effective and entrepreneurial role.

Perspectives on Europeanization

The new pluralism

In the views of many observers the impact of the EU is not just an amalgam of policy responses and short-term strategies to obtain extra public funds. Rather, European-level institutions and policies transfer ideas and working practices in a manner that moves local decision-making away from national and hierarchical forms of politics toward more negotiated and interdependent practices that blur the impact of tiers of government and involve a wide range of interest groups (Benington, 1994; Benington and Harvey, 1994; Goldsmith, 1993; John, 1994b). Goldsmith (1993) argues that Europeanization closely links to economic interdependence, which drives sub-national authorities into closer relationships with each other and the EU. Benington contends that Europeanization means greater pluralism in power relationships and the emergence of a less institutionalized context: 'The emerging pattern of European policy-making often seems to involve a pluralistic melting pot of public, private, voluntary and community organizations and interest groups, drawn together in issue based rather than institution based policy arenas' (1994: 33). European regulation creates uncertainty and unexpected possibilities for participation in coalitions. Above all, Europeanization is about the politics of networks that erode the existing pattern of government in tiers, creating a form of governance based on interlocking spheres of influence. The effect is a 'paradigm shift' in the nature of representation and participation. Benington recognizes this pattern already exists in other local political systems in Europe, but he suggests that even they are being transformed, in particular by the learning capabilities and lobbying of transnational networks composed of many sorts of public and private authorities which are concerned to lobby and exchange information. These learning and lobbying networks, Benington argues, are necessary in the context of the single European market as many local and regional authorities need to develop strategies to respond to the economic disruption caused by concentration of wealth and activity in Europe's central core. Benington presents an optimistic picture of the political relationships. He has an almost chiliastic vision as there is little that stands in the way of the coming revolution. Whilst his approach is consistent with the governance perspective, he uses terms such as pluralism uncritically. Even though influential writers have seen the EU's politics as more open than at the national level (Mazey and Richardson, 1993; Streek and Schmitter, 1991) and even pluralism has revived in popularity in the 1980s, it is hard to accept the proposal for more pluralism without at least some critical awareness of agenda setting and the power of EU institutions.

The ladder of Europeanization

John (1994b) provides another Europeanization perspective through his examination of local government management and internal structures. John suggests that Europeanization is a stepped set of activities with sub-national and regional authorities gradually ascending a ladder (see Figure 4.1). He divides the steps into stages that reflect the degree of choice local public bodies have over their activities. The more action the local authority undertakes, the greater the interplay with European ideas and practices and the higher they ascend the ladder. Some of these activities, such as responding to regulations, are compulsory and so are minimal in character (steps A–C); others are associated with the search for European funding, reflecting the financially orientated local authority (steps A–E). The next stage of networking (steps A–G), although closely associated with obtaining finance, can involve more exchanges of ideas. However, it is only when councils start to incorporate European ideas into their policies that they reach the final, fully Europeanized stage (steps A–I) (Figure 4.1).

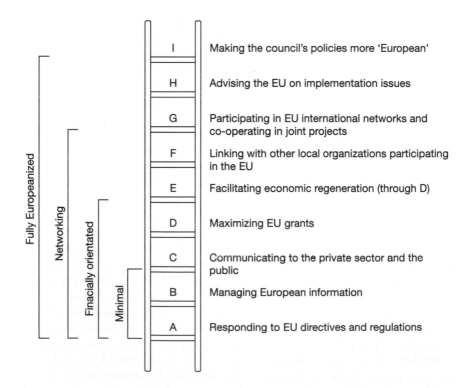

FIGURE 4.1 *The European function (John, 1994b)*

John's ladder contains much that is familiar in the discussion about Europeanization, such as the focus on partnerships and on networking discussed by Benington. What is new is the final stage. He argues there is a more fundamental transformation that goes beyond short-term instrumental behaviour whereby local policy-making becomes an aspect of EU politics. European ideas and practices transfer to the core of local decision-making as well as from local policy-making arenas to the supranational level. The European function is a means whereby public authorities can innovate and initiate policies and programmes in the context of transnational co-operation and EU policy-making.

John's scheme contains many similarities, with the more general literature on the Europeanization of public decision-making (Harmsen, 1999; Ladrech, 1994; Mény et al., 1996), which covers mainly national policies, such as on tax (Radaelli, 1997), and examines state autonomy in industrial (Kassim and Menon, 1996) and social policies (Hine and Kassim, 1998). There is also work on the Europeanization of regional governance (Benz and Eberlein, 1999; Thielemann, 1999). The emerging body of research seeks to find out the extent to which domestic policy choices have been constrained and shaped by European policy.

Multi-level governance

The other perspective about the role of sub-national politics in the EU is called multi-level or multi-layered governance (Hooghe, 1996a, 1996b; Marks, 1992, 1993; Scharpf, 1998). As with the triadic and the Europeanization perspectives, it starts from the presence of three levels of political organization in the EU – the European, the national and the local – suggesting that the interaction between them constitutes a new form of politics. Research using the multi-level governance framework discusses the possible emergence of the 'third level' (sub-national) in European politics (Bullmann, 1996; Jeffery, 1996a). Unlike the two earlier perspectives, there is much restraint in the use of multi-level governance, which is a deliberate reaction against the rhetoric of the 'Europe of regions'. Some regions adopted the slogan and it was for a short time advocated by the Commission, especially by its former president, Jacques Delors. A 'Europe of regions' implies that national institutions and powers will weaken under the growing power of the European state and that regions and cities will take their place in the sun as legitimate Europeanized political bodies with direct access to the European policy-makers. Instead, the multi-level governance approach acknowledges the changes in Western European governance without assuming that nation-states are going to decline in importance. Proponents examine the importance of the policy networks between the levels, suggesting that complex interdependencies and exchanges between the actors constrain the exercise of power. The main proponent is Marks (1992, 1993), who argues that the growing activity of regional and local policy-making occurs away from the negotiations over treaties. Sub-national bodies influence the EU political process through their everyday interactions with other levels of government, their role as a conduit of information on EU affairs and their responsibility for implementing EU policies. They have influence because the everyday work of the EU rather than grand events helps form institutions. Marks defines multi-level governance as 'a system of continuous negotiation among nested govern-ments at several territorial tiers – supranational, national, regional, and local – as a result of the broad process of institutional creation and decisional reallocation that has pulled some previously centralized functions of the state up to the supranational level and some down to the local/regional level' (Marks, 1993: 392). He regards the dispersion of power to sub-national decision-makers as irreversible because they have become part of the European governing system. He examines European regional policies to support his case.

Not all accounts of European policy assume the growing influence of sub-national government. Drawing on realist accounts of international relations, some writers argue that the nation-state remains dominant over both policy formation and implementation. What affects the autonomy of sub-national authorities is the predominant and legitimate role of national governments in the implementation of EU policies. Anderson (1990) argues that national governments act as 'gatekeepers' on European public policy, particularly over decisions concerning the implementation of programmes within the ERDF. National governments have the say over which public or private body gets the funds. Whilst sub-national governments are not powerless when faced with central government decisions, European policy outcomes tend to reflect the pre-existing balance of power in central–local policy networks. Bache (1998, 1999) elaborates this framework with his terms of 'flexible gatekeeping' and 'the extended gatekeeper' whereby sub-national actors participate in but do not affect EU programmes as they are mainly under the control of the nation-state.

The comparative context

Institutional differences

There is no shortage of perspectives about the effects of Europeanization; but much less comparative research exists, especially studies comparing the differences between sub-national governments. An understanding of the contrasts is essential because different sorts of institutions administer EU policies depending on the territorial distribution of functions within a nation-state, even though the EU assumes a level playing field across Europe when formulating its policies. In some countries, such as France, the field offices of central government departments have the main responsibility for implementing EU policies; in others, such as in the United Kingdom, much falls to local authorities. Local and regional authorities with few EU responsibilities have less incentive to lobby as they are less affected by supranational policies. Not only does the formal division of powers vary in each nation-state, but so do the rules, norms and institutions. As would be indicated by a new institutionalist approach (for example, Thielemann, 1999), European regulation and programmes are processed in different ways according to national contexts. The other difference is between levels of economic development. Regions adversely affected by European economic integration have more of an incentive to become Europeanized than prosperous ones.

The most important institutional difference is between federal and other states as regions or states in the former share powers to decide EU policy whereas national governments elsewhere may decide European policy issues without reference to the wishes of sub-national authorities. It would be expected that Europeanization shifts the balance of power between states and the federal level because EU membership is a major constitutional change. It consolidates or reinforces existing relationships in non-federal states because the EU vests ultimate responsibility for implementation at the national level. The division between types of constitutions is an over-simplification because there are few classic unitary states. The United Kingdom was a union rather than a unitary state in that it formally and informally divided powers between the constituent nations of the Union. Since 1997 the fiction of indivisible executive power has been virtually abandoned with the devolution of power to the Scottish Parliament, Welsh Assembly and Northern Irish executive. Whilst the UK parliament is sovereign in theory, in practice the British state has ceded powers. Nor are federal states uniform. Some reserve the most important powers to the national level; others, such as Belgium, decentralize extensively. Never-theless, the distinction between federal and other states has implications for the impact of Europeanization.

Europeanization in federal countries

A literature has emerged on the effects of European politics and legislation on the operation of the German federation (for example, Benz, 1998; Burgess and Gress, 1991; Goetz, 1995; Jeffery, 1996a; Malanczuk, 1985). The German constitution reserves external relations to the federal government, which means that, as a result of EU membership, it represents and parti-cipates in matters exclusively reserved to the states, such as in education and issues relating to the media. Rather than leading to a crisis of the federation, however, the co-operative principles that govern intergovern-mental relations have informed a series of institutional reforms to ensure the participation of the states in European affairs. In 1992 Germany changed its constitution to provide for the participation of the *Länder* in the co-ordination of EU representation, effectively giving the states a right of veto on European matters. Germany successfully influenced the treaty negotiations at Maastricht to ensure that delegates of the *Länder* could sit alongside national representatives at council of ministers' meetings (Article 146 of the treaty). The *Länder* also lobbied for the Committee of the Regions to be another forum for the articulation of their interests, though they have been disappointed by its performance (see below). The federal and state governments share responsibilities for European affairs and some activities have been devolved, such as the administration of the structural funds (see below), which varies across Germany. The German federal system has adapted rather than been restructured by the constitutional challenge of European integration (Benz, 1998), though not without some heated conflicts between the Commission and the *Länder* over the implementation of European policy, such as state aid to industry (see Thielemann, 1999).

Similar constitutional adaptation has occurred in Belgium. Europe has propelled the decentralization and federalization of the country. The constitutional impact of the EU has been less marked in quasi-federal Spain (Molina, 2000). However, Europeanization has centralized decision-making. Also with the system of asymmetric federalism regions have different sets of powers. The regions have not been able to mobilise so strongly to retain their powers or to share in national decision-making, though a co-ordination committee established in 1988 discusses European policy issues.

Constitutional change in the UK

There has been much less constitutional impact of the EU in other countries. The changes have occurred far more incrementally in the implementation of policy, but constitutional issues are not far from the surface. For example, the ratification of the Maastricht Treaty in 1992 led to a constitutional debate in the UK. The government proposed that the wording of the Maastricht Treaty permitted the government to nominate representatives for the newly created Committee of the Regions who need not be from sub-national government. Surprisingly, on 4 May 1993 Parliament defeated the government on a vote in the House of Commons to amend the legislation introducing the treaty and required the selection of locally elected representatives.

Constitutional issues are not far from the surface over Scottish and Welsh devolution. Whilst the parliament and assembly are still subsumed under UK representation, the Treaty of European Union allows regions to be represented alongside national ministers in the Council of Ministers. So far this facility has not generated a cross-European demand, with only Belgium and Germany using it. Even before devolution, some Scottish ministers, such as for fishing, went to the council, but this was under the umbrella of the UK. However, it is likely that the Scottish and Welsh governments will seek to have their own representation as they become more experienced and self-confident. The main influence is at the sub-national level through the Europeanization of policies and organizations, the administration of the structure funds and representation in Brussels. The chapter now turns to these issues.

The Europeanization of policies and organizations

The Eurolog survey

Most research on Europeanization is based on evidence from one country and is not systematically comparative. The one explicit study was led by Goldsmith and Klausen (1997), who pioneered the *Eurolog* survey carried out by a team of researchers using the Europeanization perspective. The team sought to find out about sub-national governments' attitudes toward EU integration, with reference to the institutional environment, administrative capacity, and organizational and institutional developments. Whilst the results from the survey were incomplete, the authors have enough information to draw firm conclusions about the contrasts across Europe. Their findings show that local and regional authorities have increased their involvement with the EU, but that the response has been patchy. They develop a four-fold classification of responses – counteractive, passive, reactive and proactive – to categorise the authorities, which is similar to John's (1994b) ladder. They find that most authorities are passive, suggesting that the impact of the EU is at best patchy or limited to a few active local governments. They are the 'bright stars' that exist among the many 'black holes' of responses to European integration (Balme and Le Galès, 1997). Dynamic local administrations, such as in Milan, Manchester, Birmingham and Barcelona, and some regional governments, such as Nord-Pas de Calais or North Rhine–Westphalia, have stronger relationships with European institutions which have been driven by politicians committed to the ideal of political integration. The incentive is political since some cities and regions wish to place themselves in European policy-making circles. For this purpose they set up European units in their organizations, appointed specialized staff and opened offices in Brussels. These pioneering local and regional governments led the integration process from below. The research qualifies the idea that European policy and ideas transform the whole of sub-national government. The partial influence they describe is consistent with other evidence and common sense. It would be surprising if all local and regional governments across Europe raised the European flag on top of their council chambers. Yet the response to the EU is consistent with the definition of governance outlined in Chapter 1. The move to governance implies more variation in sub-national systems than before. The question that remains is whether there are enough stars to illuminate the galaxy.

Variations in Europeanization

Goldsmith and Klausen stress the common sub-national responses to European integration because their categorisations apply irrespective of the system being studied. The way Europeanization gives incentives to some authorities and not to others is cross-national and is not structured by such divisions as between northern and southern Europe. Nevertheless, they find clusters of countries. In Germany, France, Spain and to some extent Britain, municipalities regard the EU as a means to bypass their central or federal governments whereas there is less political imperative in other systems. Though this division crosses the north–south divide, some of the more traditional patterns reassert themselves on other dimensions. Professionalized and bureaucratized local authorities in the northern group tend to have a bureaucratic response to European policy, as in Denmark, Norway, Sweden and the Netherlands. Successful routine administration of EU matters exists, but there is little entrepreneurial action. The Netherlands is more engaged than the others as initiatives exist in the border regions and about a third of authorities are in the 'active' category (Wolters, 1997). Whilst involvement is growing, it is limited to concern with the structural funds (Boeckhout et al., 1996). Nordic and Danish local authorities tend to respond when there is the political will. Most of the reaction in Denmark is from local authorities in and around Copenhagen and in the Western part of the country (Klausen, 1997: 28). Norway, on the other hand, which is outside the EU, is not active on European matters, which reflects the parochialism of some Norwegian localities (von Bergmann-Winberg, 1997), though Holm-Hansen (2000) discusses the role of some local authorities in European networks such as RECITE and INTERREG. In Germany, as in much sub-national matters, there is a great deal of variation. Some of the *Länder* are active. So too are the *Kreise* in the border regions when they administer cross-national European programmes (Wollmann and Lund, 1997). Without a direct financial incentive, there is little interest from sub-national authorities.

As in other analyses of comparative central–local relations, Britain and Ireland are odd cases in the northern group. Ireland is highly centralized. Local governments only perform a limited set of functions and so are not greatly affected by European policies (Coyle, 1997). The country is one region, so the regional authority becomes the nation-state. Central government runs most things related to Europe. In the UK, the centralization of the 1980s produced many initiatives and a great deal of networking amongst local authorities though with little involvement of the private sector (Goldsmith and Sperling, 1997). Ironically, the centralization of the 1980s under the Conservative government produced a counteractive Europeanization as local authorities sought a new role and engaged with more sympathetic political actors at the supranational level (John, 1996b). The devolution of power in Scotland and Wales since 1997 was partly assisted by the way in which regionalist/nationalist parties played the European card (John, 1999).

The tradition of professionalism amongst local authorities produced an effective organizational response with specialized European units and the emergence of a cadre of European officers. In 1992 the Local Government Management Board found that 43 per cent of local authorities had a European liaison officer in post (Mills, 1994). In 1996 about three-quarters of authorities had allocated formal responsibility for European issues to one or more specialist officers (Martin and Pearce, 1999). Nevertheless, local authorities vary in their responses. The leading ones, such as Birmingham, Manchester and Kent, which first became Europeanized, are still ahead of the field. Others lag behind along a continuum where the end point is complete inactivity. Martin (1998) gives an sceptical interpretation. His team's research shows that local authorities tend to be dominated by central government agendas. Their piecemeal and instrumental approach to European affairs reflects their dependent status rather than a broadening Europeanization. At best local authorities seek to be well informed on European matters, but do not have much capacity to influence policy (Martin and Pearce, 1999).

The Goldsmith and Klausen (1997) team find there are contrasts between active and passive local authorities in the south of Europe, though this pattern does not distinguish these countries from others. The legacy of clientelism in Portugal makes it hard for local government to engage with Europe, though there are signs of change in response to the progress of democratization, where some of the more dynamic municipalities have taken advantage of the opportunities (Da Silva et al., 1997). Italy has a weak response, which is surprising given the high degree of elite and mass support for European integration; but the history of centralization, a traditional bureaucracy – at both central and local levels – weak local government finance, party influence in the administration and a low level of training of local government personnel impede an effective response, except in a few dynamic regions and cities (Ercole, 1997). Nevertheless, there has been some response from Italian cities, such as Naples, which have used European programmes to modernize their local policy-making framework, such as in planning (Nanetti, 1999). France experiences high activity from the regions and a strong variation between the communes (Balme and Le Galès, 1997). There are some notable Europeanized local administrations, which are often based on the regional capitals, but many medium-sized cities facing economic problems do not have the resources to invest in European liaison. One astonishing result is the lack of interest and knowledge about European affairs in Belgium, showing that proximity to Brussels has no impact on Europeanization in that country (de Rynck, 1997). What is striking about this collection of studies is how the north–south dichotomy does not account for Europeanization. Local and regional authorities vary in the way they respond to the EU.

European programme partnerships

Interpretations of partnerships

Researchers regard the formal and informal partnerships between central and sub-national governments over the formulation and implementation of EU funded programmes and projects, such as over the ERDF, as key tests of the implications of Europeanization and multi-level governance theses. The Commission pushed through reforms that require central government to consult with local and regional authorities. Before 1984, as Hooghe (1996a: v) writes, 'the European Commission wrote a cheque, and each national government largely decided whether to involve sub-national authorities in designing and implementing projects'. The EU has required central governments to consult with public and private organizations over their regional development plans since 1988. But central governments usually decide projects and implement them. The detailed contract in each region, the Community Support Framework (CSF), is decided in negotiations between the Commission and the member state. Local authorities play a greater role in the next stage, the negotiations for the Operational Programmes, which detail the specific projects because the EU needs information about the programmes and seeks to make its programmes more legitimate (Marks, 1996a: 404). Finally, the EU requires local authorities to be consulted over the implementation and monitoring of the Operational Programmes.

The literature presents subtly different accounts. Anderson (1990) argues that partnerships should be understood only in national contexts, but Marks makes the reforms a key part of his argument. Both authors present evidence. Anderson uses two case studies, from Germany and the West Midlands in the UK. In the UK local authorities were largely passive, allowing the central state organizations to lead, to formulate the projects and to make sure the UK took up its share of European funds. Anderson notes the dominance of the federal government in Germany; yet his cases of North-West Rhineland and Saarland and some local authorities started to lobby Brussels directly and were able to access non-quota European funds, a finding supported by Conzelmann's (1995) study of North Rhine–Westphalia. The main difference between the countries derived from their institutions: German sub-national authorities had more independence in the sub-national system than those in the UK. Anderson observes little change in ideas and the norms of the policy-makers. He shows how actors seek to maximize the benefit to them from Europe within the limited room for manoeuvre they possess. Marks (1992) examines the reforms of the funds, arguing that even in Britain where the central government resisted the 1988 reforms, local authorities are able to represent their interests in the partnerships: 'once policy networks linking sub-national governments to the EC have been created, there is no certainty that they can be dominated by national government' (1992: 217). Marks (1993) reports how Commission officials visit the regions and actively mobilize input from local government administrators. He implies that the large bi-annual partnership meetings are the place where there is full consultation (Marks, 1993: 396–397). The implication is that even though central governments control the funds, they are involved in full and effective partnerships over their administration. Marks argues that the concept of partnerships may become a guiding principle of EU politics, ensuring that territorial interests participate in policy-making.

The UK and Ireland

For more centralized states, like the UK, research cannot sustain the idea that the partnership regulations involve the full participation of local and regional authorities. Even Marks realizes that partnership practice is shallow in France and the UK (Marks, 1996a: 406). There is little collaboration in the early stages, and Whitehall maintains its grip even in the monitoring stage (Bomberg and Peterson, 1996: 25). For example, central government often prevented local authorities from appointing their own representatives to the monitoring committees. Even within the nation-state there is much variation and most studies conclude that the Scottish Office had good relationships with the EU before devolution (Bache et al., 1996). Some studies found that the Commission has been able to shape the programmes, particularly by encouraging alliances between local authorities, such as over the creation of regional strategies (Burch and Holiday, 1993; Conzelmann, 1995; McCarthy and Burch 1994; Martin, 1998), as occurred in the North-West of England.

Other countries also have a centralized experience of partnerships just like the UK. Laffan (1996) describes how the Irish central government tightly controlled the administration of the funds before 1988. Subsequently it incorporated local authorities into a working and an advisory group, but largely maintained its 'gatekeeper' role. Other small countries, such as Greece (Ioakimidis, 1996), have a similar pattern, though again sub-national actors mobilize in response to the procedures of the Commission.

France

France has a centralized approach. The administration of the ERDF falls to the regional planning agency, the DATAR (Délégation à l'Aménagement du Territoire et à l'Action Régionale), with more detailed implementation matters handled by the regional prefectures. In addition to their role in the partnerships, local communes shape the policies through the informal influence of the leading mayors. The organizational provisions of the 1988 reforms were implemented by the contractual rules that the French state introduced to govern the relationships between central and local public authorities. European funding enhances the role of the central state, which takes on the gatekeeper role and creates more complex networks whilst leaving the elected regions weak (Balme, 1995; Balme and Jouve, 1996). Few networks emerge just to handle the structural funds. As Conzelman's (1995) case study of the Nord-Pas de Calais shows, the DATAR and state agencies remain as the key decision-makers. Not all accounts of sub-national relationships take such a negative view. Smith (1995) finds there are variations according to region as some are more active and innovative than others, a finding that follows Balme and Le Galès' (1997) stars and holes metaphor. Smith (1998) argues that researchers need to understand the conditions when Europeanization sometimes increases the autonomy of sub-national actors and at other times does not.

Belgium

More dramatic effects occur in countries that divide powers between the centre and locality. However, it is hard to disentangle the changes arising from European rules on partnership from more general shifts in inter-governmental relationships. For example, responsibility for regional policies in Belgium has been delegated to the regional level since 1980. In 1989 and 1993 the Belgian state gave most national powers to the regions (Hooghe, 1995a). Regional partnerships and direct Commission involvement flowed from the decentralization of power. The most that can be said is that the reforms of the funds strengthened regional autonomy as Commission officials used their contacts with decision-makers to influence the course of events (de Rynck, 1996). The gatekeeper role falls to the regional governments themselves, which have considerable autonomy in the manner in which they include their sub-national actors. The unit of analysis drops to the region, which becomes equivalent to the nation-state in this case. Sub-regional actors seek access to regional decisions in a similar manner to the way that regions lobby the central government in other countries.

Germany

There are clearer effects of the reforms of the funds in Germany, though the unification of East and West makes a conclusive judgement harder to make than before. Nevertheless, researchers agree there was a gradual shift in responsibility for decision-making from the federal state to the *Länder* in response to the reforms of the structural funds in 1984 and then in 1988 (Anderson, 1996). Whereas the central state received and allocated European funds, the arrangements meant that the sub-national authorities became involved in the preparations of CSF and in the monitoring committees. Inclusion was easy because the sub-national authorities were already involved in interlocking co-operative arrangements over regional policy matters, so that they had the expertise and contacts to participate effectively. Anderson (1996) concludes there was little change in central–local relationships despite these responses to the legislation. Bonn retained much control after unification since the new *Länder* lacked administrative capacity. However, the designation of the former GDR as an objective one region allowed formerly excluded state and federal actors access to the decision-making process. As with Europeanization more generally, some regions become important, such as North Rhine-Westphalia, which became influential in the design of its structural plan (Conzelman, 1995). As elsewhere in Western Europe, the results of EU regulation have been complex. Whilst the balance of power remains more or less as before, there have been subtle re-orientations within the policy networks.

Spain and Italy

Spanish regions already played a role in European funding through their involvement in the first Spanish regional development programme; but the 1988 reforms increased their direct participation (Morata and Muñoz, 1996). The requirement for monitoring and evaluation spawned a complex set of committees, mainly involving the regional authorities rather than the social partners and local authorities. The monitoring committees tended to be large and cumbersome, as in other countries; the participation of locally elected representatives was limited. The government's refusal to have a single CSF for each region also restricted the activities of the autonomous communities. Though the regions can influence the programmes in objective 1 and 2 areas, their influence is limited by their dependence on the central government for funds (Held and Velasco, 1996). The emerging federal Spanish state has not been transformed by European rules on partnership. A similar pattern exists in Italy, where, despite a rhetorical commitment to the values of the EU, central government maintains control over decision-making (Grote, 1996). The regions have nevertheless gained some access to the policy-making process as they have developed more capacity to formulate European projects and non-state actors, such as private firms, have been drawn into decision-making, mainly into informal networks, and researchers regard Emilia–Romagna as an example of the development of dynamic public and private networks based on EU programmes (Bonaduce and Magnatti, 1996; Leonardi and Nanetti, 1990). Garmise (1995), using the example of Prato, Tuscany, shows how the EU has allowed partnerships to stabilize. The decentralization of the Italian state in the 1990s complements this trend.

Summing-up the European partnerships

Taking the countries together, and dividing partnership into the four stages of: 1) regional development plans; 2) formal contracts, the Community

Support Frameworks (CSFs); 3) Operational Programmes and; 4) implementation and monitoring. Marks (1996) argues that regional governments are influential at the start of the sequence but much less at the end and that the countries vary significantly. In part these variations reflect the balance of power, the constitutional arrangements and the allocations of functions and finance between the tiers of government in each nation-state; but they also depend much on political factors. An example is the Flemish province of Limberg, where the Christian Democrat government was resisted by the socialists at the regional level.

Partnership is but one element of the participation of sub-national authorities in the European project. Given the patchy experience, it is not the arena where influential practices and behaviours are likely to emerge. The implementation of the reforms of 1988 has not increased the participation of sub-national governments in European public policy as their involvement tends to replicate the existing relationships between central and local political institutions. When taken with small coverage of EU programmes – about 40 per cent of the population of member states – their effect on sub-national government as a whole is probably limited. Nevertheless, as the many examples across Western Europe show, national governments are not just gatekeepers and constructive relationships emerge when the Commission becomes directly involved with local and regional authorities. As Smith (1998) discusses, sub-national authorities need to take the initiative.

Lobbying the EU

The litmus test of the Europeanization and the multi-level governance theses is whether local and sub-national authorities have mobilized to influence European public policy. There are two necessary steps in the argument. First, sub-national government needs to be organized and active to be internationalized; but, second, local preferences ought to be incorporated into the European policy process. If only a few local authorities lobbied Brussels, then the term Europeanization would not capture the overall experience of sub-national government. Moreover, if the activities of local authorities in their associations, offices and campaigns are only symbolic, then the claim that a new form of politics has emerged would be unfounded. The academic literature (for example, Marks 1992) often notes the expansion of territorial representation, but does not assess its impact, and thus does not conclusively show that a system of multi-level governance has emerged.

Research should review the extent to which lobbying occurs, note the comparative differences and seek to evaluate its effects. The first two objectives are straightforward as it is relatively easy to ascertain the amount of effort sub-national governments put into European policy matters. The difficult objective to evaluate is the third because organizational and group influences on policy-making are notoriously hard to research. The presence of interest groups in the arenas of decision-making do not necessarily show their impact on policy outputs and outcomes (John, 1994c). Moreover, as Salisbury (1990) comments, a growth in the activity and number of interest groups may reveal a decline in their influence as they may jostle for position rather than monopolize public decision-makers. Finally, studies of the impact of interest groups need to examine the influence of those who are being influenced. As Christiansen and Dowding's (1994) study of UK central government departments shows, policy-makers may cultivate the involvement of interest groups to achieve policy objectives that they agreed long before the interest group became involved in policy. In other words, interest groups may be more useful to the Commission than the other way round. What researchers may observe is how European policy-makers use local and regional authorities as pawns in their internal battles and as useful assets in their quest to build the legitimacy of the EU. Rather than being a part of European governance, sub-national governments may be short-term allies that the Commission and European Parliament can discard when debates about policy move on. The conclusions that can be drawn from the research summarized below are limited, though it is possible to offer some insights.

Formal representation

The starting point for understanding the influence of sub-national government on EU policy is the operation of the representative organizations of local and regional government. There are several. The Council of European Municipalities was formed in 1951 by a group of local government leaders who wanted local government to help the reconstruction of Europe. The title was changed in 1981 to the Council of European Municipalities and Regions (CEMR). The organizational map is not coherent as there is competition with the Standing Conference of Local and Regional Authorities of Europe (CLRAE). In addition, the International Union of Local Authorities (IULA) also takes a representative role. Finally, there is the Assembly of European Regions founded by nine interregional associations in 1985, which now represents most of the European population. Research on lobbying shows that these organizations have an important role to play, particularly the more formal delegations, such as those that pressed for changes in the treaty in the EU's 1996 Intergovernmental Conference (John and McAteer, 1998). Largely because of the problems of agreeing a common strategy across Europe, bodies like CEMR have not been effective. Conflicts between sub-national authorities from different countries are a common occurrence.

The Brussels offices

The second sort of activity is the setting up and management of offices in Brussels. They have permanent addresses with full-time representatives and support staff; they serve as a source of intelligence for the participating local authorities; and they are the base from which they carry out lobbying campaigns. They express paradiplomacy: the real and symbolic presence of sub-national organizations outside the boundaries of their national state. In 1985 there were only six regions with offices; by 1999 there were more than 160 (*Financial Times*, 22.1.99) and 167 in 2000 (see Table 4.1). They include representation from all of the sub-national systems from Western Europe (Jeffery, 1996b; John, 1994d, 1995).

Local authorities in the UK have taken the lead in setting up the offices. The UK remains the country with the largest number because of its fragmented and non-regionalized sub-national structure, because its local authorities tend to prefer organizational responses to new policy issues, and the offices became part of a sub-national strategy to bypass central government in the inclement years of the 1980s and 1990s. Despite these drivers of reform, however, the UK offices have modest aims and recognize the dominance of central government (Jeffery, 1996b), which is the same as other countries with strong central governments, such as Denmark (Klausen, 1997). Some representation is dominated by regional or state governments. The German *Länder* staff their offices amply, reflecting their wish to build a coalition of regional governments across Europe in response to the changes in intergovernmental relations brought about by the EU (Jeffery, 1996b). Although regions dominate representation from France, their presence is largely symbolic, representing their aspiration to a European role rather than indicating they have a large stock of legitimacy and political resources to deploy in Brussels. Yet some cities use their representation more effectively than others (Balme and Le Galès, 1997).

In contrast to the effects of partnerships, the north–south pattern emerged over the offices. The more bureaucratized and professional local authorities in the north tend to set them up whereas representatives from other systems do not need to engage in formal lobbying as they rely on their informal contacts. Local authorities in the south of Europe also suffer from financial constraints and the suspicion of their central government ministries. However, the regionalization of these systems has altered this pattern of relations, with many more Italian and French offices opening in recent years. Consistent with the government to governance thesis, there is now more similarity between countries in the use of the offices, with larger countries having more of them (see Table 4.1).

Marks et al.'s (1996) quantitative exploration of the presence and size of the Brussels' offices substantiates the qualitative account. They find that local and regional authorities do not set up offices in response to the amount of resources in the region or locality; instead, the key factor is political, namely the amount of autonomy sub-national governments have to act

TABLE 4.1 *Regions and localities with offices in Brussels in 2000*

Member state	No. of substate offices in Brussels
United Kingdom	26
Germany	21
Spain	19
Italy	18
France	17
Denmark	12
Austria	11
Sweden	10
Cross-Europe	8
Netherlands	7
Finland	7
Belgium	5
Greece	3
Ireland	2
Portugal	1
Total	167

Source: Committee of the Regions
http://www.cor.eu.int/KeyCont/RepresentationBrussels.htm (as at 20.11.00)

outside the nation-state, findings elaborated by Nielson and Salk (1998). As more autonomous actors are more affected by European policy, so they invest more resources. Because there is no longer such a variation in the pattern of local autonomy, the extent of representation no longer follows the north–south divide. Acquiring representation is one of the games some sub-national authorities play to outwit their central governments.

Transnational networks

Linked to the offices is the participation of sub-national bodies in transnational networks across Europe. These networks are based on common interests, such as second cities in the Eurocities network, founded in 1986 at the initiative of Rotterdam to connect the large cities across Western Europe (Ercole et al., 1997). These networks may end up having formal arrangements and take on the characteristics of a lobbying group. Other initiatives are based on functional interests, such as the MILAN network, based on the motor industry. Not all of these networks emerge from the sub-national level as the European Commission sponsors networks to connect together the participants in Community Initiatives, such as under the RECITE (regions and cities in Europe) programme, launched in 1991. Even some bottom-up networks are heavily influenced by the Commission, such as European Regions of Industrial Technology. Other networks come about through relationships between border regions, again often sponsored by the Commission as an adjunct to the cross-border,

INTERREG programmes I and II, or others that are more independent, such as the Conference of Peripheral Maritime Regions (CPMR).

The significance of these networks is that local authorities participate in a range of activities and exchange ideas and practices as well as seek to influence European policy. They are an aspect of Europeanization at the local level whereby local authorities link with a wide range of actors and groups, and transfer ideas to the locality. In Benington's (1994) view, these networks transform local politics because information turns into political power.

The Committee of the Regions

The EU set up the Committee of Regions and Local Authorities in 1991. There was considerable optimism during its creation and the first year of operation in 1994. The German *Länder* appeared to give the body effective leadership and could have influenced its success through their political power in the strongest European state. In the context of new and strong regional governments across Europe, the Committee seemed able to develop into a legitimate political institution. As Loughlin notes (1996), commentators tend to be polarized about the effects of the Committee. Some academics are pessimistic (Christiansen, 1996; Jeffery, 1995), whilst others and the practitioners tend to be more optimistic (Meehan, 1997; Milan, 1997). It is hard to judge both accounts, as the former tend to erect high standards for such a young institution whereas the latter base their optimism on nothing other than the possible effects of time.

The difficult first few years of the Committee may mean that it will never gain legitimacy and recognition in European policy circles. Regions and local authorities have split over important policy issues. Then the *Länder* lost interest in European affairs when they became immersed in their domestic problems (Jeffery, 1996a). Farrows and McCarthy's (1997) study of the formulation and impact of opinions shows conflicts between the three interests – authorities in north versus south, the federal countries versus the rest and type of authorities – making it is hard for the Committee to formulate proposals. They indicate how the Committee proliferated the numbers of its opinions in many areas of public policy and that it has not managed its internal decision-making process well. The danger is that, without formal power, the Committee will become as ineffective as the Economic and Social Committee, another consultative body. On the other hand, during the 1996 intergovernmental conference, the Committee successfully argued for a separate organizational status from the Economic and Social Committee. Many of its conflicts with the European Parliament subsided. As Meehan writes (1997), the symbol of regional representation may in the end create formal rights. McCarthy's (1997) later research comes to the same conclusion: whilst the Committee's formal impact on EU policy outputs has been minimal, its value lies in its unique resources which could have potentially important implications for the exercise of power at the sub-national and supra-national levels.

Lobbying campaigns

The lobbying of the EU provides the strongest test of the Europeanization thesis. If sub-national government can influence EU policy, then local politics is part of a wider international system of decision-making. If the answer is in the negative, then the account of local government remains much as before, with central governments deciding most international issues. This argument may even apply in federal states, because federal institutions regulate the state's European matters in these countries.

The question of influence is important to the multi-level governance framework. The argument for such an influence is that there is evidence that local and regional governments participate in the consultation process and play a role in the informal networks in Brussels. Many scholars note the mobilization of sub-national interests (Hooghe, 1995b). However, there is less concrete evidence that sub-national activity influenced EU decision-makers; rather EU decision-makers used the lobbies to legitimate policies, to help implementation or as an aid in battles within Brussels.

The lobbying over the reforms of the structural funds in 1993 showed that the lobby groups were pawns between those in the Commission seeking to retain the existing system and others wanting to give a more urban and less regional focus to the distribution of the funds (John, 1996a). The Commission often sponsored groups, such as RETI, which was composed of groups and organizations from areas in regions suffering from industrial decline (McAleavey and Mitchell, 1994). John and McAteer (1998) show that the impact of the sub-national lobbying campaign over the intergovernmental conference was ineffectual, largely because sub-national governments' views did not cut much ice with the Commission and the European Parliament, which were also seeking to influence the proceedings.

As many writers stress (for example Mazey, 1995), the nation-state remains vitally important in the European context, which means that local authorities and regions need to follow its agenda rather than fight their own campaigns. The main examples of sub-national influence have been where expert lobbies pass information to the Commission so that it can manipulate national governments, as when sub-national authorities in the UK gave details of the government's decisions so that the Commission could threaten to implement the additionality requirements of the structural funds (John, 1996a; McAleavey, 1993). Even when the Commission and sub-national governments successfully ally and have the backing of law, national governments can subvert these manoeuvres by their control over the implementation of policy. For example, the UK government continued to flaunt the additionality rules after backing down in 1991 (Bache, 1999). Other situations where lobbying can be effective are when a regional group puts together a case for favourable treatment during the reforms of the funds, though sub-national actors sought to nudge rather than to lobby national and European actors (John, 1996a). By comparing campaigns it is possible to find out when sub-national actors have successfully mobilized or not, though no such study has carried this out (but see John, 1994c). Again, as with so much of the Europeanization of sub-national government, and of the move from government to governance, the experience is variegated and contingent; sometimes sub-national governments are influential whilst at other times they are not.

The future

Much of the literature on Europeanization and multi-level governance appeared between the late 1980s and the late 1990s. Academic interest reflected the massive expansion of the powers of the EU following the Single European Act 1986 and then the subsequent increase in resources the EU directed into regional policy initiatives. Following from a time when the European Community policy-making had fallen into abeyance in the 1970s and early 1980s, there was optimism about the European project and many debates about what course the path to European integration would take. Sub-national governments willingly engaged with this discourse, invested symbolic and financial resources in European affairs and sought to influence policy. However, the political environment at the turn of the century is somewhat different. First, there has been a backlash against European integration in countries such as Denmark and the UK, with strong anti-European movements elsewhere, such as in France. Secondly, some of the key sub-national actors have lost interest in the European project, in particular the German *Länder* (Jeffery, 1995). Thirdly, the legislative explosion of the 1980s and early 1990s came to a halt, partly because of opposition in some member states and a deliberate choice by Commission actors to invest energy in implementation and to research for a new wave of policies. There is no longer the tranche of directives coming from Brussels. The main driver of European integration is monetary union, but so far it has affected central governments' spending decisions rather than local governments' roles as service provider and regulator. Fourthly, the expansion of the funds halted in 2000. Moreover, there was an extensive reform in 1999, which has concentrated the areas receiving the funds, narrowed down the objectives to three and reduced the number of Community initiatives to four. The reforms transfer resources away from Western Europe, affecting authorities that were previously mobilized, and also continue the re-nationalization of regional policies begun in 1988 (Bache, 1999). If sub-national authorities in the UK mainly mobilized, for financial reasons (Martin, 1998), then the diminishing likelihood of getting funds will reverse the trend toward Europeanization that occurred in the early and mid-1990s.

However, the agenda should not be taken to mean that the era of sub-national mobilization is at an end, merely that European integration moves in cycles rather than as a linear trend. First, not all sub-national mobilization is financial in character, as local authorities have sought to influence EU policy and their leaders gain benefits from international liaison, such as travel junkets. Some British local politicians, for example, have sought to enhance their political careers by involvement with the Committee of the Regions. Secondly, there is likely to be a new round of regulatory measures on taxation and further efforts to harmonize the single market following the introduction of the Euro. As with the measures of the 1980s, sub-national authorities will take a great interest in them. Thirdly, the inclusion of central European states into the EU will bring new sub-national actors into the decision-making process. They will benefit from the redirection of the structural funds and have an incentive to participate in European policy. Rather than there being a limitation of Europeanization, its centre of gravity moves eastwards. There should be less financially orientated lobbying from countries that used to benefit from the funds, such as the UK, and more participation of countries from central Europe. Fourthly, the constitutional reforms occurring in many European countries create incentives for sub-national elites to mobilize. The devolution of power sets up or strengthens regional-level authorities and leaders of these bodies that wish to link to other European actors. The move to directly elected mayors in the UK, Germany and Italy creates powerful politicians who compete for resources and seek to influence policy across Europe. It is likely that the early part of the twenty-first century will find local authorities taking part in the next wave of European integration.

Conclusion

The literature on sub-national politics and the EU diverges between those who see the changes as transformative and others who regard them as slight and transitory. This division extends to all the related literatures on Europeanization, multi-level governance, European partnerships and the Committee of the Regions. As with any new development, there are pessimists and optimists, so such a division of views is not surprising. But it is not clear what the standard should be with this topic because the debate about sub-national mobilization contrasts or closely links to other theories of the EU which make writers either inflate the importance of the inter-actions that exist or, in reaction to the inevitable disjuncture between promise and reality, downgrade the importance of European liaison. The issue for governance is not so much about comparing the influence of sub-national actors with other European institutions, but to work out the implications for local politics within nation-states. Empirical studies do not appear to confirm either a sanguine or a pessimistic view. The EU changes but does not radically transform central–local relationships; moreover, Europeanization and sub-national mobilization are patchy. As with the other elements of governance, Europeanization promotes the gradual re-orientation of governing systems. With the variety of responses and their diversity across Europe, Europeanization breaks down the north–south divide of local government systems. Given the tendency for European integration to move in cycles, the early years of the twenty-first century should see new directions of sub-national mobilization and Europeanized policy-making.

5
Privatization and the New Public Management

Many of the trends this book discusses concern the external relationships of local public bodies. The chapter on regimes, for example, focuses on the relationship between the business community and local political leaders and bureaucrats. The main theme is how institutional fragmentation generates an extended network of policy-makers. Whilst such changes are the most obvious aspect of a move from government to governance, the transformation rests on two pillars: one is external to public organizations; the other is internal to them. These two aspects of change complement each other. Just as the field of local politics has become more networked and interdependent, so organizations have become more internally differentiated. Local governments have broken down their internal barriers, contracted out some of their functions, flattened many of their hierarchies and sought to be more entrepreneurial in their styles of management. When thinking about local decision-making, the terms flexibility and complexity describe the internal management of local organizations as much as their external relations. Both internal and external reforms complement each other in the way they drive the reform of local political systems. Governance is as much about public management as coalitions. Indeed, observers may claim the reforms of the internal structure of local government and other public bodies are hard to reverse whilst public–private partnerships and policy networks are often unstable.

It is not enough to show that local governments and other public organizations have reformed, since it is possible to find evidence for a wide range of organizational innovations. To support the argument of this book, the evidence needs to show that the changes have a logical and empirical unity and that they relate to and constitute the move from government to governance even though there is substantial variation according to nation-state and place. Whilst this task is hard with the politics of networks and regimes as they frequently vary, common policy problems and the role of the private sector make coalitions and networks recognizable in cities such as Milan, Lille and Barcelona even though the members of such networks have different functions, powers and sets of ideas. The task of comparing management reform is more difficult because it is about the functioning of institutions that are highly distinctive. Moreover, the intellectual ideas about management reform since the 1980s, those of the New Public Management (NPM), often lack intellectual consistency and do not appear to be a coherent programme. Notwithstanding the powerful criticisms of NPM, the chapter argues that the radicalism of its ideas and their rapid adoption into management practice complement the Europeanization of local government and the emergence of regimes. The chapter first reviews the management structure of traditional local and sub-national governments before moving to consider the impetus and direction of NPM.

Management structures in Western European local governments

The traditional framework

Organizational structure forms an important distinction between northern and southern local government systems. The welfare states of Western Europe decentralized functions to local governments whose bureaucracies developed hierarchical structures to administer public services. Large numbers of personnel deliver services directly. Specialized bureaus provide support for the front line staff. Directors and middle managers co-ordinate the organizations. Such a structure is similar to Mintzberg's five elements to an organization: 1) the controlling apex, the top management and company board; 2) the middle management; 3) the operating core; 4) the technocrats; and 5) the service departments and ancillary services (Mintzberg, 1983). The in-house approach easily described traditional local government organizations with their departments divided on the basis of function, the hierarchical bureacracies, control by committees and specialized departments providing support (Leach et al., 1994).

In the UK, where local government takes up about a third of public expen-diture and about 10 per cent of GNP, local government is an important branch of the welfare state. The model was that many local services are drawn into the organizational structure of the elected local authority or set of local authorities in tiers of administration. These bodies have at their head a political authority, a council of elected representatives that votes on policy and may delegate responsibilities. The elected council is sovereign, but it does its work in council committees. Because of the strength of local political organizations, if one party gets a majority of seats it can control the whole business of the council. The lack of direct political authority and a weak political leader of the council, who draws from among the ruling party group, means that the centre of the local authority was weak. Power was decentralized to committees that correspond to the service divisions of the council, such as social services, housing and education. The chief officer of the council used to be the clerk, who was usually a lawyer and had the formal role of co-ordinating council business. Because parties control voting, the councillors who sat on committees are generally loyal to the ruling party group or powerless members of opposition parties. Committees tended not to decide many policy matters themselves. The political and bureaucratic leadership drew up the business of the council beforehand and managed the agenda internally for presentation and approval. Power rested with the ruling group and with the permanent staff of bureaucrats in each service division. In traditional bureaucracies, directors of the service divisions are important posts.

In a large part of the post-war period local authorities took a highly hierarchical structure based on these empires. Their authority, which was largely reinforced by a growing professionalization of qualifications and organizational cultures, meant that officers who worked in a service, such as housing, would have trained as housing officers, have housing qualifications, go to housing conferences, moved either upwards within the authority or across local authorities, but always within their sector. The result was little contact between the different divisions of the authority, and cultures and ways of working varied according to the nature of the task. Cross-authority services tended to be weak, such as the chief executive's office, department of finance and the legal department. Hierarchical sets of structures were often insulated from each other. The culture was slow moving and did not reward merit. Public sector unions were powerful.

Management reform

Management reforms hit local authorities in the 1960s and 1970s, influenced by developments in the private sector. Scientific management models and central planning systems led to proposals to create large corporate local authorities, which influenced the local government reorganization of 1972. The most significant change was recommended by the Bains Report of 1972, which promoted the introduction of chief executives, research units in local government and new management techniques like Operational Research. Though the changes created more of an effective organization at the centre, they left the municipal empires intact and reinforced a system of hierarchical management.

Just as in the UK, many systems for local management were reformed in the 1960s and 1970s. Many northern European countries reduced the number of territorial units in response to the expansion of welfare states and central government demands for efficiency (Dente and Kjellberg, 1988). The effect of the modernization of local government was that management became even more hierarchical and co-ordinated by special management units from the centre, based on specialized advice and scientific policy analysis. The interest for students of management change is that this change occurred just before the fragmentation and de-centring of public organizations of the 1980s. Such a quick turnaround might appear to be consistent with a move between Fordism and post-Fordism or between government and governance. Given the argument that the transformation of local government depends on long running trends in the economy and in the evolution of scientific knowledge, it seems ironic that in the period before the change, central and local government reformers were intensifying the Fordist hierarchical model.

One consequence of the reorganization of local governments in northern Europe, such as in the Netherlands, was that they acquired a professionalized structure much like the UK pattern described above. The Netherlands had a 'monist institutional setting' (Hendricks and Tops, 1999: 135) since power flowed from the Burgomeister downwards. Such hierarchical structures were similar to those in other parts of northern Europe, such as in Germany (Dangschat and Hamedinger, 1999), which had a similar organizational form (Gunlicks, 1986). There are sources of variation, such as in the extent to which bureaucratic culture reflects a legalistic approach to administration and the role of the core executive.

Bureaucratization could never proceed far in the southern European counties because of the small size of many municipalities. In France, for example, many municipalities have fewer than 200 inhabitants. Nevertheless, the larger communes developed bureaucracies to administer services such as social welfare. Whilst elected local government lacked a functionally specialized local bureaucracy, the institutions of the central state provided the equivalent form. In education, the decentralized bureau, the *rectorat*, takes a classic organizational pattern, with a strict hierarchy (Cole, 1997). However, a good description of the pattern of administration needs to encompass the extensive contracting out of service provision to private companies and parapublic organizations (Lorrain, 1987, 1991).

The basic legal principle derives from the French revolution: individual private ownership is a human right. So private ownership and private business may trump public ownership and business in the commercial and industrial fields, which means that a public authority can do business (sell goods or services to its own community within the restricted limits of public interest criteria) only when no private enterprise acts in the area and when it is in the public interest, such as to promote public health and safety and equal access to services. Many companies formed in the late nineteenth century in response to local problems, first for water distribution and then for other services (Lorrain, 2000). They expanded greatly in the 1950s and were joined by a new organizational form, the semi-public company, the mixed economy society (*l'économie mixte*). The longevity of these companies and the complexity of their structures are a reminder that contracting out of services and complex interorganizational forms are not purely aspects of the transition from government to governance. In the UK many private companies also provided services until they were nationalized by local authorities or made part of publicly owned national companies in the 1930s and 1940s. The existence of such companies in France meant the bureaucracy did not take such a classic form, as indicated by the Mintzberg scheme.

As in other matters, the rest of the southern group partially resembles the French pattern, with weak communes and highly developed central states. Italy's communes are small as well. In the south they did not supply many municipal services, though in the north they provided education and health care (Dente, 1991: 110). In countries that had been ruled by centralized and undemocratic regimes until the late 1970s – Spain, Portugal and Greece – local bureaucracies were not that developed (Christofilopoulou-Kaler, 1991). Since the late 1970s, local bureaucracies have expanded as the centre has given communes political independence and more services. But it would not make sense to call these organizations Fordist in their structures. They were too closely linked to central government organizations.

This historical discussion neatly follows the institutional divide between countries that developed their welfare states and gave local authorities the task of administering them and those places where local government organizations were small and undeveloped. The move toward governance may involve two related but different processes. In the north it concerns the restructuring of traditional bureaucracies along the lines predicted by NPM; in the south, it involves the re-elaboration of complex forms of bureaucracy and private sector organizations. Given that the pressures for reform affect service-orientated bureaucracies and existing management systems, the reform impetus may affect the bureaucratized and state dominated countries of France, Italy and Spain much less than the UK, the Netherlands and the Nordic countries.

The New Public Management

There is an international movement to reform public administration (Kickert, 1997; Lane, 1997). Governments throughout the world reformed their public bureaucracies often in the name of the New Public Management (NPM), though with great variation across and within countries. Whilst NPM seems to have a clear set of doctrines, once it is looked at more closely its apparent clarity starts to dissolve and to turn into a set of slogans and contradictory reform programmes. Whatever the case about the coherence of NPM, public sector management has experienced a long period of change since the early 1980s, and continues to do so. The question for social scientists is how to understand current management practices and ascertain their consequences.

Traditional public administration

It is useful to recall the old public administration. This task might seem easy at first as the image is of the progressive era, with the importance reformers placed upon the formal principles of public administration: clear hierarchies and public values underpinning the exercise of power and the attempt at neutrality. There was a long career pattern and the assumption that public sector values matter. Underpinning the system was a justification of the role of the public sector which rests on different principles from business. Public provision is not about markets; a range of values may apply to public policy, and the public sector responds to the political direction of democratically elected governments. Another important value is professionalism where specialized forms of knowledge and expertise govern policy-making. But what was covered under the old public administration was actually a large number of practices – some to do with hierarchy and control, some to do with the values of bureaucrats and others to do with the autonomy of the bureaucracy and professionals. The key principle was that markets do not have a place in public administration and that the values of public service are important even when taking into account the long traditions of private sector provision in some countries.

Factors leading to change

So why did this framework change, particularly in the UK? The first factor was the long-running debate about failures in key services, such as education and policing, that led to the questioning of the authority of professionals and trade unions and encouraged bureaucrats and politicians to seek new solutions and to be receptive to the rhetoric advocating wholesale reform. The second factor was fiscal austerity caused by rising costs and demands to reduce taxes in many Western countries in the 1970s and 1980s. The third factor was the emergence of more populist political movements manifesting themselves as critiques of bureaucracy and waste in government. The fourth factor was the growth of public choice ideas in academia that gradually affected the think tanks and then the views of politicians, particularly those of a right-wing persuasion. The fifth factor was the wave of private sector reforms in the 1980s that led to structural change in many large financial corporations. These changes were fed into the public sector by consultants that had both private and sector practices.

It is not possible to consider NPM without discussing Osborne and Gaebler's *Reinventing Government* (1993). It is important, however, to be careful not to claim that this book alone influenced world reforms, nor did it sum up the whole of governments' programmes for change. Much happened before. Also it is mainly based on the USA. But it is important none the less as it was the management guru book for the public sector. It tried to put all the modish ideas of the time together and sought to influence managerial practice and government reforms. It saw itself as the equivalent to Peters and Waterman's *In Search of Excellence* (1995). The authors had undertaken many consultancies with the public sector. The book makes many predictions of a shiny future that awaits public management if only reformers seize on the main ideas. It laments the continuing state of public administration that is still locked into the assumptions of the progressive era and makes the argument for entrepreneurial government. The book argues that it has been a long time since the last reinvention; so now is the time for the new era.

According to Osborne and Gaebler, entrepreneurial government questions the values of traditional bureaucracy and believes that the public sector can be transformed by the power of leadership, the introduction of market mechanisms and a focus on results and decentralizing power. Traditions of progressive administration are not suited to such a fast-changing global world. NPM sees itself as a new paradigm based on entrepreneurial government, the need for risk-taking and for government to be like business. Its catch-phase was 'steering not rowing' and it argued for decentralization.

There are several elements to the NPM doctrine. First, it focuses on leadership by giving power to entrepreneurs/managers, ending red tape, limiting hierarchy and formulating mission statements. Secondly, it advocates market mechanisms, such as competition in the public sector, contracting out, privatization, the exercise of consumer choice and decentralization within bureaucracies. Thirdly, it believes in results-orientated public administration, focusing on outcomes rather than processes, putting the customer or consumers first, measuring outcomes and introducing performance related pay systems. Fourthly, it argues for the decentralization of power to citizens and away from traditional bureaucracies. It was widely adopted by US and UK politicians and it became a synonym for competitive government.

NPM across Western Europe

The implication for local governance in Western Europe is that NPM ideas diffuse both across nations and to the sub-national level. The claim of universalism is that any administrative system would be subject to such changes. Whilst in part internal organizational reforms are a pillar of the transformation from government to governance, the NPM version is strongly reductionist and does not greatly take into account the variations in sub-national governing systems. Indeed, it is possible to mount a severe attack upon the claims of NPM. In the view of Pollitt (1993), NPM has had a brief existence, which followed from the earlier neo-Taylorist reforms, but was undone by its contradictions and vagueness. NPM is a fad that contains all the rhetoric of markets and entrepreneurialism, but has everything else stirred in, so it can appear as anything to anybody. Hood (1995) argues that traditional public administration systems are varied anyway; there is no global convergence to one model of administration as management practice remains locally distinct. Moreover, some systems have not changed. Institutions and context count for more than global theory. NPM is an incoherent amalgam of arguments that do not hold together. Moreover, culturally different variants of NPM can be identified. Osborne and Gaebler's types become in effect a 'public management for all seasons'. Some countries with large public sectors engage in cost cutting. Many NPM reforms are unstable and become unpicked, especially when the negative consequences kick in. Hood has a powerful critique, but it seems to hover between accepting that NPM is powerful and dismissing it.

The implications of these critical perspectives is that research should find no coherence to management reform. An alternative approach is to acknowledge that managerialism does have a powerful set of ideas about competition, measuring performance, thinking about incentives and reforming the hierarchical structure. The introduction of the doctrine means that similar but not identical management reforms appear; they adapt and change over time; they change at different rates and in contrasting forms in Western European countries. Some countries are receptive to the reforms, such as those in northern Europe. Others, with stronger state traditions and entrenched bureaucratic routines, do not adapt so fast. But it is possible to observe management reform in Western Europe just as in the rest of the world. The task of the rest of the chapter is to see if the cynics are right and to find out the extent of management change that has transpired.

Management changes at the sub-national level

The UK has experimented with a wide range of management reforms since 1979 (Leach et al., 1994; Stoker, 1999). Whilst there is continuity, such as the continuing division of bureaucracy into services and a corporate focus in some local authorities, these reforms have transformed the internal structure of local authorities, revolutionized executive leadership, created a new set of organizations that local authorities need to deal with and shifted the culture of local government, though with some considerable variation both within and across local authorities. The most important change has been the contracting out of services to the private sector or to other organizations promoted and compelled by central government since 1980. Contracting out is one of the mechanisms to increase competition or establish a market-like mechanism in the provision of public services along with internal markets and charging. It is important not to confuse tendering with privatization. Contracting out is a mechanism to transfer services from direct state provision to another organization. The contractee need not be a private company, as it can be a management group or even another public organization, such as a another local authority. The purchaser specifies the activities in a formal document, makes the contract and monitors performance; then the provider delivers the service. There are a variety of ways of carrying out contracting out, in particular through the terms of the contract, the extent of monitoring and the degree of competition.

Modern contracting started from experiments by Conservative controlled local authorities in the late 1970s and early 1980s. The first bodies the government reformed were direct labour organizations in the 1980 Local Government, Planning and Land Act and local public transport from 1984. Then the Education Act 1988 introduced a form of contracting out, with schools holding budgets. The Local Government Act 1988 required the tendering of further local services, such as leisure. Contracting out is a major change in the management of local authorities since it removes the direct providing element from local authority bureaucracies and changes the shape of the Mintzberg diagram. As some of the evidence suggests (Walsh, 1995), there are some long-term effects of contracting out on the management of public services. Not only were there cost savings, but local government revamped its management structures, tightened its organizations and moved away from highly entrenched routines that were dominated by the demands of public sector trade unions. After 1997 the Labour government continued this approach to public management.

Changes to the financing of local services

The government introduced the Private Finance Initiative in 1993. It turned many capital projects into private sector financed ones where central government gradually repays the loan from the private sector whilst it uses the service. More directly there was the privatization of local authority assets, the most important of which were council houses since 1980. These direct sales have partly been superseded by transfers of local authority owned housing stock to housing associations that are not private landlords, but are associations that manage social housing.

There was a series of measures, the most important of which was the delegation of budgets to schools, which transferred power away from local education authorities to schools themselves. The local education authorities had to court schools rather than direct them because they now depended on schools deciding to buy services in. The effect of these reforms was to break up the traditional bureaucratic structure of local government and transfer elements of it to other organizations. These changes are an essential part of the move to governance where there is management in more open, decentralized networks.

Less discussed are the more informal changes introduced to public management. In particular, the measurement of local authority performance, such as school league tables, has become common practice. Many measures have been promoted by the Audit Commission, created in 1982, which was not just about managing the UK audit service, but took on a role to promote economy, efficiency and effectiveness in local government and other public services. It is important to realize that these measures have long-term effects within local authorities. The results have shattered the old management culture. Local government is faster, leaner and more flexible, though observers need to be wary of the ways in which organizations and their cultures adapt to ideas and frameworks and manage to retain their power by learning new languages, tricks and ways to access resources. Management fashions are powerful partly because authorities compete with each other. Moreover, officers view closely their counterparts in other authorities. It makes sense for managers to adopt the latest reforms to advance their careers and the status of their authorities. On the other hand, just as in the rest of Europe, public bureaucracies resist change or find ways of adapting to it. Even in the face of major reforms of their organizations, local government maintains its values and practices, often weakening the effects of the reforms (Lowndes, 1997, 1999).

Many reforms came from sub-national government. First, the delegation of budgets to service providing units was pioneered by local government in the 1980s, such as by local education authorities. Secondly, there has been the decentralization of service provision pioneered by Tower Hamlets and Islington, which was part of the Liberal Democrat Party's mission, but became widespread. The idea is to place services in a 'one-stop-shop' that can deal with all the client's needs and problems. These programmes have management costs. Thirdly, management experiments, such as the client–contractor splits in many local authorities, effectively divide members of staff into two groups.

No other Western European country has reformed its system of sub-national government according to the dictates of NPM as much as the British. Even countries that have been enthusiastic followers of management fashions have reformed central or state structures first with sub-national governments following rather than leading the reforms. The relative slowness and diversity of management change in the rest of Western Europe could support the idea that the UK has been exceptional in its public policies and institutional reforms, reflecting the dominance of right-wing governments during the 1980s and 1990s, the weakness of the state in Britain and the influence of ideas from the USA. If anything, the rapidity of management change seems to show how Anglo-American and limited are the ideas in the governance debate. The review below probes the extent to which management change in Western Europe complements what may be observed in the UK.

The Netherlands

The strongest case for the application of NPM ideas is from the northern group. NPM took hold in the Netherlands during the 1980s under the influence of the Anglo-Saxon countries, reflecting the willingness of Dutch reformers to engage with UK and US ideas (Hendriks and Tops, 1999). Municipalities experimented with business practices and contracting out (Snape, 1995). There were some prominent examples, such as the municipality of Tilburg. As elsewhere, the impetus to reform was fiscal austerity; municipalities considered reforms that would increase efficiency. A culture emerged that was critical of the hierarchical methods of delivering services and accepted modern business practices. Reforms of the organizational structure of the local authority sought to divide its structure between the central 'holding authority' and product divisions. The central bureaucracy developed specialized instruments to review the production and delivery of services. Municipalities tried to create a risk-taking culture. Finally, local authorities reviewed their activities to see if they needed to be performed. As Hendriks and Tops report, the reforms led to more energy and innovation in Dutch local government, but by the 1990s the zealous programme waned as local politicians and reformers experimented with measures to rediscover the role of the citizen in local politics and administration, and new forms of consultation (see Chapter 8). In the meantime NPM ideas receded into the background. However, other commentators note that the 1990s also saw the application of NPM ideas in local policy, especially in its implementation by the municipalities (Denters et al., 1999). In Ireland the government has recommended that local authorities adopt a framework of performance indicators and that the central government should not have such detailed controls over local government (OECD, 1997).

Germany and Switzerland

German local authorities have reacted more slowly to NPM ideas (Hendriks and Tops, 1999). In the 1980s there was resistance to the market ideas that local administrators and politicians associated with right-wing governments of the UK and the USA. These ideas appeared to undermine the values and character of the German administrative system based on the rule of law. Continuity and stability characterized the country's system of public administration (Benz and Goetz, 1996). Reforms started to emerge in the 1990s, challenging the bureaucratic model of administration, partly affected by reunification and fiscal austerity (Reichard, 1997). These measures started at the local level with experiments in privatization, functional decentralization, transparency in financial administration, budgetary reform (for example, global budgeting), defining products, quality management and one-stop-shops. A few pioneers, such as Duisburg, Cologne, Offenbach, Hanover and Nuremberg, introduced new policies, with many other local authorities following suit. Local councils contracted out services and searched for efficiency savings. They sought to measure outputs. They also borrowed from earlier experiments in the Netherlands, especially from the city of Tilburg (Hendriks and Tops, 1999), as well as developing a less market-orientated version of NPM, the 'new steering model', pioneered by the national association of cities and applied in cities, such as Berlin (Schröter, 2000). From a slow start, Germany has embraced NPM ideas rapidly (Wollmann, 2000), though the application and debate take a different form from elsewhere. The German reforms appeared as a result of fiscal austerity rather than central or state level imposition. The reforms have not been driven by a neo-liberal agenda, but have derived from experiments and discussion amongst practitioners. Finally, there has also been municipal privatization, such as of the municipal water industry, adopted because of the massive capital expenditure needed (Reidenbach, 1997). There has been privatization or contracting out of telecommunications and waste management. Similarly, in Switzerland, municipalities, such as the city of Berne, have experimented with new public management ideas, such as defining the outputs of the service and incorporating reports of the satisfaction of users (OECD, 1997). A number of other cities, such as Lucerne, Zurich and Winterthur, have adopted a similar set of reforms.

Scandinavia

Nordic countries show the differential emergence of NPM ideas. They have resisted full privatization, but have sought to improve the commercial foundations of their organizations (Lane, 1997). Local governments have wanted to move away from the Weberian form of bureaucracy and have experimented with internal markets. The countries of Sweden, Norway, Denmark and Finland embraced NPM ideas cautiously. Sweden shows some emergence of market ideas and managerialism in the 1980s as the Social Democrats moved away from their support for traditional bureaucracy. At the local level, municipalities adopted a business model, sought to break up their bureaucracies and contract out services (Wise and Amna, 1993). Cities set up procedures to manage by objectives and introduced the purchaser-provider model (Montin, 1992, 1993, 1995). In many cities, such as Stockholm, the impetus was financial. The local authority needed to make budget savings (Almquist, 1999). Many authorities introduced quality management schemes. Also, central government seeks to monitor performance through inspections.

There is a different story in Norway. In the 1970s, many Norwegian municipalities were reformed according to the ideas of corporate management (Baldersheim, 1986 cited in Bukve, 1996). Later in the 1990s, central ministries required local authorities to provide information, but there is no move to monitor performance systematically (OECD, 1997). Norway has not developed its auditing functions as much as other countries, such as Sweden. However, it has adopted charters and guarantees to enshrine the rights of individuals to specific services.

Denmark also found it hard to adjust to the legacy of local government reforms of the 1970s. There have been some debureaucratization reforms

under the influence of the centre-right governments of the 1980s that sought
to simplify regulation and to reduce planning controls. Governing bodies
for schools and other schemes for user participation emerged in the 1990s
(Torpe, 1992). Also there has been an attempt to merge private and public
sector principles in institutional design by transforming public organizations into private sector companies (Lane, 1997). Overall, the Danish local
authorities managed to escape some of the NPM reforms, though the
Ministry of Local Government publishes quality standards which are used
to inform local decisions. There has been some development of performance
initiatives at the local level (OECD, 1997) and local authorities have focused
on Total Quality Management (TQM), decentralization, and instituting the
influence of users, such as parent boards for schools).

Finland has experienced NPM reforms that seek to move to results
orientated management and the use of market mechanisms, though the
state has held back from monitoring local government because of the
consitutional protection and belief in local self-government (OECD, 1997).
Some municipalities have developed standards of service quality.

France

In France, as Lorrain (1997) points out, privatization has generated much
less debate than in the UK, but there have been profound changes none the
less, many initiated by the private sector. Business has enhanced the role it
plays in French public administration, such as over water production,
cable and transport. As Lorrain argues, this development has been helped
by the decentralization reforms and the retreat of the state. With the retreat
of central government, mayors turned to the private sector for partners
(see Chapter 3). During the 1980s and 1990s extensive privatization of
locally owned public utilities occurred. What happened in France is that an
already fragmented and partially privatized form of public management
has been extended and that private sector ideas and practices have
influenced the public sector, creating what Lorrain calls the para-public
sector. The nationalized industries that operated at the local level became
organized more on market principles and policy-makers addressed the
cross-subsidization of public services. Yet the application of NPM ideas
to public sector organizations has been relatively gradual, both at the central
and local levels. Whilst the state has re-conceived the role of public
organizations, the system of contracts that emerged in local policy and other
areas was not a revolution in public policy. Rather, it was a restatement of
the hierarchy and authority of the central state (Le Galès and Mawson,
1995). France's powerful system of public law conflicts with the NPM
doctrines of efficiency and flexibility (Guyomarch, 1999).

Spain

Like France, Spain has a tradition of private sector provision by companies founded in the late part of the nineteenth century. There are some large companies, such as Formento de Constructiones y Contratas (FCC) and Societatad General de Aguas de Barcelona (SGAB), now called Grupo Agbar. Spain also has a tradition of state provision of services that were nationalized or taken from municipal authorities during the twentieth century (Fernàndez, 1997). Since 1975 Spain privatized or contracted out many local services, such as water, public transport and waste collection. As in other countries, waste collection and street cleaning have been extensively contracted out. There has also been a transfer of responsibilities from direct control by the municipality to syndicates. Such efforts may also be observed in Portugal, where municipalities have privatized their water supply and waste management services (*Financial Times*, 8.11.95).

As in France, the progress of NPM reforms in Spain has been limited by the power and salience of the traditional bureaucratic state whereby municipalities are subject to strict legal controls and have their foundation in law (Calderon and Cabrera, 1991). The numerous regulations limit the flexibility municipal organizations have in responding to change. It also means that bureaucrats have limited discretion and are subject to rules of financial accountability. More generally, there has been less support for management change in the Spanish state than elsewhere in Europe, partly because of the expansion of the public sector and because of low academic and expert interest and knowledge about public management (Boix, 1996).

Nevertheless, some municipalities have experimented with new forms of organization. Since 1979, Barceclona City Council has introduced a decentralized administration to improve services, promote the use of new technology, encourage citizen participation, bring management closer to the citizen and act as an agent of social policy (Amoros, 1996). Over time, the council focused more on the administrative tasks of decentralization rather than on political objectives. Decentralization assisted the introduction of new technology. It also led to a rationalization of staff activities and an improvement of information storage and retrieval. A further example of management change was the attempt to reduce the amount of regulations constraining (and also empowering) local officials, such as those in Valencia, or creating one-stop-shops for citizens to interact with different services in one place (Mateo, 1991).

Italy

Italy's experience of privatization and NPM differs from France and Spain, since there is less of a tradition of providing services privately. Many functions were provided in house, such as cultural and social services; others, such as water, refuse collection and disposal and transport, were provided by semi-autonomous communal agencies. Moreover, the move to more flexible forms of service delivery has been much slower and incremental than elsewhere. As Dente (1991) writes, fiscal pressures on local government and the expansion of demands upon local services provoked something of a rethink. Moreover, central government required local authorities to seek ways of providing services more efficiently and there were severe constraints in replacing staff. Dente describes the gradual road to private provision, with the initial search for temporary staff, then working with a 'service co-operative', followed by buying products, such as school lunches, with the final step a contract with a private organization. Dente notes the slow pace of change in the 1980s and also the caution public authorities have shown when contracting services out because of fear of handing over control to the Mafia. Italian elites showed no ideological commitment to privatization and contracting out. Since that time the growth of the importance of business people in Italian politics has meant more public commitment to business practices. Strong mayors have pursued privatization policies. In Trieste, for example, privatization has been advanced with the selling off of land and contracting out of municipal services (Somma, 1999). The city's mayor, Illy, trumpets the idea that local administration should become like a business concern.

Conclusion

This survey of developments in management and in public ownership shows the diversity of experiences at the local level in Western Europe. The variation encompasses the managerial revolution in the UK and the Netherlands and the weaker trends elsewhere. As with other developments discussed in this book, the UK can seem to be the odd country out, with a centralizing central government and pro-market policies. Both Conservative and Labour enforced NPM ideas as well as privatizing and contracting out services. Elsewhere in Western Europe the changes have been slow and more voluntaristic. This aspect of governance appears to be an Anglo-Saxon idea, with only the Netherlands keen to imitate this pattern. Whilst commentators agree that the changes in the UK have been more centralized than elsewhere (Batley, 1991; Stoker, 1997a), the contrast is more a question of degree than a fundamental distinction. As the chapter discuses, many changes in the UK were bottom-up and the writ of central government is never as extensive as it appears. Moreover, developments in the rest of Western Europe belie such a distinctiveness as the public management reforms in Germany, Sweden and France show. Municipal privatization has been a universal phenomenon as resource-poor local governments have been attracted by the cost savings and promises of investment.

If NPM and municipal privatization is not just a British phenomenon, the second set of arguments would see it as a feature of 'northern' local government systems. The argument is that the large welfare bureaucracies are particularly vulnerable to reform because of the demands of service efficiency and the prior prominence of hierarchical bureaucracies. These countries have a tradition of reforming local government boundaries and organizational structures in the interests of efficiency and subscribe to professional forms of administration. It is no surprise that some of these, such as the Netherlands and Germany, leap on the NPM bandwagon. In the south, in contrast, the strong central state is hidebound by legal rules, procedures and the established baronies of the professional corps. Local bureaucrats and politicians are less focused on the quality of services and are less likely to find reforms attractive. The evidence suggests that NPM reforms found their natural expression in some northern countries, but did not transfer to the classic southern countries. But the analyst must be careful. Within the northern group some countries have been faster than others to adopt NPM. Germany took to the ideas much slower than the Netherlands. There is a differential rate of reform within the Nordic group. Nor is NPM much in evidence in southern local government systems. It diffused to France, Italy and Spain. The attraction of municipal privatization is Western Europe-wide and cannot be restricted to the north. Rather than a strict north–south divide, a variegated pattern has emerged.

The adoption of these ideas is particular to contexts. Ideas cross nations and between levels of government. Reformers adapt them to fit in with their own systems of government. Ideas may also engage with older practices. In Scandinavia many of the management reforms followed on from the previous experiments with private sector ideas in the corporate management revolution. Such national variation and recycling should not be seen as evidence of insubstantial cultural forms that only hold together through a belief in myth. When speaking of new forms of governance, as earlier chapters discuss, identical forms of management practice are unlikely to emerge; rather, central–local government systems develop in ways that reflect their heritages. There is no contradiction between arguing that institutions and context count and observing a marketization of management and enterprise in local government.

Such management change complements the fragmentation and multiplication of organizations. Just as public bodies have to negotiate a more complex external environment, they have become more complex and lose their centralized structured. By breaking down the hierarchies and becoming like post-bureaucratic organizations (Barzeley and Armajani, 1992), local government depends more on interpersonal networks and becomes more unpredictable. In this way one of the traditional foundations for stable policy-making and routinized administration becomes weaker, leaving the way open for more active and innovative forms of administrative and executive leadership.

6

Institutional Formation and Regionalism

Institutions and governance

So far this book has focused on the non-institutional factors that have led to local governance, such as economic competition, cross-national networks and reform ideas in the public sector. These factors would appear to indicate that governance is intrinsically non-institutional in character. Indeed, the definition of governance in the first chapter suggests that the new modes of governing are a reaction to more institutionalized forms of politics. However, the focus on networks and regimes does not imply that institutions and their evolution are not part of the changes to sub-national politics. Moreover, one of the basic elements to governance is the changed character of institutions themselves. Fragmented organizations and micro agencies require networks between them to ensure that decision-makers can make policy effectively. Institutions do not disappear; they become more complex. In particular, there is a tendency for institutions to operate on more territorial levels than hitherto. At the smallest territorial level, micro agencies, with their small client bases, have been given greater autonomy; on the other hand, meso or middle tiers of government have emerged to operate between the various units of local government and the institutions at the centre. Even central government becomes more effectively organized at many territorial levels, with the spread of special purpose agencies and the strengthening of departmental and regional tiers of field administration. The state becomes more differentiated in its local, regional and national dimensions. Whilst institutions remain important, their relations to each other become more complex. Local agencies and authorities have to find different ways of operating to respond to faster policy changes and there is a greater linking of policy sectors as public problems become more complex.

Institutional reform

There is also an interaction between institutional processes and the networks of informal politics through policy challenges and reform of political institutions. On the one hand, networks are shaped by political institutions; on the other, the leaders of political institutions and reformers respond to decision-making networks and to the difficulties of making policy. Institutions count because of their working practices and cultures – the degree of freedom that they allow bureaucrats to negotiate and make decisions, the rules of the game that allow interest groups, such as businesses, to have access to decision-makers. For example, institutions comprise the arrangements about the delegation of authority to public–private partnerships. The other institutional response to complexity is to reform the territorial organization of decentralized government. Central governments have created new tiers of government, re-allocated responsibilities between territorial organizations and democratized administrative authorities. The paradox is that the factors that cause nation-states to reveal their lack of uniformity may be the same ones that lead them to create ordered political institutions to try to manage the complexity. Regional and/or middle-level governments derive from the forces that give expression to the territorial dimension to nation-states, such as new forms of political mobilization; at the same time, central governments create tiers of government to impose some order and integration over the many organizations that occupy the space between the primary units of local government and central government ministries. The further paradox is that the new tiers of government themselves become part of the matrix of local governance because each organization seeks to operate at every territorial tier. At the local level, representatives from central and middle-levels of government argue alongside local government for their preferred policy positions; similarly, at the middle levels, central and local levels of government compete with the regional authorities. Into these spheres of activity it is possible to add the multi-level activities of interest groups, such as businesses and trade unions. Moreover, the EU organizations discussed in Chapter 4 complete the interactions of each tier. The interplay between the forces of complexity and institutional formation is the theme of this chapter.

Meso or regional government?

The chapter explores the progress of these middle-level institutions and evaluates their progress to comprehend the way territorial interests affect the organization and policies of the state. To avoid a linguistic trap, the book refers to the meso or middle level of governance as regional or as regions. Even though a strict definition of regions would refer only to the level below that of the nation state, they are often thought to be the political institutions that operate between the local and national levels. Rather than the emergence of a similar level of regional government, governance implies the reconstruction of organizations at several territorial levels. It is also difficult to follow Keating's advice of seeing regions as a confluence of political, social and economic spaces, largely because it is plausible that such a confluence varies across nation-states and need not overlap. The term meso also adds some flexibility when comparing across nations, so it may be easier to compare Spanish and French regions, for example. But even after Sharpe's (1993) formulation, the term failed to gain currency, particularly as regions and regionalism became slogans of new political movements and academics and commentators commonly use the term. So the chapter uses the term region in the place of meso, even though there is no major difference in the meaning the terms.

The factors behind regionalization

As with the rest of governance, the factors behind the regionalization of the state are complex. A broad classification of the causal mechanisms helps the discussion. In keeping with the idea that some factors drive the change and others respond to it, the chapter follows other authors (for example, Keating, 1995b; Sharpe, 1993) by dividing the forces for the regionalization of Western European states into 'top-down' and 'bottom-up' factors. The former derives from more technocratic considerations that circulate in central government and also in some local elite circles. They are about the wish of the institutions of central government to have more efficient forms of territorial organization. Here the concern is to find the best means to deliver services and to co-ordinate the various levels of activity. There are certain functions, such as strategic planning, transport and regional economic development, that local government cannot effectively perform, so creating a need for an intermediate tier to co-ordinate matters. In addition, the long-standing argument about the advantages of large local government areas re-appears in the regional government literature. Regionalists assert there is a link between the efficiency of service provision and the size of local government units because of economies of scale (Sharpe, 1993: 9). As well as these technocratic considerations, top-down regionalization can have more political aims, such as to pre-empt and to contain bottom-up regionalism. Bottom-up regionalism is a political force, expressing itself as a demand for more autonomy for areas that lacked an institutional outlet to express their identity. These areas were often former nations conquered by nation-states or places with looser but still salient forms of identities. The creation of regional government is top-down in character, but the bottom-up descriptor suggests the centre's choice is constrained by regional mobilization.

'Top-down' regionalization

Rational and functional factors

Territorial organizations served the interests of the state in the nineteenth and twentieth centuries. State bureaucrats and politicians found it efficient to decentralize administration into territorial units and to subdivide the tasks of the state; it also made sense to respond to diversity by creating separate authorities that can target populations whilst at the same time maintain the fiction of a uniform state. Central governments also found it practical to ensure political organizations link to administrative units. Regional governments can foster the legitimacy of centrally inspired policies, control local political elites and ease the political pressures on the centre. The functional pressures driving state organization are imperfect; they are guided by cultures and fashions. None the less, behind each complex reform, state actors seek to organize the territorial administration more effectively.

The size of the public sector has not been constant. The state's expansion during the twentieth century caused sub-national authorities to increase their responsibilities and their shares of public spending and gross national products (Sharpe, 1988). Local governments and public authorities have increasingly provided services that require high capital investment and complex bureaucracies staffed by professionals. At the same time, populations have spread across territories in suburbs and conurbations so they need more complex forms of local government organization than that provided by just city administrations and rural authorities. The pressures to provide services efficiently have driven some countries to re-organize their local governments, to sweep away small municipalities and to create large authorities to administer both town and country.

The UK has been a victim to this rational–functional form of administration. Not only did reformers in the 1960s and 1970s wish to create local government units to run local centres, suburbs and their environs, they sought to identify the most efficient local government size and reorganize local government with this principle in mind. The Redcliffe-Maud Commission, which reported in 1969, recommended a minimum population of 250,000. Yet even the research of the Commission could not find a clear association between size and efficiency, except for some specialist services. The consensus of the literature is that there is no clear relationship (Travers et al., 1993). Some studies show that per capita costs rise (Boyne, 1995); others show a variety of effects (Martins, 1995; Newton, 1982). The obsession with finding the most efficient size has receded in the UK. The local government reform of 1972, which imperfectly implemented the Redcliffe-Maud proposals, became discredited. The two tier system was partly dismantled by the Local Government Review in 1993. The Conservative government of 1992–7 flirted with introducing smaller local government units, but in the end it gave up trying to impose a uniform structure except in Scotland and Wales.

In the rest of Europe such ideas about local government efficiency have been powerful if less pervasive. There has been a massive reduction in the number of local authorities. Between 1950 and 1992, Council of Europe data show that three countries reduced the number of local authorities by 80 per cent and six by 60 per cent or more (Council of Europe, 1995). Predictably, the northern group reorganized its local governments whereas the communal basis to southern local governments remains today. Though there have been amalgamations of communes in France, usually through annexation of smaller communes by the larger ones, there are still over 36,000 left. The contrast between municipal reform in northern and southern Europe seems to confirm the north–south pattern this book seeks to question. Sharpe (1993) argues that the emergence of regional tiers of government in the 1970s and 1980s was the state's response to the difficulties of reforming the primary level of local government and so fits a functionalist explanation. Whereas central states in the north could happily reform their local government systems, southern states had to create new tiers of government to administer services effectively. There is some truth in Sharpe's assertion, because many of these authorities, such as those in Spain, now administer the welfare state which emerged in the 1970s. However, the change is not as neat as this argument implies. In many southern countries regions take on non-service-based functions, such as strategic transportation and planning, whereas the provision of services either remains a central government function or becomes a local government one where the field units of central government have become democratized, such as the departments in France. Moreover, technocratic modernization was mainly a feature of the 1960s and 1970s, and had slowed down by the 1980s (Dente and Kjellberg, 1988). In the north, similar pressures to create new tiers of government have emerged. The reality is that, even with variations from country to country, similar forces in the north and in the south of Europe have caused the structure of subnational government and administration to become more complex and multi-tiered, with many functions shared between the tiers of government. Thus the functional modernization of the political system is an important background to the reform of the periphery, though the main causes for regionalization lie elsewhere.

Regional planning

The second factor is the legacy of regional planning, which was the attempt by nation-states to direct the location and growth of their main industries, subordinate to national plans. Such planning emerged in some Western European states in the aftermath of the Second World War. The exemplar was France, with its indicative planning regime, imitated in Belgium, Italy and the UK (Hayward and Watson, 1975). The life-span of this form of regionalism was not long, as many of these plans did not fulfil their targets and were undermined by new policy initiatives. But there were some long-term effects on the organization of the state. The first was to embed thinking about the regional aspects of central policies into the procedures and routines of the central state. These ideas emerged from time to time in subsequent public decisions. The second was to create regional boundaries and some sort of regional organization within the state which could become the basis for political regionalism later on. The clearest example was the French administrative regions created by Debré in 1962 that were based on the boundaries of the Vichy regime. The administrative reformers agreed several boundaries that did not reflect the traditional regions or nations of France, such as Provence, partly to prevent them gaining any regional identity and from becoming the focus of regionalist movements. The historic nation of Bretagne is split in two and there is the 'non-entity' region, Centre. Despite the efforts of the reformers, some of these areas became the focus for political regionalism of the 1970s and then formed the boundaries of the elected regions created in 1982 and 1986.

The UK is a similar example of the link between administrative and political regionalism. Central government created standard regions in 1954 based on administrative units of the 1940s and, with some modifications, they were used mainly to collect regional statistics and formed the boundaries of some government organizations. In spite of a myriad of boundaries from which to choose (see Hogwood, 1996), these regions became the focus for the government offices for the regions (GORs) created in 1993 that continued, with some revisions and an amalgamation, to be the boundaries for the Regional Development Agencies of the Labour government elected in 1997. The slow development of administrative regions created a regional level of governance that helped central states to create democratically controlled regional bodies.

Regional functions

The third factor is the emergence of special functions for the regional level. These are different from the welfare services administered by larger local government units, such as health and education. They derive from the need to co-ordinate and manage strategic policy sectors, such as planning, transport, training and economic development. These functions appear in different combinations at the regional level, reflecting a functional need for a strategic tier of administration that differs from central government ministries and also from the regulative and/or service providing role of local government. These functions do not amount to indicative planning and the direction of transport, with the government providing all the funds for infrastructure projects, but reflect a demand for some co-ordination and bring together the many public, quasi-public and private sector organizations that occupy the regional space. The demand for integrated planning, economic development and transport networks partly reflects the loss of power of the state because economic competition and EU rules limit state intervention.

The importance of economic development powers of regional authorities has occupied a special part of the literature. The argument is that regional authorities need to attend to the soft side of economic development, such as to manage the complex networks in regions and the public–private partnerships. New regionalist writers (Amin, 1994; Cooke and Morgan, 1998; Keating, 1998; Scott, 1996, 1998) stress the emergence of regional economies that are partly independent from national governments. Others focus on the changes to the economy as another driver to new regions, particularly the decline of traditional industries and centrality of rapid information transfers in economic enterprises. These writers often suggest that effective regional government is the most attractive way to manage regional economies, whereas sceptics (for example, Harding, 2000) argue that is does not matter whether a tier of government is elected or not so long as regional co-ordination and policy-making takes place. Just in case it might be thought that changes in economies and their management are moving Western Europe toward a Europe of regions, there is a sceptical literature emerging that questions the extent to which regional development is at all independent from national economic performance (Dunford, 1998). Some writers think that the new regionalism is nothing more than the rhetoric of government policy-makers, regional elites, self-interested academics and consultants (Lovering, 1999) and overlays complex patterns of institutional formation that vary from place to place (Tomaney and Ward, 2000). A study of Baden–Würtemberg claims that attempts to mobilize regional political and economic actors in a network failed because of the power of global economic forces (Koch and Fuchs, 2000).

The crisis of the state

The third set of top-down factors are more political in character and link with the 'bottom-up' factors discussed below. Reformers are keen on more tiers of government because they deflect pressures from the central state and can be used to off-load troublesome public problems. Fiscal pressures are important and central governments are keen to transfer responsibilities for service provision to new or old agencies but also to cap their budgets or allocate them weak tax-raising powers. The UK has had some examples of this practice. In 1990 central government allocated the responsibility for community care to local authorities, with relatively little financial compensation. In Denmark, during the 1970s and 1980s, the government transferred responsibilities for social security to the municipalities and gave regional planning, primary health services, care for the handicapped and disabled, secondary schools, environmental quality and public transport to the counties. Another example was the revival of regional governments in Italy in 1970 where it suited the Christian Democrats to transfer functions, such as hospitals, housing and transport, to these authorities (Mény, 1986). The sub-state level has become the preferred body to administer health services, as in Italy, Sweden, France and Germany. In many cases the transfer of functions has been associated with the creation and/or democratization of intermediate tiers of government, as in France.

The European Union

The fourth top-down factor is the EU. Chapter 4 sets out the impact of the EU on sub-national governance. Regional governments and organizations play an important role in implementing EU policies, particularly programmes, such as the ERDF. The word regional appears in many guises in EU institutions and policies, such as the ERDF, the Committee of the Regions and the Directorate-General for Regional Policies. Moreover, policy-makers prefer the slogan 'Europe of Regions' to a 'Europe of cities' or 'Europe of local governments'. It would appear that stronger European integration means a greater role for regional government (Keating, 1998). Indeed, it is possible to set out some of the causal mechanisms. Regional policy acts at levels above local government as programmes apply to the economic performance of large territories often wider than cities or counties. Moreover, there is a synergy between the activities of regional governments, such as planning, transport and economic development, and a cluster of policies on transport links, high technology and planning measures promoted by the European Commission. Regional governments, which usually have had economic development functions, have often applied for European funds; they regard themselves as leaders of sub-national partnerships and have pioneered the setting up of offices in Brussels. In turn the Commission has sought to deal with the largest sub-national units, partly because they are almost as important as federal governments in Germany and Belgium. Commission officials find it easier to deal with regions as they do not have to respond to the multiplicity of communal and municipal administrations. It is significant that the EU's classification of sub-national authorities into NUTS (nomenclature of units for territorial statistics) puts NUTS1 as the regional level, such as standard regions, though they amalgamate some regional authorities, such as those in Spain and France. Because of the link to other regionally based policies, such as land use planning and transport, central states have integrated the administration of the regional funds into regional field agencies. The regional prefecture in France co-ordinates the partnership; in England, the government offices for the regions have the responsibility. These strengthened regional bodies form alliances with the regional governments if they exist, and/or the public and private bodies and partnerships that form the regional space, themselves forming a level of regional governance.

As well as these practical links, it is important not to dismiss the rhetorical impact of regionalism as advanced by EU policy-makers. Whilst the slogans are largely empty of content, they find a ready audience with regional elites seeking to mobilize their followers; and they suggest alternative arenas of political action than the nation-state. The most enthusiastic supporters of regionalism in Western Europe are the ethnic regions or former nations contained within modern state boundaries whose leaders are keen to become European politicians. Parties seeking the independence of their territories from the nation-state use the European project to advance their cause, hence the slogan of the Scottish nationalists – 'Scotland in Europe' – denotes Scotland as an independent small state with institutional protection and international representation supplied by the EU. Nevertheless, as the previous chapter indicates, the prediction of a uniform Europeanization of the sub-national level is unlikely to be substantiated as a variegated pattern has emerged. Instead, there is likely to be sporadic regional mobilization as a result of European integration.

Moreover, the regional aspect to EU policies is more apparent than real. The Committee of the Regions has strong representation from both local authorities and regions. Regional policy does not necessarily connect to regional entities since the areas eligible for EU funds are determined by measures of economic deprivation that can be of any size and may cross sub-national government boundaries. Many purely urban areas are eligible for funds and there are concentrations within and across regions. Recently EU regional policy has focused on urban issues. Urban lobby groups in Brussels are as active as regional ones and have a Europe of the Cities as their slogan.

'Bottom-up' factors

Regional mobilization

Renewed territorial political movements have successfully challenged the legitimacy and institutions of modern states. Whilst the top-down measures led to incremental adjustments to administrative and political structures, it was the conventional and unconventional strategies of decentralist parties and organizations that have been the spur to reform. The devolution reforms in the UK, which are the first moves toward a federal or quasi-federal state, would not have occurred without the long campaign of the Scottish National Party and the demands for regional autonomy from within the Liberal Democrat and Labour parties. Similarly, the ethnic challenge to Franco's regime was the main factor that led to the decentralized constitution of 1978. Even though the demand for France's regions appeared to be technocratic in character, political elites have articulated the decentralist agenda.

Regional mobilization has several linked causes. The first is the re-awakening of regional/national/ethnic identities within nation-states. As many writers stress (for example, Harvie, 1994; Keating, 1998), nation-states imposed universal values and institutions over territorially diverse areas. Underneath the apparent uniformity, there are many identities and interests. They can include many former nations, such as Scotland, Brittany, or areas that national governments and elites conquered or absorbed into national states. In some countries, such as France, these territories were wholly integrated into the one and indivisible state (Hayward, 1983), having the same territorial organization as the rest. In Franco's Spain, regional languages and the expression of culture as well as political organizations were banned. Italy too suppressed its regional identities, particularly during the fascist period. Even though regions were enshrined in the constitution of 1948, they were repressed by the stifling central bureaucracy and centralized political parties who feared that the Communists would gain control. Other unitary or quasi-unitary states were less relentless in their centralizing impulses. The UK rather than an English state emerged from an ambiguous political settlement that enshrined the all-powerful legal doctrine of parliamentary sovereignty backed up by economic and military might. But constitutional understandings allowed for separate national identity and administration in Scotland, maintained some national institutions in Wales and provided for devolved government in Northern Ireland. Ironically the doctrine of Unionism sustained the ethnic nations of the UK and legitimated the social institutions that underpinned ethnic identities. This regime led to an oppressive, intolerant and violent form of rule in Northern Ireland, but overall it sustained the tradition of decentralizing power in the so-called unitary state. Elsewhere countries like Belgium never developed a national identity, preserving polarized communities and separate territories. The government of divided societies in Belgium and the Netherlands meant that the all-mighty power of the central state was more of a fiction than a reality.

Territorial identities are not usually just a historical throwback to the pre-industrial era; regions and nations continually reinvent themselves (Anderson, 1983). Aspects of regional cultures, such as many Scottish customs, were inventions of the nineteenth century. The region of Padania in Italy is a fabrication by the Northern Leagues to describe an area of the basin of the Po river, but the area never existed as an administrative or political unit (Giordano, 2000). The assertion of regional identity is both economic and political in inspiration. Regionalists appraise spatial inequality within the nation-state and address such matters as the distribution of government finances. But regionalism can also be a critique of centralization of power in the capital. Ethnic regionalism or nationalism usually blends with a defence of working class occupations or rural interests; the movement supports decentralization within the nation-state.

There are variants of regional mobilization. The strongest resembles ethnic nationalism, often meaning the wish and assertion of independence from the nation-state. This form of politics usually centres on former nations that were never fully integrated into the industrial and financial networks of modernizing states, so have the residues of language and culture and a perception of being left out, such as the Basque country in Spain and France, and Wales and Scotland. Movements based on national identity can embrace extremist politics, such as the Irish Republic Army (IRA) and Euzkadi Ta Akatasoma (ETA).

The perception of economic difference can work the opposite way as the more developed regions of the country articulate their ethnic interests as a way of loosening the economic burdens of supporting the rest of the country. Catalonia and Flanders are clear examples, but echoes of the politics of economic superiority appear in the demands of the Northern Leagues in Italy. The call for independence can often be mollified by the introduction of regional autonomy as the central state seeks to buy off regional elites with substantial political autonomy and/or beneficial financial transfers or careful playing the international arena, as in Northern Ireland.

In tandem with nationalist movements, a weaker form of regional mobilization has emerged. Certain regions of Western Europe retain their regional customs and accents that remain in the cultures of media organizations and whose values are articulated by elites in local government, business and the quasi-public sector. The manipulation of cultural symbols by regional elites becomes more prominent when there has been some form of regional decentralization or the promise of it generated by more assertive regions, such as Catalonia or Scotland. These actors know that regionalism is a card they can play to gain resources and autonomy, especially when they are in competition with more powerful nationalist movements. Economically insecure places, such as the north-east of England and north-east France, start to develop political movements and campaigns at the same time nationalist movements take hold in other parts of their countries.

Democratization

The second factor is the force of democratization, which emerged in the 1960s and gained energy in the 1980s and 1990s. This movement of ideas emerged from the long-term socio-economic factors that caused groups to mobilize in defence of their identities as well as their interests.

Democratization represents the extension of the equality and rights to groups based on common values and beliefs as well as on economic interests. Even though territorial movements are different from each other, what is striking is that they emerged at a similar time in the 1970s and beyond. There is a link between Irish nationalism, the disruption of stable consociational democracies in Belgium, Cyprus, the Lebanon and elsewhere, the rise of Basque nationalism, the renaissance of Italian regionalization in the early 1970s and the emergence of regional demands in France. The rise of identity politics coincided with a reaction against the centralization of many southern European states. These movements were a direct counter to the authoritarian regimes in Spain, Portugal and Greece, particularly as much of the opposition in Spain was led by the regionalists. The resurgent Spanish democracy enshrined regional tiers of government in its constitution of 1978. In other countries the reaction was not so marked. In France during the 1960s, progressive political groups became more critical of the centralized and bureaucratic state and proposed decentralization away from Paris. It is significant that De Gaulle should step down from office in 1969 after failing to win a referendum on regional government rather than at the hands of the Algerian nationalists or from the onslaught of the New Left. Regional government became a key aspect of the left's programme. The Socialist party in the 1970s advocated decentralization as part of its platform. When the Socialist government was elected in 1981 it was no surprise that it made regional government a key part of its decentralization reforms. In Italy, there have been successive waves of democratization and regionalization, stretching back to the provisions of the 1948 constitution, which were rediscovered in a bargain between the Christian Democrats and the left in 1970. In the later period, after a period of disillusion, there was the revival of demands for regional government after the collapse of the Christian Democrat regime. Dramatic events often provide the spur to regionalization when an existing government system falls into disrepute and there is an opportunity for regional elites to press home their advantage. As Wright (1984) comments, the political crisis in Italy in 1969 provided an incentive for central elites to reform, as did the abortive coup in 1981 in Spain. The forces of democratization, ethnic identity and regionalism have advanced in combination across Europe.

The role of regional elites

The final bottom-up factor closely intertwines with the rise of identity politics: the interests and strategies of regional elites. These elites are composed of the leaders of regional political parties and the regional organizations of national political parties, the local government politicians, bureaucrats in local government and in state field agencies, leaders of the regional sections of the private sector, representatives of interest groups, members of the media and leaders of social institutions, such as churches.

They articulate the demands for regional government and usually they and their organizations benefit from the transfer of power from the centre to regional governments. When satisfying the aspirations of their followers, they create a role for their organizations and more employment, offices and financial rewards for themselves. There is an incentive to manipulate regional/nationalist symbols to maintain regionalist identities. As Wright (1984) points out, once regionalists' demands have been met, there is an automatic incentive to pursue them further. The genie has been let out of the bottle.

The reforms to the central state, such as the transfer of functions to the EU, privatization, market reforms and the setting up of new agencies create opportunities for the regional elites to carve out functions and responsibilities for themselves. The change in the strategies of the state since the 1980s gives them opportunities to outwit central governments. It is not clear whether the elites always prefer independence for their territories. Elites may prefer some decentralization and transfer of responsibilities but wish to remain under the umbrella of the nation-state. A compact between the national and regional elites may lead to the off-loading of functions from the centre to the regions to the interests of both. The other set of crude interest-based factors is the need for offices and posts, particularly for the politicians. The creation of tiers of government may be a way of rewarding and pacifying party followers. If regions administer functions that are politically sensitive and local politicians are bought off by these posts, the centre can effectively divide the periphery and still control the functions of government indirectly. The smaller number of regions are easier to control than the multitude of local authorities or a powerful political class based in the cities.

Comparing the factors across Western Europe

The combination of bottom-up and top-town factors would appear to indicate that regionalism and regionalization are powerful tendencies in Western European states. Functional logics, the EU and ethnic mobilization are the most salient factors. Indeed, the purpose of setting them out so strongly here is to argue against a narrow particularism which can easily dominate comparative Western European studies. The particularist claim is that the historical experiences, administrative structure and identity politics are so different as to make regionalism and regionalization entirely distinctive in each state. The art of comparison would be to observe the differences. As with any cross-national phenomena, there are many variants. The degree of ethnic mobilization varies from state to state; there are contrasting starting point, such as the extent of the division of powers; the traditions are vastly different; and there are unique historical junctures, such as the politics of the late 1960s, the end of authoritarianism in the 1970s, the arrival of socialists in French governments of the 1980s and the democratization waves of the 1990s. How can these regional reforms be compared? This chapter claims that, just as with the emergence of regimes and a Europeanized local polity, the development of regions is patchy and contingent. There is no emergence of a universal tier of regional government, but more the development of new and varied levels of administration, which appear at different times. As with the development of local governance as a whole, the development of regions or middle tiers of government is messy and erratic. This variability of regional governments becomes all the more evident when their detailed pattern and performance is examined.

The progress and performance of regional governments

Criticisms of regional governments

Much of the literature on regional government discusses why they emerged; few studies assess their performance. So far this chapter presents an optimistic picture whereby new organizations and movements have searched for and developed a role in formerly centralized political systems. As these regional governments' performance can be examined over a long period of time, a more critical literature has appeared (Le Galès and John, 1997; Le Galès and Lequesne, 1998), and some reaction against the critique (Rogers, 1998). Le Galès' argument is simple: the evidence of fifteen years of regional governments in Western Europe shows that regions are not going to dominate sub-national politics; instead, differentiated governance has emerged in most Western European states, without regions becoming the winners. He writes that 'whereas 15 years ago, there was every reason to believe that regions were going to become an essential level of government, this evolution did not take place' (Le Galès, 1998b: 240). Regions are not the key institutions that drive economic development. The economically active regions often do not coincide with institutional boundaries. Areas of economic activity either cross over regional boundaries or economic development policies are carried out at the sub-regional level. Moreover, regions are not the key actors in Western European governance; rather there is an interdependent multi-layered experience. Le Galès (1998b: 244) notes the weak institutionalization of regions in countries like Portugal, Ireland, Greece and in Scandinavia, with the partial exception of Sweden which has a weak regional level. He argues there is no inevitable development in countries that have regional governments, and rational functional arguments have become increasingly irrelevant. Le Galès (1998b: 245) discusses the example of the Netherlands (see also Toonen, 1998), where regionalist pressures exist but where central government has not introduced an elected regional tier. Then a complex pattern of regional governance has emerged in England, and the French state increased in complexity. Le Galès cannot deny the importance of regional governments in Spain and Belgium and the continuing importance of the German states, but notes their varied institutionalization (1998b: 246–248).

It is possible to acknowledge the strength of Le Galès' arguments without being so dismissive of the achievement of regions. Le Galès erects some high standards for these organizations in some countries, like France; but does not discuss this standard in other countries, such as in Belgium and Spain. Whilst not wishing to deny variations in the size and function of regional authorities, it is possible to be fairly relaxed about the ways in which middle-level government emerges in each country, particularly given the varied starting points. Le Galès' analysis is correct, but he draws too many negative inferences from the evidence he surveys. The varied experience of regional government across Western Europe is evidence for the move from government to governance because reformers have given up the quest to be uniform. In a similar way, evidence exists for the varied occurrence and performance of city administrations. There is no need to pit cities against regions, although these entities will jostle for position in the complex layers of institutions.

France

Some of these arguments appear neatly in France, where the creation of twenty-two elected regions has been an important reform, as they have powers in economic development and land use planning, control aspects of secondary education, higher education, training and transport. Though they do not challenge the unitary character of the state and have few powers and functions when compared to their counterparts in Belgium and Spain, their creation marked a change of direction of the French state. As a critique of their performance, Le Galès and John (1997) compare the optimism of the first years since their creation in 1982 with their poor performance later, arguing that the administrative nature of their political boundaries, their weak powers and low budgets attenuated them as organizations and as policy-making bodies. They also have a low level of political legitimacy since important local politicians do not wish to serve as regional councillors. When the French state limited the number of elected offices politicians could hold, powerful mayors retained local communal leadership and their national offices, dropping regional representation. Moreover, local elites use the membership of regional assemblies to reward political followers and turnover has been high (Négrier, 1999: 135). Although regions were expected to take on a key role in economic development and co-ordination, the French state moved away from *dirigiste* planning. Departments and the main communes were the winners in the decentralization reforms of 1982 and 1983. The critical view is that the regions do not have vast budgets, they have reduced expenditures in their key area of intervention, economic development, and face competition from other units of government.

Whilst Le Galès and John provide a welcome correction to the rhetoric of regionalism (see also Balme, 1995, 1998; Balme and Jouve, 1996; Le Galès, 1994), it is important to assess the contribution of regions to public policy-making. As acknowledged by Le Galès and John, some regions are forward-looking policy-makers, such as Bretagne, Nord-Pas de Calais and Languedoc–Rousillon, which have pioneered economic development policies. Most regions have financed and planned higher education expansion, lobbied Brussels and developed policies on culture, though they have failed in training. The experience has been varied and non-uniform. Whilst the regions have not lived up to the expectations of the optimists, some have been successful and have pioneered intervention in some policy sectors. Rather than demonstrating the weakness of regionalism, the French experience displays one of its most recent characteristics – the development of asymmetric patterns. Territorial unequal political institutions are not destabilizing; in contrast, they have become part of the way in which sub-national governance adapts to variation in activism, ethnic mobilization, economic development and competition between authorities (Keating, 1998). Moreover, regions show some signs of settling into the French political system as they gradually find a role. Even the public has grown to approve of regions, as revealed in regular opinion poll surveys.

The UK

The term asymmetric now applies to the UK. Administratively and culturally it was always so. Separate arrangements existed for adminis-tering the various parts of the UK, particularly when the Scottish and Welsh offices started to gain functions and when devolved government in Northern Ireland was in existence. In practice, however, there was much homogenization of policy across the administrative systems, particularly between England and Wales. The asymmetric character of the British state was hidden from view, being part of its customs and conventions rather than being stated in constitutional documents. Moreover, across England, which covers about 83 per cent of the population of the UK, central state departments imposed a uniform local government structure and a grant regime that aimed to equalize spending need

Much of the pattern of decentralization changed in 1997 when the Labour government introduced its devolution proposals – a parliament with slight tax-varying powers for Scotland and an assembly for Wales. Then the Good Friday agreement led to the power-sharing executive in Northern Ireland, which was formed in December 1999. What had already existed in administrative practice became manifest in separate political arrangements, which divides powers between the central state and the regional adminis-trations. The UK parliament in theory remains sovereign, but in practice regional governments will be hard to dislodge. Just as in a federal state, there will emerge a whole series of disputes about powers which will need to be resolved by the courts (such as the Judicial Committee of the Privy Council in the Scottish case), bureaucratic bargaining or through the political parties. The disputes so far have been few, though well publicized, such as in agriculture, but they are bound to grow as the devolved governments start to exercise more autonomy over policy-making.

Asymmetric regionalism, however, has two main consequences that change UK government and politics. The first is that the central state has to reorganize itself to deal with both England in some capacities and the UK in others, making the central administration partially regionalized (Hazell, 1999) and affecting the work of Parliament (Hazell, 2000). The other effect is on the territorial distribution of power in England as there is an administrative logic and political demand for some equivalent arrangement as in Scotland and Wales (Bradbury and Mawson, 1998; John and Whitehead, 1997). The institutionalization of the English regions has developed, partly in train with the fortunes of Scotland and Welsh devolution. By the mid-1990s, there had emerged a complex matrix of regional governance composed of local authorities, government agencies and interest groups that articulated the interests of the standard regions (Mawson, 1998a, 1998b). Moreover, in 1993 central government integrated the regional organizations of four central state departments into the government offices for the regions (GORs) and created a new civil service post, the regional director, to run them, which had the effect of legitimizing political action in these regional spaces. In 1998 the Labour government created Regional Development Agencies based on the nine regions; then it set up regional chambers as quasi-corporatist bodies to articulate regional interests. Here the development of regional government remains, with the lack of identity and unwieldy character of some regions being an obstacle (John, 1998b). The next step is some form of elected regional government, but with limited powers. The northern regions might acquire powers first, creating asymmetric regionalism in England as well as across the UK.

Spain

Spain is another country that has a diverse experience of regional government. After the death of Franco regional political movements pressed the state to introduce regions because of the territorial basis to the anti-Franco movement and the reaction against centralist rule. Such was the political pressure that the three 'ethnic' regions, Catalonia, Galicia and the Basque country, moved ahead to an *ad hoc* form of self-rule in 1977, a practice that the government extended to other regions in the 'State of the Autonomies' (Estados de las Autonomías) in the 1978 constitution (Tamames and Clegg, 1984). The Constitution retained the unity of the Spanish state, but gave substantial autonomy, in particular legislative competencies, to the regions. The constitution allowed regional administrations to absorb the central bureaucracies. The regions have many functions, such as town and country planning, regional roads and railways, the implementation of environmental policies and regional economic development.

Commentators make a great play on the development of asymmetric regionalism. Here they refer to the provisions of the 1978 constitution that allow for each of the seventeen autonomous communities to adopt regional powers, and indeed only the three ethnic communities voted for it. Rather than remaining like English regions in the context of Scotland, Wales and Northern Ireland in the current UK, the other regions of Spain soon demanded powers. In 1981, the Autonomic Agreement (LOAPA) speeded up autonomy for non-historic regions and by 1987 virtually all the powers in the statutes of autonomy had been granted to the regions. This provision was extended in 1992 by the Autonomic Agreement, which transferred identical competences within a five-year period. The significance of the Spanish case for asymmetric territories, such as the UK, is that regions that are left out will demand their place in the sun. As elsewhere there is a mutually supporting relationship between institution building and identity. Regional/nationalist identity has always been strong in the historical regions. But once some regions acquire powers so elites in other regions wish to follow (Keating, 1998: 91).

As in other countries, the regions have developed their role and have adapted to their environments rather than following a pre-set path of development. Some regional leaderships, such as of the Socialist party in Andalucia, started with ambitious plans for autonomous economic development policies, but these policies have gradually moderated as regional elites have sought to integrate decision-making into the policies for the whole country. The regions have some autonomy, and seek to exercise it, particularly in relation to their supportive publics. But both centre and periphery are locked together, even in conflicts that are often adjudicated in the courts. Whilst Spain has some quasi-federal elements, it is not a federation as it lacks some key features such as full regional representation in the second chamber of the national legislature (Spain allows only 44 out of 252 senators to be appointed by the autonomous parliaments). It retains a high degree of formal centralization, with a powerful central bureaucracy (Cuchillo, 1993).

In terms of explaining regional policy decisions, it is important to examine party politics in the regions and at the national level, and understand the complicated games played between the two levels. The system is also characterized by a high degree of competition between the regions, usually for legal and financial resources from the centre (Colomer, 1998). There is also competition and conflict between the leaderships of the main cities and regional administrations. The result is what Colomer calls non-institutional federalism, which sounds like an oxymoron, but captures some of the character of decentralization. The regions have gained a slice of income taxes that began with Catalonia, which the government extended to other regions.

Some writers believe that there is a pragmatic spirit that informs the strategies of national and regional elites. Taking the example of the Olympic

Games in Barcelona in 1992, Hargreaves (2000) argues that both sides co-operated to ensure the success of the games, indicating an emerging pluralism. The project played to both Spanish and Catalan senses of identity. Critics would suggest the Olympics is an unusual event as it confers large benefits on all and so is not a good measuring rod to judge the integrity of the nation-state.

Like over other countries that have decentralized, observers divide about the future of the Spanish state. Some argue that radical forces break up its unity, which will lead to a further round of decentralization reforms; others believe that regional politicians are happy with the extent of decentralization and play the regionalist card to access more resources. The flexibility of the system means it can adapt to any political pressures, but at the same time there is integration and a high degree of legitimacy. As some writers note (for example, Garcia, 1998), Spanish policy-makers make the best of the adaptability of the system so that they can temper solutions for each problem.

Italy

Italy is a further model of regionalization. Regions and former nations dominate social, political and economic life, from regional cultures and dialects, the organization and factions in political parties and the success or otherwise of regional economies. But, at the same time as there is massive regional diversity, the central state retains its control over many aspects of administration and policy-making. Centralization has been challenged by successive waves of regional mobilization, particularly among the political classes, which came to a head in the 1990s. The first wave was during the constitution-making phase of the late 1940s when there was a reaction against the centralist period of fascist rule (Cassese and Torchia, 1993: 94). However, with the exception of the special statute regions of Sicily, Sardinia, Val d'Aosta, Trentino–Alto Adige and Friuli–Venezia–Giula), the regional provisions were never implemented, partly because the Christian Democrat government feared regions would become controlled by the Communists. By the 1960s economic prosperity and an anti-centralist culture changed the agenda as a generation of bureaucrats emerged who were more at ease with democracy. Decentralization became one of the platforms of the new left which invested much hope and optimism in regional governments.

From the 1970s central governments implemented the regional government provisions and Italian regional governments gained the functions of health and agriculture. Yet most Italian regional governments were not successful entities, partly because most decisions continued to be controlled by the central bureaucracies in Rome. The theme of Putnam's *Making Democracy Work* (1993) and of the earlier research for the book (Putnam et al., 1983) is the link between civic traditions and the success of regional government. Thus some regions failed to become effective and open governments. The last phase was the break-up of the Christian Democrats in a wave of corruption scandals and the parallel growth of the Northern Leagues. These developments have made an impact on regional conscious-ness, something that has been surprisingly weak in Italy (Keating, 1998: 93). The Italian leagues peddle an anti-statist, anti-southern populist rhetoric, and argue for succession, though in practice they support a federalist solution (Giordano, 2000).

Portugal and Greece

Regionalization does not extend to all of southern Europe. The countries of Portugal and Greece have not developed strong regional structures, partly because their elites, located in strong centralized bureaucracies, have not been willing to relinquish power. Portugal has some history of regionalization of the state in its national plans (Merloni and Vecchio, 1987), but these structures existed purely for administrative convenience. After the end of the dictatorship, title VIII constitution of 1976 provided for the creation of regions, composed of representative of the municipalities. At first they were not implemented owing to the conservatism of the central administration and because the Christian Democrat centre feared control by the Communists. Now regional assemblies have the power to monitor and supervise the activities of a regional executive body (junta regional). The junta has powers over regional planning and development, though in the main regional policies are managed by the central government divisions, the *Comissoes de Coordinaçao Regional*. In 1998 the government put the proposal to have elected administrative regions to a referendum. But the proposal fell, largely because the political parties did not support and campaign for the reforms (Mira, 1999) The latest reform was the creation in 1991 of self-governing metropolitan areas of Lisbon and Oporto (Pereira, 1995).

   Greece has a similar history of administrative centralism, largely because it is in a part of the world where ethnic tensions are potentially explosive (Featherstone and Yannopoulos, 1995). The prefectoral authorities, the *nomarchia*, were partially democratized in 1995 and groups of them form the thirteen regional councils. These regions are not elected bodies, but comprise representatives from central government and local authorities. The development of regionalism and regions is weak, since the regions' powers are advisory. The government created them to respond to EU funding programmes rather than from bottom-up pressures.

Germany

It is hard to compare regions and regionalism in federal states with those elsewhere, especially in countries that have stable and embedded forms of decentralization, such as Germany. The incentive to decentralize does not exist as much in a federal system as elsewhere and bottom-up regional pressures are often institutionalized. The German mix between an entrenched constitutional status for the states, requiring the sharing of powers, and a complex pattern of policy networks and interdependence between levels of government, creates both institutional and informal constraints on political action that absorb the demands for reform of the territorial structure of the state. Moreover, the norms of consensus and the powerful interlocking policy networks, the system of joint policy-making – *Politikverflechtung* (Scharpf et al., 1978) – ensures that the demands posed by Europeanization and economic competition lead to gradual adjustments in the machinery for making policy, as Chapter 4 demonstrates with respect to Europeanization. Unlike other countries, the demands such as the autonomy of certain states, like Bavaria, tend to be expressed in central–local conflicts rather than in demands to reform the system as a whole.

Such a pattern of intermediation does not imply that the German pattern of intergovernmental relations is smooth, that policy-making does not suffer from conflict and confusion or that these tensions have not grown in recent years (Scharpf, 1988). Whilst the federation has suffered from the strain of reunification and demands from the states to repatriate responsibilities lost to the federal or Western European levels, what is striking is its resilience and adaptability (Jeffery, 1999). At the same time and consistent with trends in the rest of Europe, German regional governments have rediscovered the importance of territorial difference and the fashioning of policies designed to respond to economic competition. Rather than a centralizing federation, decentralist pressures and the forces of complexity and differentiation reshape the German political system as elsewhere. Moreover, regional networks and organizations between the state and local government have emerged within German states for land use planning and economic development (Benz, 1998: 114), largely because areas of regional economic activity do not coincide with the boundaries of the *Länder* so that these forms of co-operation are either within state boundaries or across them. These informal regional arrangements are an indication of the pressures for institutional reform within Western European political systems whilst at the same time they show that major institutional reform does not happen so easily in a strong federal system. Where co-operation is voluntary, the partners to city regions, for example will act in their short-term interests, such as between the city state of Berlin and its surrounding hinterland, Brandenburg (Hauswirth et al., 2000).

Belgium

Belgium presents an example of radical change. Here bottom-up factors have led to the reconstruction of the state. Belgium has moved from a centralized unitary state to a federal one in just over two decades. The existence of the two main ethnic communities has driven the change (Delmartino, 1988). Originally the Flemish were excluded from elite positions within the state. Very gradually the Flemish gained the use of their language in education, the courts and in administration, which led to the granting of cultural autonomy for the three linguistic communities in 1970. In 1980 three regional communities were created whose powers were extended in 1993. The main political reforms occurred in 1988 and 1993 which created federal arrangements and ended the hierarchy between federal and regional laws (de Rynck, 1996; Hooghe, 1995a). Two aspects of policy-making are affected. The first concerns language and, more broadly, culture. It gave rise to the communities, a concept that refers both to the people and identity, in this case language and culture. Belgium has three Communities based on language: the Flemish Community, the French Community and the German-speaking Community. The second main state reform was inspired by economic concerns, since the regions wanted more autonomous power, and gave rise to the three regions: the Flemish Region, the Brussels Capital Region and the Walloon Region. The country is further divided into nine provinces (10 as of 1 January 1995) as well as the 589 communes. The federal state retains foreign affairs, defence, justice, finance, social security, and aspects of public health and domestic affairs. The regions and communities are entitled to run foreign relations themselves in those areas where they have responsibility.

The high degree of decentralization in Belgium is the logical end point of regional decentralization. If it goes further, then Belgium may break up and become separate nation-states, with perhaps a confederal solution for the multi-ethnic capital city of Brussels. Artificial features hold together the state: the impossible solution to the government of Brussels, the presence of the monarchy as a national institution and the EU, since Belgium has to come together to make its vote (even if sometimes the country abstains when the regions cannot agree). The conclusion to draw is that Belgium has become stable since the state remains intact even if hollowed out, suggesting that states, such as Spain and the UK, can devolve power but retain their integrity. The trends toward multi-layered government imply that the nation-state changes its character rather than dissolves. It becomes one player alongside communes, provinces, regions and communities as well as the other actors in the framework of governance.

The Netherlands

Regionalization does not extend across the whole of Western Europe. Consistent with the north–south divide, many Northern local government systems have retained their local government structures. These states have reformed local government whilst keeping regional and/or provincial structures weak. In the Netherlands there is a complex set of administrative and decentralized structures at the meso level (Toonen, 1993). Twelve provinces exist, but they have few functions. Provincial authorities control environmental management, spatial planning, energy, social work, sport and cultural affairs, yet they are not responsible for much public expenditure. Elites have made a considerable effort to reform sub-national structures, leading to a set of proposals to create regional governments, but these reform efforts came to nothing and the complex form of administrative regionalism remains (Toonen, 1998). The main demand for regional structures does not come from territorial identification, which is weak or hidden in Holland, but from the need to administer the system more effectively. As a consequence, there is no political drive for reform. The Netherlands is changing its governing structure in other ways. More powers and duties are being devolved from central government to the provinces and municipalities with the aim of reducing bureaucracy. Other small countries do not engage much with regional experiments. There is little demand for regional government in Ireland because the whole country can act as a region for European funding purposes, for example. But the government set up non-elected regional authorities in 1995, mainly for co-ordination and planning purposes.

Scandinavia

Regionalism has not been such a force in the Scandinavian countries as elsewhere. There are strong regional identities, as in Norway, but the institutions that administer the welfare state remain strong. Many countries have a two-tiered system of local government, such as the counties and municipalities in Norway (Hansen, 1993a). This two tier pattern replicates across Scandinavia (Hansen, 1993a). With such embedded local government systems, these countries have strengthened their local governments and have sought a clearer division between the functions of each tier of government. It is possible to identify a small group of countries that adhere closely to the 'northern pattern' because they have the means to deal with the functionalist pressures for regionalism, have not been a victim of institutional experimentation, such as in the Netherlands and in the UK, and have not had to regionalize in the face of ethnic and territorial mobilization. Nevertheless, in 1995 a parliamentary Commission proposed a new type of directly elected government with regional development functions in addition to the powers of local councils. Also, since 1994 Finland has regional councils which are joint municipal authorities, which are composed of associations of municipalities. The councils take on the functions of regional development and planning.

Conclusion

The diversity of the experience of regional governments suggests that national particularity defines the experiments since the 1970s. Whilst reformers introduced regional authorities in a similar period, they emerged for different reasons and have a varying character. The regional experiment in France was modest and fitted into the existing framework of administrative deconcentration; it did not upset the powerful local baronies in the communes, and regional governments struggled to find a role in the system. The weak progress of Italy's regional governments indicates a similar prognosis, though the massive changes in Italian politics since the early 1990s suggest that regions may yet find their place in the sun. Spain, on the other hand, has pushed ahead with a more fundamental trans-formation of its political system. Under pressure from the ethnic regions, it created asymmetric political institutions, which became more uniform in response to the desire for the other regions to catch up. Progress has been more modest in the other Mediterranean countries, such as Portugal and Greece, that have found it hard to shake off the legacy of centralist rule. Meanwhile, one country, Belgium, has introduced radical reforms that almost challenge the integrity of the state. Other countries have tried asymmetric models but without any constitutional provision for the other regions to catch up. The UK has moved from informal administrative decentralization to a form of asymmetric government where the nations of Scotland and Wales have some legal and practical autonomy from the rest of the United Kingdom, but have different powers from each other; there is a confederal arrangement for Northern Ireland but with a high degree of centralization, and a lack of regional government in England. Yet the UK central government retains control over finances and other key policy instruments. Meanwhile, the extent of regional institutional formation has been weak in the other northern countries. This variation suggests national particularity rather than a universal trend.

In spite of the contrasting institutions at the middle level of governance, states are responding to similar public problems. Their leaders and reformers attend to economic competition, accommodate ethnic identity and make provisions for strategic planning and transportation even though the common factors emerge in different combinations and strengths and change in salience over time. The attempt to solve a similar set of problems feeds into the policy-making process where different organizations and office holders try to perform functionally equivalent tasks. The impact on the organization of the state is similar in that formerly simple demo-cratic territorial organizations are being replaced by more complex and overlapping sets of structures as governments search for new solutions and institutions to deal with public problems. The new regional governments also interact with the existing deconcentrated state institutions and regional interest groups. They also intersect with the matrix of local organizations in such a way that there is no neat distinction between the local and regional levels. Each is so embedded in each others affair's as to make a continuum of networks and interrelations between overlapping actors.

When described in this way, governance is similar to what Keating (1998) calls a variable-geometry Europe and a differentiated political order. As he writes, 'if there is to be a model for the state, it is likely to be asymmetrical, a national and European mosaic more akin to the pre-modern Europe than the uniform nation-state of the nineteenth century' (Keating, 1998: 188). As other chapers of the book show, the differentiation of institutions and networks is a feature of governance because local particularities and multi-level problems become more evident than under government. The breakdown of unitary administration is especially evident when states adopt asymmetric patterns of regional government because the varying institutional solutions offer different services and bestow different rights to the supposedly equal citizens within a liberal democracy.

7

Leadership and the Local Executive

In local politics there is a tension between fragmentation and co-ordination. Political leaders and institutions try to counteract the complexity and diversity inherent in local social and economic life. The argument of the chapter, which extends the claims of the others, is that the existing tension between diversity and co-ordination in local politics becomes more marked under conditions of governance because the stable environment under which political leaders governed for so long has shifted to one of fragmented institutions and rapid policy change. Solutions normally adopted by mayors or by ruling party groups no longer work so neatly as before.

Pressures for reform

The shifting framework of institutions and the emergence of new policy problems have several effects. The first is pressure on the institutional structure itself. Local government has a political executive, like in any political system. It may be hidden from view or explicitly stated in legislation. Power may be vested in a directly elected or appointed mayor or in a cabinet, which itself is concretized by formal and informal contacts between the executive and the legislature, local bureaucracy and to central government organizations. In normal circumstances the institution of the executive processes political demands from the locality, manages the interests of the bureaucracy and negotiates with central state bodes, which have great power but lack knowledge about how to implement their policies. In this brokering position local executives have much freedom of manoeuvre to reward their interests and those of their followers. They can also follow relatively autonomous policies. But with the growing importance of local economic competition, greater demands from different cultural groups, more pressures from central government to deliver policies, more competition between local authorities and impositions from energized regional authorities, the challenge of leadership becomes much greater than before.

The reform movement

To counter fragmentation, a reform movement has emerged to give greater power and legitimacy to elected leaders by consolidating their power by either strengthening directly elected mayors or replacing more collegial and party-based forms of decision-making with mayoral leaderships. Much of this chapter examines the pressures for reform that lead either to mayors being introduced or to stronger powers for existing ones. Although there are different systems of sub-central government, the question arises as to whether they are being subjected to similar pressures associated with internationalization and local competition or whether these reforms only appear similar. This chapter, like the others, examines the argument that the reforms make sense only when taking into account the differing national contexts, where legal rules, organizational routines and contextual rules of the game determine and process the outputs of government.

The character of political leadership

The second set of changes concern the character of political leadership itself. Here the strength of political leaders and their capacity to solve political problems is at stake. Leaders vary in the extent they can think of and implement successful policies, in their personal skills and in their ability to manage organizations. From the perspective of governance, leaders vary in the extent to which they can deal with institutions horizontally and respond to fast-moving agendas. In part the changes at the local level throw up the politicians who are best able to survive in office; in part, political leaders consider new ways of doing business. Even traditional leaders, the boss politicians, become more adept at managing wider coalitions and new networks. Here the topic of this chapter links with the discussion of regimes in Chapter 3. The argument is that the fragmented character of local areas, with their competing micro localities and range of territorial interests, leads to the demand for more coalition-based politics. Only strong leaders are capable of leading such partnerships and have the balance of skills necessary to sustain them. When making this argument, this chapter restates one of the classic truisms of political leadership: the personal skills of persuasion are the essential skill of high office (Neustadt, 1960). This idea, however, has been articulated more in the US political system where fragmented government is the norm, whereas studies of leaders in Western Europe have tended to examine either the relationship between leaders and followers (Burns, 1979) – reflecting the importance of party politics – or the importance of institutional arrangements (for example, Rose and Suleiman, 1980). By stressing the importance of personal factors, researchers recognize that fragmented institutional structures need more North American-style politicians to give charismatic but practical leadership to localities and cities.

Local government leadership

As with so much of the discussion of sub-national government in Western Europe, the starting point is the classification system of central–local government systems, in particular those that indicate clusters of countries in the north and south of Western Europe. Comparative studies have found that political leaders of southern systems play a particularly important role in the articulation of interests and the balance of power. Tarrow (1977), in his classic work, *Between Center and Periphery, Grassroots Politicians in Italy and France*, discovered that the mayors of the primary local government units, the communes, exercised a brokering role between centre and locality. Mayors had close contacts to the other local political actors and citizens; and they used their gatekeeper role to access resources from the centre. Strong mayors occurred in post-Napoleanic states where the primary units of local governments were small and had few functions. Their legal discretion was low, but leaders had good access to the centre (Page, 1991; Page and Goldsmith, 1987).

France

Such an account corresponds with the classic accounts of French politics and central–local relations where the *cumul de mandats* have allowed local politicians to be both local and national politicians at the same time and so exercise power at both levels (Gremion, 1976; Kesselman, 1972; Worms, 1966). Research stresses the existence of many cross-cutting networks of relationships between political and economic actors (Crozier, 1964; Crozier and Friedberg, 1977; Crozier and Thoenig, 1975). The principal ones are between elected politicians (usually mayors) and state officials (generally prefects and their officials). Important too is the legal status of the mayor as an officer of the state – and writers refer to the 1884 law that standardized the status of communes. It is difficult for a French party to dislodge a mayoral incumbent, which can lead to the creation of mayoral dynasties. The local political party often becomes subservient to the town hall, which is central for the distribution of local patronage. Other political personnel, such as the powerful position of *adjoints* (assistants), are selected by the major – a decision usually ratified by the first meeting of the new municipal council – and the mayor is usually assisted by a series of *cabinets*. Mayoral patronage extends into the local administration. This system of local power remained untouched for over 150 years and survived experiments with municipal socialism in the first decades of the twentieth century and rapid urbanization later on (Borraz, 1994).

Italy

Tarrow found that the Italian system also corresponded to the clientelistic model. As with France, there is a large number of communes (varying between 7,000 and 9,100 over the past century and a half). Local mayors are often important figures within their political parties, rather than acting as administrative brokers as in the French case. But they play a similar role by mediating between centre and locality. Yet the form of political representation is different. The municipal councils are elected on a proportional basis every four years. Then a majority coalition takes shape in the council and elects a mayor. In effect, the mayor is indirectly elected and emerged because of an agreement between the political parties rather than necessarily being the most popular candidate, even though there have been some remarkable figures in post-war years, such as Dozza in Bologna or La Pira in Florence (Somma, 1999).

Although mayors are formally first among equals in their councils, they have remained powerful politicians who have used the fragmented local party systems to their advantage. They manipulated the unstable structure of the coalitions in the Italian party system to promote their objectives. They also directed the *giunta*, which is a collegiate body elected by the council and which comprises the heads of administrative departments. Because of the extensive bargaining between political parties, it has been in the smaller communes where mayors have dominated, whereas they have had to cede to the power of the bureaucrats and the political parties in larger places.

Spain

It is possible to find similar relationships outside the two countries Tarrow studied. Spain has a similar primary local government structure to France and Italy, with about 8,000 communes in 1985. As was the case in Italy, mayors are appointed from the elected council if the municipality has over 100 inhabitants. In the period of the *cacuiqismo* in the late nineteenth and early twentieth centuries, there was an extensive form of local clientelism, but this practice was blocked by the Franco regime (Clegg, 1987), though many mayors maintained informal contacts with the central state. Local governments emerged with freedoms in the post-Franco period; but they had few functions and resources. Moreover, they have been overshadowed by the increase in the power of the regions.

Portugal and Greece

Portugal follows a similar pattern. It too has a communal level. There was a centralized pattern of administration, as before the revolution of 1974 the mayor was appointed by the central government and was its representative (Pedroso de Almedia, 1991). There is a municipal executive, elected directly by the population, with a chairman who is the candidate with the most votes. Both Spain and Portugal do not follow a typical southern pattern, with the Spanish system not unlike British local government before the reforms of 2000 (Stoker and Travers, 1998). In Greece, the leaders of the list in the municipalities over 5,000 people need to receive 50 per cent of the vote to be elected mayor. Then there is a second ballot a week later. The mayor takes on executive functions and is assisted by an executive committee composed of three to five councillors (Christofilopoulou-Kaler, 1991).

Belgium

The final 'southern' country is Belgium which has a communal structure that has been in place since 1836 (Delmartino, 1991). Although mayors are formally appointed by the king, they are the person who heads the list of candidates of the party that gains the largest share of the vote in the municipal elections. The mayor represents central authority in his functions over local policing and civil defence. The council proposes the candidate for the mayor and nominates the executive members. Southern systems do not entirely correspond to the power broker as envisaged in Tarrow's analysis as they have elements of collective decision-making characteristic of the north.

Scandinavia

There are considerable variations in the structure of the executive in northern states, particularly the Scandinavian countries that are supposed to be the defining examples of more collegiate forms of government in strong welfare systems. Swedish municipalities are run by an executive committee drawn from the ranks of elected members. Because of the proportional electoral system, there is often coalition government, which leads to the commissioner presiding over an executive committee of several parties. In Denmark, since 1919, the mayor is chosen from among the other members of the council and since the reforms of the 1970s is elected for the whole term of office and chairs an executive committee of the council (Bogason, 1991). The office has power to decide business, which is delegated to committees. So Denmark is a good exemplar of the more northern pattern of collective decision-making. In Norway there is no strict executive body as administrators carry out the decisions of the council. But the municipalities and counties have boards or executive bodies that are empowered to make decisions (Council of Europe, 1992). There is a mayor who chairs this body and who has a term of office for four years. Any municipality can decide to have a parliamentary system of self-government – when the political body exists instead of the chief officer and is elected by majority ballot. As in other countries, mayors like to place themselves above party politics; they tend to be political veterans who are influential in the policy-making process (Goldsmith, 1991: 25). They have to work in a multi-party context and to seek consensus among the different parties in the council. In Finland, there is an executive board whose members are appointed for a four-year term. The political head is the chair of the council. Another important figure is the head of administration, the municipal manager, who can be elected as chair of the council.

Germany

At first sight it appears that the former West Germany showed a neat north–south divide. Because the states have the final say in the organization of local government, there were variations in the executive structure. Most writers group these systems into four types that reflect the history of occupation by allied powers after the Second World War (Bullmann and Page, 1994; Stoker, 1996). They were, first, the Magistrat form, a Prussian form of local government that was found in the city authorities in Schleswig Holstein, Hessen and Bremerhaven and in parts of the city-state of Bremen. Here the council formally vested power in the municipal executive – the Magistrat – which consisted of paid officials as well as elected representatives. The Magistrat drew up the policy and oversaw its implementation. The mayor chaired the Magistrat, but not the municipal assembly. Secondly, the leadership form that existed in the Rhineland–Palatinate had genuine 'southern' influences as it derived from French influence. Here the town council elected the Burgermeister who did not have a seat on the council. Thirdly, the south German form in Bavaria, Würtemberg and Baden, which developed in the nineteenth century, gave more power to the Burgermeister who was directly elected, chaired the municipal assembly, took the executive role and had emergency powers. Fourthly, in North Rhine–Westphalia there was a collective form of decision-making that resembled the British system. This legacy is not surprising as it was introduced following British occupation after the Second World War. After 1989 a fifth system entered on the scene from the *Länder* that were part of the former German Democratic Republic. This was a hybrid between the Burger-meister system, the south German model and the Magistrat system whereby the Burgermeister headed the administration for a four-year period of office. Within Germany therefore a variety of systems diverged between collective decision-making, more prevalent in the north, and systems that gave more power to the individual decision-makers, in the south. The southern systems offered more visibility to the mayor; whereas those in the north allowed for more flexibility and clearer programmes for the electorate to choose (Bullmann and Page, 1994: 52). Later the chapter describes how these systems are changing as a part of the move from government to governance.

The Netherlands and Britain

Other northern systems are more straightforward. The Netherlands resembles other countries by having a Burgomeister, though the Crown chooses the occupant. The Burgomeister chairs the municipal executive and serves for four years (Council of Europe, 1999). The British system was that the leader of the party group became the leader of the council. This office is not formal but exists because of the reality of party politics and the discipline of groups on the council. The council was the authoritative body which delegated its power to committees rather than to an executive.

British leaders, by tradition, lacked visibility and formal power. Rather than holding office, they headed the party group and derived their power from the control the party exercised over council business. Leaders were selected by their party groups of councillors. Leaders had to keep the group loyal or else it might vote into power another of their number. The legal framework vested power in the elected council and its committees, so it was up to the political party and its leadership to organize council business and to ensure council officers follow its decisions. Leaders could not depend on a stock of local legitimacy to act authoritatively. Rather than assuming a preordained role, they had to build the relationships by their own efforts. Some critics suggest the executive was headless and unaccountable because it is unclear who exercised power (see Young, 1994 for a summary of the debate). Other critics believe the leader was too weak, a tendency that became more marked over time (Norton, 1978).

On the other hand, it is important not to underestimate the power of British leaders. They head large and powerful organizations and they are the most prominent democratically elected individuals in local areas. Moreover, they exercised these resources through relatively disciplined political parties. Indeed, British local politics has had many strong, even ruthless local political leaders: T. Dan Smith of Newcastle in the 1960s, Herbert Morrison in London in the 1930s and 1940s (Donoughue and Jones, 1973) and John Bradock in Liverpool in the 1940s and 1950s (Baxter, 1972). Whilst leaders became less colourful and powerful in the 1970s, resurgent local public figures emerged during the politically turbulent period of the

1980s. On the left there was Ken Livingstone who led the Greater London Council, David Blunkett in Sheffield and Ted Knight in Lambeth; on the right, Dame Shirley Porter in Westminster and Paul Beresford in Wandsworth were also powerful and charismatic. The conclusion to draw is that in Britain, as elsewhere in Europe, the power of parties allows leaders a good deal of latitude, even though British party groups can easily oust leaders (Leach and Wilson, 2000).

Comparing practices across Western Europe

In this review of executive structures, the chapter shows a rough north–south divide as predicted by the comparative local government literature, at least in the period before the 1990s. In general, practices of strong individual leadership exist in the south, with power and legitimacy vested in the office and person of the mayor who often acts as a broker between central and local actors and is often a powerful national politician as well as being the local boss. In contrast, the simplified picture of the northern local authority is where collegial processes appear to predominate, the decisions of the elected council as a whole are legitimate, there can be collective cabinet-style of government and the leader is the chair of this cabinet. In theory, the former system is well placed to represent local interests. Mayors deploy their personal contacts to extract favours for the locality from all-powerful central government organizations. At the same time the central state invests mayors with responsibilities and duties that do not emanate from an electoral mandate. The mayor becomes a visible manifestation of both local and national interests – and has power accordingly. In the northern model decisions are made more collectively, are closer to party interests and linked to the different services of the council. The leader needs to ensure the consent of the different parts of the organization. It is easy to undermine this simple view. The account of the south best fits Italy and France. But even in these countries mayors often represent small communes and do not have much clout. Until recently, Italy's mayors could not claim a monopoly of power. The mayor is in a weaker position in Spain and Portugal, having been undermined by decades of authoritarian rule. There are a variety of practices in the north, from collective decision-making to where the mayor has extensive power. Nevertheless, as with other matters, the stereotype illuminates rather than accurately reflects the structures and the exercise of power.

The move to governance

The reform of public services

The political executive has experienced intense strain in previous years. The first is that the pace of reform of public services and institutions has increased rapidly since the 1970s. Most Western European countries have reformed their institutions of local government by adding powers and tiers of elected authorities – as in France – or by reforming the legal framework for service delivery – as in the UK. Central and state governments have sought to improve the quality and performance of public services through the tools of NPM (see Chapter 4). Local political leaders can no longer rely on running their baronies without much interest from central government politicians, regulators and civil servants. They have to take note of the extensive reforms of sub-national government. The Europeanization of sub-national government has placed further responsibilities and added to the number of organizations a local leader has to deal with.

Secondly, fiscal austerity has been a reality of local politics since the 1970s (Newton, 1980): increasing responsibilities for providing services, an inadequate local tax base and the declining willingness of central governments to provide the finances to pay for services. In contrast, there have been some brief periods when central government off-loaded functions and created governments in some states, such as France, in the early 1980s when, for a brief period, local government enjoyed central government beneficence. Also places varied to the extent to which they experienced fiscal austerity (Mouritzen, 1992). Scandinavia has not experienced fiscal strains, except Finland in the early 1990s and Sweden in the early to mid-1990s.

Thirdly, municipal leaders have to compete with many other sources of authority. The prime source of conflict has been with the regions that have their own politicians and compete with resources and functions with local government. The many public and semi-public organizations need to be co-ordinated, and usually this task falls to the most prominent and legitimate person in the local area. Municipal leaders find themselves at the head of partnerships and try to give them unity and coherence. As with the other changes, this role places a strain on municipal leaders as they have to be coalition builders as well as party bosses, managers and lobbyists. Yet the enhanced role is an opportunity as well as a cost, since it gives leaders a chance to reinvent themselves as champions of the wider community, to re-engage with business and other private elites and to mobilize communities in the face of economic change. As Stone comments (1995), good leadership comes out of difficulty and from the need for challenge and vision when times have become hard. This comment draws attention to the two sides of the problem of executive leadership – the person and institutions – and the argument that reform of the latter could lead to better persons and opportunities in the main office.

Fourth is the familiar driver of economic change. The large enterprises and public sector organizations that provided stable employment in many localities have now been wiped out or reduced by economic competition. The loss of traditional industries and the search for investment provide practical challenges for local leaders. They also cause a political crisis because many social-democratic party supporters were employed by these industries. Such a change in economic fortunes means that the leader has to please both traditional supporters and show a wider constituency that they are not outdated dinosaurs but modern politicians reaching out to new and old citizens. Internationalization necessitates potent local solutions. Both citizens and elites are happy to transfer their anxiety to their leaders. The mayor become the booster, such as the leaders in former industrial North American localities who helped their economies draw in investment (Judd and Parkinson, 1990).

Fifthly, there have been changes in political culture and behaviour. Chapter 1 reviewed Clark and his co-researchers' argument that there is a post-industrial political culture where the old left–right issues do not have such salience as before (Clark and Hoffman-Martinot, 1998). The implication of challenges to hierarchy, the plurality of values, the influence of ideas, such as environmentalism, and the power of new social movements, is that mayors cannot act so freely as before and recruits must appeal to new groups and articulate a broader, more liberal set of issues whilst at the same time not disturbing the institutions of the market economy. The new agenda of politics is driven by these long-running social forces. Some leaders adapt; others cannot. As with the changes in the economic context of local politics, the crisis may enhance the power and status of the elected leader. On the other hand, new conditions may call for demands to reform the institutions of leadership, particularly where collective forms of leadership appear to hold back the autonomy, impair the legitimacy and inhibit the creativity of the person at the top. Elite political cultures also shape the opportunities and beliefs of local political leaders as leaders are drawn from the membership of local elites and need their loyalty.

Leadership change

France and Britain

In the light of economic pressures and new challenges for policy-makers, the practice of leadership in Western Europe has become more high profile and dynamic even within the existing structures. Leaders have seized the economic development agenda with gusto. John and Cole's (1999) study of networks in France and Britain found that dynamic leaders had emerged in the four localities they had studied. These politicians sought to widen the agenda, to engage with business and to introduce new policies whilst seeking to please their traditional supporters. They learnt that old practices of doing business within political parties did not work, and that they needed to build more coalitions outside their political parties. One example was the northern French city of Lille, the principal city in northern France. The Lille Urban Community (CUDL), an inter-communal grouping, has eighty-five communes. The commune of Lille is the main centre and its leader has been the dominant politician in the area. Leader since 1973, Pierre Mauroy also displayed an acute awareness of the need to build governing capacity and to forge alliances with private and voluntary sector interests mainly because heavy industries collapsed in the early 1980s. Closer co-operation between the Socialist town hall and local economic interests was an important part of his strategy. Mauroy drove this alliance. He played a personal role in promoting major economic development projects, such as the international rail link, the new train station and the Euralille commercial and business complex. His leadership overcame the parochial loyalties of the many communes in the Lille metropole. John and Cole found a similar pattern in Rennes, though there were more challenges to the leadership. In the UK, in the period before the reform of the local executive, they found leaders who aspired to be strong mayors and to lead an economic development coalition, but floundered on their lack of power, the ease with which they could be deposed by their supporters, the lack of a permanent career path and the need to move to take national office.

Economic-style leaders have emerged in other localities. In France Michel Noir was a powerful boosterist leader of Lyons (Harding et al., 1994). There are other examples of French mayors taking on an entrepreneurial role (Le Bart, 1992), such as Alain Carignon of Grenoble. During the 1990s, however, many of these prominent leaders left office in disgrace, often from corruption scandals. Mayors rediscovered their interest in exclusion and social policy. In the last years of the twentieth century they sought to balance these interests with economic development projects. More fiscally conservative mayors sought to be populist and neo-liberal (Clark and Inglehart, 1998: 26). Some UK leaders aspired to the roles John and Cole found in their study. The leader of Manchester sought to bring a coalition together to bring the 2000 Olympic Games to the city. Birmingham, under its leader Dick Knowles, developed a economic strategy based on attracting EU funds. Indeed, there is a link between the role of leaders as entrepreneurs and their aspiration to be European politicians. Leach and Wilson's study of England finds that leadership has become much more prominent since 1980 (Leach and Wilson, 2000).

Italy

Many current Western European local politicians increasingly seek to be charismatic. Francesco Rutelli swept into office in 1993, after the 'tangentopoli' or 'bribesville' scandal that shook Italy's political system, with a platform of tackling corruption. Declaring bureaucracy to be the main obstacle, he developed a populist strategy. He cut the number of steps needed to get a building permit from twenty-six to four. Rutelli has been responsible for the clean-up and modernization of Rome for the Vatican's Jubilee year and reclaimed 100 piazzas for the use of pedestrians. However, not all of this is because of his personality, as the political influence of Italy's mayors has been magnified since they became directly elected.

Spain

There are similar sorts of politician in Spain. The leadership in Barcelona used the Olympics of 1992 to regenerate the city (Garcia, 1991). Many of the potential conflicts the games could have caused in Spain were alleviated by the charisma of the mayor of Barcelona, Maragall (Hargreaves, 2000). Joan Clos, mayor since 1997, has sought to rejuvenate the city. Barcelona hosts the 'Cultural Olympics' in 2004 and will have a high-speed rail link with France, an expansion of the port and airport and regeneration of one of the most run-down areas. The last point is particularly important, as the activities of leadership have been directed to flagship economic regeneration projects, with little attention to the poorer areas of the city. The problem is that the conflict between the socialist-run city with the region is paramount. The region is controlled by the centre-right regionalist nationalists, yet they are highly proximate to each other. In the Placa Sant Jaime the socialist-run city hall faces the Generalitat – home of the regional government. Mayors are powerful in the Spanish system, and are becoming more so; but they have to depend on the activities of other majority coalition partners (Stoker and Travers, 1998: 22). Much depends on their ability to wield influence above party politics and to have a direct relationship to the citizens.

The Netherlands

It is not surprising that localities in France, Spain and Italy developed more powerful leaders; what is more interesting is that mayors have become more charismatic figures in Northern local political systems, such as Holland. The mayor of Rotterdam, Bram Peper, presided over regeneration and growth in Rotterdam for more than a decade, though he gained a reputation for corruption, allegedly using the city's credit card as his own. But the port of Rotterdam flourished despite the scandal. It now rivals Amsterdam as a cultural centre, and the city hosted the final of Euro 2000. His successor, Ivo Opstelten, tried to clean up the town hall after the misbehaviour of his predecessor.

Germany

The growth in party politics in Germany meant the party leader, who is also the leader of the council, has tended to grow in power and importance (Bullmann and Page, 1994), leading to conflicts with the formerly powerful chief executive officers and the party politicisation of the bureaucracy. High profile mayors have emerged, such as in Frankfurt. Here the mayor has to deal with the highest debt of any German city. The conservative Petra Roth became Frankfurt's first directly elected mayor in 1995. However, the

Christian Democratic Union lacked a majority in the local council. The mayoral elections of March 2001 had Petra Roth as the favourite for re-election, but the CDU funding scandal has tarnished her reputation. Other countries have seen the growth of the local executive role, such as in Belgium (Delmartino, 1991: 337). On the other hand, many muncipalities retain low amounts of prominence for locally elected leaders, such as in Switzerland, for example, where political leadership has always remained weak (except in Geneva), largely because of the influence of its powerful communal traditions (Clark et al., 1989).

These examples from the UK, France, Spain, Italy, the Netherlands and Germany suggest that change is in the air. Leaders in contrasting institutional systems have sought to be local boosters, to lead development coalitions and to break free from the constraints of party hierarchies. They have felt less constrained by party ideology; they have developed popular policies and initiatives whilst at the same time seeking to please business leaders.

Institutional change

The same pressures on political leaders also affect the decision-making systems. There is a cross-European movement to reform the executive structure of local government. Experts, pundits and politicians think that systems of collective decision-making are not up to the job. The challenges of contemporary decision-making require stronger leadership but that the institutional rules prevent the person in office from asserting power and developing effective policies. Collective forms of decision-making and party lines of control trammel many leaders. The reasons are similar to the ones that have encouraged stronger leaders to emerge. There is the familiar grouping of factors of public service reform, municipal competition, fiscal austerity, economic internationalization and cultural pluralism that cause political elites to demand stronger powers for the person who has to pull together the shifting framework of competing interests and to rise to the difficult challenges. To these factors must be added cross-national policy learning. New structures have spread across Western Europe as some countries and municipalities have experimented with new forms of leadership. As important has been the transfer of ideas about the economic policy agenda. Political leaders have gained a reputation for delivering prosperity to their localities. The EU and its research projects on urban policy have also been influential in changing views about local politics.

Scandinavia

One of the best-known reforms comes from Scandinavia. The most discussed has been Norway's experiment with cabinet forms of management, such as in Oslo (Baldersheim, 1992; Hambleton, 1999, 2000; Myrvold, 2000), which was also replicated in Stockholm. In 1986 the city of Oslo set up a cabinet system that abolished its existing local government committees, marking a radical change from the existing consensual system that tended to fragment decision-making to the service departments. Party politicization and financial cutbacks have also undermined the consensus (Baldersheim, 1992: 23). The cabinet is elected by a majority vote of the local council and comprises seven members. It implements the resolutions passed by the local council, and individual members of the cabinet manage their departments. It is a majoritarian rather than multi-party cabinet that concentrates power in the hands of the ruling group. Policy can be driven through the council. Observers conclude that the new system did not produce radical change, but that the cabinet allowed decision-makers to act more strategically, strengthened lines of accountability and fostered the scrutiny of the administration, but polarized public and media opinion. The example shows that the pressure to increase executive capacity need not result in the adoption of directly elected mayors. Nevertheless, Scandinavian executive systems have experienced pressure in recent years. In Finland, a reform in 1993 enhanced the ability of the municipal council to dismiss its council manager. The number of dismissals has increased since that time.

Germany

The most striking example of reform is Germany after the unification of East and West, where the variegated pattern described earlier in the chapter gradually gave way to directly elected mayors (Elcock, 1998; Bullmann and Page, 1994; Stoker, 1996; Wollmann, 1997). The reforms aimed to strengthen the hand of executive leadership and to wrest power away from the bureaucracy. Stoker (1996) notes that there has been a demand for more democratic involvement and also some party political competition between the states on the issue. The pioneer was Hessen in 1991, which had a referendum supported by 90 per cent of the vote. During the 1990s the North Rhine–Westphalian Ministry of Interior proposed a merging of the chief officer post with that of the Burgermeister to respond to the policy challenges. Reformers looked to Bavaria for a model (Grunow, 1992: 52). Once some localities adopted elected mayors, others felt they needed to imitate; and once the bandwagon started to move, municipalities did not want to be left out. In addition, once the East German states joined the federation, institutional reform moved up the political agenda. Executive structures had to be thought out amid other reforms.

The reforms modify rather than replace each system. The assembly remains important as the Magistrat must agree the proposal and lay it before the assembly. Skilful leadership can overcome these limitations. The Burgermeister in the Rhineland has greater control over the cabinet than in the Magistrat system. Direct election leads to more power for the leader. Where there is a strong cabinet, as in the Magistrat system, direct election of the political leader can exacerbate conflicts. The most radical change is in North Rhine–Wesphalia and Lower Saxony, where Burgermeisters have been directly elected since 1999. The leader and the assembly are elected for five-year terms.

Italy

The reforms of leadership in Italy parallel those in Germany (see Stoker, 1996). In 1993 a law introduced directly elected mayors as part of a general move away from proportional to majoritarian electoral systems. The reform took place in the context of the rise of personality politics at the centre, the decline of the old parties in the face of corruption scandals and the emergence of regional autonomous movements in the north. It was one of the most wide-ranging changes in Italian local government even though it built on an existing rationalization of the system in 1990 (Rolla, 1992). But the reform has stabilized the existing system and has made it less prone to crises. The mayor has been given a leading role to make policy and the assembly finds it hard to exercise control, particularly as votes of no confidence are rare. The reform has helped mayors increase their already significant national standing. Prominent examples include Rutelli in Rome discussed above, Cacciari (Venice), Formentini (Milan), Bassolino (Naples) and Orlando (Palermo). The mayor's outlook has altered in character, partly as a result of institutional and party change and because they increasingly draw from the private sector or rely on private sector support (Somma, 1999), particularly in northern localities, whilst the south has retained party politics and its clientelistic practices.

The UK

As in all things sub-national, the UK is the most dramatic example of institutional change. For a century and a half there has been almost no interest in the topic of executive leadership and the local political system remained entrenched in a legal framework where parties and the leadership are invisible and informal. In England since 1991 the debate has shifted rapidly from one where the government frowned on political action in the Widdicombe Report (Committee of Inquiry into the Conduct of Local Authority Business, 1986) to 1997 where the incoming Labour administration promised to reform the executive structure and to introduce an elected mayor in London. The agenda started to shift slowly. An important early precursor was the Maud Committee's (Committee on Management in Local Government, 1967) proposal to concentrate power in the hands of a few leading councillors, but these proposals met largely with ridicule (Rao,

1994). In the meantime the business of local government expanded beyond recognition. Leaders had to cope as full-time politicians, but without the salary and powers commensurate with the post. They tried to promote their localities, but internal political opposition and the need for a long-term and full-time career meant their terms of office either ended in failure or they stood down to take up parliamentary seats (John and Cole, 1999). In the late 1980s organizations such as SOLACE, the chief officers' association, promoted ideas about executive structure; at the same time research by academics, such as by Stoker (Stoker and Wolman, 1992), noted the public prominence and dynamism of mayors in North America and had an influence in the network of local government experts and practitioners. Many academics criticized the dominance of the party group (for example Commission for Local Democracy, 1995; Copus, 1999).

As elsewhere in Western Europe, it was probably ideas about local economic development that encouraged central government to act. The prominent Conservative politician Michael Heseltine, who took over as Secretary of State for the Environment in 1991, admired the North American local administrations and leaders that had revitalized many localities. He championed the idea in the political vacuum about local government reform that had emerged after the poll tax debacle. The consultation paper that set out the options for reform (Department of the Environment, 1991) was the start of a decade of research and commentary (for example Borraz et al., 1994; Hambleton and Bullock, 1996; Hambleton and Stewart, 2000; Leach and Wilson, 2000; Pratchett, 2000; Stoker, 1996). In the end, the Conservatives did not run with the reform agenda, but Labour picked it up because it chimed with its mission to modernize British politics. Mayors appeared to be above the political machinations and inefficiency of local government politics. They would give Labour an opportunity to claim the credit for revitalizing local government.

Mainly out of pragmatism, Labour did not promise to compel English localities to adopt directly elected mayors. In the White Paper *Modern Local Government: In Touch With the People* (DETR, 1998) the government set out its plan of allowing local communities to choose an elected mayor who appoints a cabinet of two or more councillors or a council leader elected by a council who heads a cabinet or a directly elected mayor with a council manger appointed by the local council. The government had reviewed the workability of many options in North America and in Europe. They were also aware that local councillors resisted changes to the system, but by the time the Act was passed in 2000, many had started to believe in the advantages of a cabinet model which would abolish many committees in a similar way to the Oslo experiments and set up overview and scrutiny committees in their place. Some local councils, such as Hammersmith and Fulham, were more headstrong and set up directly elected mayors without cabinets or local managers, particularly as public opinion supported the idea in the big cities. English local government has rapidly moved away from the model of collective decision-making that has been in place since

1836 – and has embraced a more southern European-style leadership pattern that is more visible to the public and able to broker with central government. It remains to be seen whether these structures transform the exercise of power at local level, improve dynamism in policy-making, increase the popularity of local government, improve its ability to extract resources from the centre and remedy the decline in local voter turnout.

London government

The centrepiece of the reforms was the government of London. In 1999 the government introduced legislation for a directly elected mayor and an assembly. The first elections were held in May 2000. The genesis of the reform was the abolition of the Greater London Council in 1986 by a vengeful prime minister, Margaret Thatcher, who opposed its radical policies. From that time London was left without strategic leadership, which fell to the many boards and government departments (Travers and Jones, 1997), and latterly to central government initiatives, such as London Pride. Labour had to set out a credible strategy that would meet the demand for better co-ordination, in particular from discontented commuters coping with the city's clogged transport networks and from a business sector keen to have a prominent figure to enable the city to compete with Frankfurt, Paris and New York for financial and other businesses. Labour felt it could not return to a wide-ranging authority that would provide key services. The 'modern' idea of a mayor for London was one who would act to co-ordinate and champion London rather than directly run services, and who would not symbolize a return to the capital's radical politics. When elected, the Labour government went ahead and set up the London mayor and assembly. As is increasingly common in British politics, the mayor is elected by a system of proportional representation – the alternative vote system – as is the assembly (with a top-up list). The mayor chooses his (or her) own deputy from the 25-member assembly.

The mayor's office is the central area of policy-making for the Greater London Authority, with a chief of staff, senior advisers and the major's own policy units covering all areas. The mayor has formed a cabinet and appointed assembly members to a range of London-wide authorities and boards. The assembly takes over existing funding along with its functions. It has responsibility for spending on police, fire, transport and economic development – a budget of around £3.3bn. The mayor has the task of submitting a budget plan to the assembly for approval or amendment. But the Home Secretary can overrule the mayor on police spending, and step in to set a minimum level if the minister decides the GLA has allocated insufficient funds. A London Development Agency takes over responsibility from central government for the allocation of inward investment and regeneration funds. But the mayor is not in complete charge, since a large proportion of spending on the agency and on Transport for London (see below) is met by specially earmarked central government grants. Using them for any other purpose is not permitted. The mayor is responsible for producing an integrated transport strategy and for running Transport for London, the body that incorporates London Transport, the Highways Agency's responsibility for trunk roads, the Traffic Director for London and the Government Office for London's transport activities. The mayor appoints the board of Transport for London. In time the mayor will have the power to introduce road-user charging and workplace parking levies. The mayor is responsible for strategic planning and has to produce a Spatial Development Strategy for the capital which replaces central government guidance and covers housing, retail development, waste management and regeneration. The mayor can organize city-wide action to improve the environment and will be required to produce a four-yearly report on the state of the capital's environment, develop an air quality strategy, a biodiversity action plan, an ambient noise strategy and a municipal waste management strategy. The mayor can organize city-wide action on cultural issues including arts, sports and tourism, such as a bid to get the Olympic Games staged in the capital. The mayor appoints and oversees the London Fire and Emergency Planning Authority and twelve out of twenty-three members of the Metropolitan Police Authority.

With these reforms the Labour government hoped to create a dynamic institution that would change local government. As with other consti-tutional innovations, it did not realize that one of the effects of establishing institutions and of decentralizing power was to create new rules of the game for party factions who could advance their interests. It also gave new alternatives for voters who could vote against Labour to express their dissatisfaction and to rebel against hierarchical party politics without necessarily voting against Labour in a national or other local elections. The government could not rule as before and claim the credit for decentralizing power. When power is decentralized, those who are given power wish to create their own power bases and challenge the centre.

In London as in Wales both the public and the party loyalists did not like the political manipulation that Labour followed to ensure that candidates it favoured would be selected for the top posts. Just as the Labour party leadership tried to impose its own candidate in Wales, the loyalist Alun Michael, so it tried to ensure that Ken Livingstone, MP for Brent and leader of the Greater London Council 1980–6, would not get nominated as the Labour candidate for mayor, even though he rapidly became popular with the media, public opinion and amongst London party members. Labour designed an electoral college system of Labour MPs, MEPs, trade unions and party members that successfully elected Frank Dobson, the former government minister as the candidate on a minority of the vote. In response Livingstone decided to run as an independent, which caused him to be expelled from the Labour party. But Dobson had little chance against the strength of Livingstone's popularity – which he managed to promote without a campaigning party machine. Livingstone remained ahead in the polls for the whole of the election race. In the final run-off of the two winners Livingstone won comfortably, with 57.92 per cent of the vote after second preferences were taken into account. At a stroke the monopoly of party politics in England had been broken, ushering in a new era when powerful figures – either within or without political parties – can gain electoral mandates.

It may be the case that by adopting more mainland European political institutions, such as proportional electoral systems and powerful mayors, and by being in keeping with trends of voter disengagement, the UK sub-national system may be ending its divergent course from the path of decentralization in the rest of Western Europe and joining with its neigh-bours in a more pluralistic and diverse polity. The irony may be that just as clientelistic systems become more bureaucratized and less dominated by powerful politicians, so northern systems, and centralized ones such as the UK, may be developing the politics of the personality and broker-mayor figures. Ironically Jospin government in France proposed an ending to the *cumul des mandats*, the linchpin of the system of intergovernmental relations, just before England introduced stronger mayors. But the political power of the centre in England does not disappear after the election of a charismatic politician. The formidable battery of central government legal controls over local government stay in place, as does the expectation from central government civil servants and ministers that local government must imple-ment central government policies in detail. Whilst central government appeared to give local authorities freedom to contract with whom they please in the best value regime, which is the framework that replaces compulsory competitive tendering, they imposed a large number of detailed controls over the process.

Conclusion

Leadership is crucial to local governance. The politics of decentralization, networks, participation, partnerships, bureaucratic reform, rapid policy change and central intervention need powerful, but creative figures to give a direction to local policy-making. In a time of institutional fragmentation and complexity, leaders can make the shifting framework of individuals and organizations work together. They can recreate local identities and senses of purpose in age where locality has lost its association with traditional industries and well-defined spaces of economic activity. Whilst creating the need for better leadership, the transition to governance imposes intense strains on those who exercise policy choices. They have to make sense of the complexity and cope with novel circumstances.

The institutional structures, the forms of party organization and competition and local political cultures count in that they foster certain types of leader, whether directive or responsive, and offer varied opportunities to generate governing capacity. It is no surprise that strong leaders have emerged in the southern countries of France, Italy and Spain. They already have a pattern of leadership that can respond to economic and policy challenges. The problem with leadership institutions is not so much the power they bestow on the occupants, but that there is an insufficient system of local accountability to prevent the abuse of power. In France the challenge is to revive the institutions of local democracy and to limit the negative consequences of the *cumul des mandats*. In many parts of the rest of Western Europe collective forms of decision-making have given way to systems of leadership that rely more on direct election and control over the levers of power. In large countries, such as Germany and Italy, the transformation is near complete; in other places there are more subtle reforms. In Norway, the Oslo experiments suggest more collective forms of decision-making may be appropriate. In the UK the legislative provisions for different forms of leadership implys the strengthening of executive structure will take different forms based on local choice. But historical experience indicates that once a bandwagon sets in motion, municipal competition spawns directly elected mayors.

Given the diverse national contexts it is not surprising that the reforms have been different, with more collective arrangements remaining in the north. But the experience of Germany shows that each locality and state cannot be an island in the face of municipal reform. There are functional and competitive pressures to move toward a system of directly elected leaders where once parties and coalitions held sway. Not that institutions and party groupings remain silent with these leaders, but they too must adopt different ways of doing business.

8

Renewing Local Democracy

The normative dimension to governance

Given the transition from government to governance, what are the implications for local democratic forms of politics? In the era of powerful nation-states and the dominance of ideas of representative democracy, there was little problem in identifying the advantages of local democracy. In the view of Mill (1861), local government existed to promote liberty and pluralism as well as act as the training ground for participation in national political institutions. The key idea is that locally elected people should be in charge of local matters that affect them. Local government adds to the diverse nature of the democratic polity by experimenting with new ideas and practices and representing plural interests to the potentially mono-polistic centre (Sharpe, 1970). There have been many faults in the system of representative government at the local level. Localities have been governed by hierarchical political parties and bureaucratic elites with often little involvement of the public. It might be thought that any development that moves local government away from its often hidebound and conservative nature would be favourable. Nevertheless, as local government systems evolve toward governance, there are normative implications for such a change.

The first perspective is the one the first chapter of this book offers. The breaking down of hierarchy presages a more open form of local politics that can respond to the demands of its citizens and groups. The retreat of the state may leave more of a place for local politics which was ignored and suppressed in the age when national state institutions were the prominent and legitimate form of political activity. From this perspective, it is possible to point to the pluralism implied by institutional diversity and division of powers across and within political institutions. Indications of the new pluralism are the diverse governing coalitions, the powerful and visible mayoral figures, the new parties and pressure groups on the local scene, the representation of women and the strength of regional politics. The complexity of contemporary public problems and rapid policy change may place established interests in a more defensive role than hitherto. The experimentation with public policies puts a premium on innovation and the ability to follow up initiatives that may advantage newer groups. Moreover, the emergence of multi-level governance also creates more opportunities for local input into policy as it cannot be assumed that nation-state actors monopolize decision-making.

Nevertheless, governance can weaken democracy. Whilst it is possible to be critical of government, it was clear who was responsible for decisions and that there were some means to hold decision-makers to account through elections and constitutional checks on public authority. Moreover, it is easy to caricature political parties and forget they help aggregate interests in societies and achieve political action. They may represent groups that otherwise find it hard to mobilize and articulate their interests, something that is supported by comparative research on local political parties (John and Saiz, 1999).

Even if it were possible to accept the most negative account of local representative democracy, governance may not necessarily be an improvement, and in many ways it reduces local democratic input and legitimacy. The move to governing in networks may diffuse decision-making and weaken its clarity. When it is hard to locate which body formally makes decisions, how is it possible to hold power holders to account? The issue of accountability comes to a head in public–private partnerships. When public authorities transfer decisions to autonomous boards, composed of representatives from the private sector, local government and other public bodies, the outcome does not represent the view of the locally elected public body. Elected mayors in France or councils in the UK can initiate projects and need not report back to their bureaucracies and other elected representatives, though the local authority in the UK can be held accountable for the expenditure involved. Such a privatization of decision-making is the predictable consequence of a weak public sphere. Public sector actors seek private gain and try to manipulate the levers of office for re-election. It is not surprising that the age of governance should also be the period of municipal scandal and corruption. Moreover, it is possible to criticize the rapid pace of economic development in some localities. Self-serving growth coalitions can produce cheap and ugly city centres and create redevelopments that benefit a small class of property owners and consultants. But would a more traditional form of local decision-making fare any better? It is possible to identify poor economic development in the period of the centralized French state (Savitch, 1988). In the 1960s, British local governments allied with the private sector to build cheap municipal housing whose quality has not stood the test of time (Dunleavy, 1981). Maybe the lesson is that local politicians in any era seek fast solutions and are too ready to adopt the latest technologies from the private sector.

The other aspect to local governance may have a complicating effect on local politics. Europeanization has multiple influences on the locality that are not easily observed by the general population, such as changes in the regulatory structure and on contracting out. Moreover, it may not be obvious to local participants that it is hard to change a European law without extensive lobbying over a long period of time. At the same time, local opinion leaders may criticize the high costs of European representation. When many decisions about local politics are made a long way from the town hall, local self-government appears more as an anomaly than as a core value in a democracy. The internationalization of local economies and the growing interest of central government in the performance of public service may encourage local politicians and citizens to believe that local government does not have much autonomy and therefore is of little relevance. After radical reforms to local government organizations, the local authority becomes invisible to the general population. Fewer residents work for local government. The symbol of the city does not have such a local presence on the streets, even in the form of local government municipal employees collecting the refuse. Whilst the town hall commissions the services, citizens cannot see so clearly that they pay for them.

The complexity of local political and institutional structures and policies means that citizens cannot attach public decisions to their local representatives. Whilst local representatives may be heavily involved with networks and partnerships and in European liaison, they may not be able to claim they are the decision-makers even of last resort. The essential character of the political in modern societies has receded and has been replaced by more shifting and less certain forms of decision-making, where it is harder to make authoritative decisions. When local political institutions wrap themselves up in the language of legitimacy as it is understood in a representative sense, they can only feel a sense of crisis when decisions are no longer as comprehensible within this framework.

To these factors within political systems it is essential to add other factors that may undermine the democratic credentials of local representative democracy. Population mobility, the decay of traditional social bonds and the decline of local political parties are components of the change that mean that citizens no longer have such a close connection to their local political institutions. The disengagement of citizens in the UK has reached new heights in the decline of conventional forms of local political participation, such as turnout. With the exception of Spain and France, this pattern is replicated across Europe, with Western European countries experiencing a decline in local election turnout during the last decade of the twentieth century (Committee of the Regions, 1999).

This book describes how some local political systems have responded to the demands of local governance. They have renewed the ways in which local political leaders can exercise power on behalf of local residents. The emergence of stronger mayors and the reform of the local executive are partly a response of traditional political institutions to the demands that economic and policy change have placed upon them. In tandem with the need to raise the visibility and effectiveness of local leadership are cross-European attempts to renew democratic mechanisms. Local governments have realized they have neglected the citizens in their experiments with NPM. This response does not just amount to the almost desperate attempts to raise local political participation in the UK (DETR, 1998). But there has been a more wide-ranging set of experiments that not only reform the institutions of representative democracy, but also experiment with new forms of local political participation, such as referenda, citizen juries, deliberative polls and electronic democracy. As Chapter 5 shows, the Netherlands has moved away from its obsession with NPM to renewing democracy. The diverse set of experiments is the final element to the emerging system of governance that seeks to compensate for the loss of clear lines of democratic accountability. Just as governing systems seek to re-invent new forms of co-ordination, they need to re-imagine the procedures of democratic control.

Democratic renewal and participation

The reform impulse

The rest of this chapter charts some of the many participation initiatives that have recently emerged in Western Europe. The extent of experimentation and diversity of experiences in some parts of Western countries suggest the beginning of a more wide-ranging transformation which could be transferred to the rest of the local government system in each country. The proselytism of many reformers, especially those in the USA and UK, fosters the idea that practices can transfer easily. The enthusiasm comes from the stage in the evolution of ideas where new modes of participation are in the upswing of the agenda cycle, when advocates generate ideas, innovators adopt them and others copy.

This chapter, however, does not intend to replicate the format of policy entrepreneurs. It has as much an eye to the constraints and contexts as to the opportunities. As with other public sector reform movements (for example, the NPM programme and urban regeneration projects), the evidence contains a classic methodological flaw. Studies and reports usually only convey evidence from successful initiatives and do not evaluate the causes of success and failure, which would explain whether the same outcomes would have occurred in the absence of the instrument. There is no way of knowing whether the innovators are a minority experience that cannot transfer within nations let alone travel across regions of the world or whether the participation experiment is the effect of another process occurring within a local community. In other words, the instrument is the effect not the cause of the participation initiative. Communities that are already advantaged create better participation initiatives. Top-down reformers become convinced that these schemes can be universally applied, when in fact their success may vary greatly. But reformers need to understand the relationship between individual action, incentives and the institutional structures within which individuals make their choices when they transfer policies across nations.

Examples from the 1960s

Such caution, however, should not replicate the pessimism of the accounts of participation initiatives of the late 1960s. These were cynical about the prospects of greater citizen involvement. The experiments failed to empower because of the self-interest of the bureaucrats that run them and the power of local elites. The strength of the power structures not only prevented effective participation but also replicated power relationships in the new participatory institutions. The most notorious and populist was Moynihan's *Maximum Feasible Misunderstanding* (1969), but there was an extensive set of research from a variety of perspectives (see Berry et al., 1993, chapter 2, for a review). In the wake of the explosion of US federal participation initiatives in the wake of the War on Poverty, their imitation in Europe, and the subsequent political reaction, it is not surprising that researchers became disillusioned at the same time that practitioners felt the long years of activism were wasted. The picture becomes even bleaker when researchers accept the view that business elites have become more important in the face of greater economic and political competition and the exclusion of more traditional forms of political participation, both in the USA and in Europe (DiGaetano and Klemanski, 1999).

It is not, however, the case that initiatives automatically fail or succeed but that their fate is affected by their contexts. Some environments are fixed. For example, political culture can often account for participation rates across nation-states. But other factors, such as the design of institutions and the framework for making policy, vary. Even such imponderables as political values may also be affected in the short term by the performance of governments in delivering policy outcomes and also by the effect of education programmes, such as citizenship teaching. It is not just a case of transferring initiatives, but of thinking about the effects on the citizens themselves and how they mobilize to take action.

Western European experiences

Western European experiences suggest both opportunities and constraints on participation experiments. Some of these constraints derive from the national contexts of participation; some are from cross-national trends on the general level of participation; some come from the legacy of the reform of the public sector; others derive from political factors that drive the introduction and implementation of citizen action policies.

The context is the long history of some Western local democracies, their well-developed and professionalized bureaucracies and the presence of welfare state structures in some countries, particularly those in northern Europe, which affects the quality of participation and the demand and success of experiments. But it is easy to overstate the modernization of Western states. Traditional elites, personal networks and corruption characterize some Western states as much as elsewhere. Nevertheless, the long-established nature of representational institutions has muted criticism of their effectiveness as they are regarded as legitimate and effective. Moreover, relatively efficient bureaucracies in the north of Europe operate on the basis of impartiality and equality and so also weaken the case for direct involvement of citizens. In addition, in the past experts in the various policy fields claimed a monopoly of expertise, so limiting the role of citizens. Such institutions continue to be important: as participation in Northern European states benefits from strong bureaucracies. However, the challenge to traditional bureaucracies and the decline in trust and confidence of the citizen in Europe has reduced the legitimacy and effectiveness of the traditional welfare state and representative model of consumer involvement, which is why the experiments have found so much favour. But do they involve any more than window dressing on the existing institutions rather than a renewal of the democratic process? There are three groups of countries that have differential experiences of participation initiatives.

The first is the Anglo group, which have weaker state traditions and tend to give legitimacy to private sector involvement and innovations and where the elite and public attachment to collective forms of provision is weaker than elsewhere. In Western Europe, the UK and Ireland are in this group. The second group are the established welfare states in Scandinavia and in northern Europe – Sweden, Finland, Norway, Denmark, Northern Italy, the Netherlands and Germany – which have long-standing commitments to collective provision, have institutionalized the participation of producer groups and have high stocks of social capital in the form of supportive networks, a healthy incidence of associations and high levels of trust in government. The final group are the southern European countries that lack developed welfare states, where political parties and patronage dominate participation, where there is a high degree of distrust in government and implementing policy has been difficult. These countries include southern Italy, Spain, Portugal and Greece. The nature of citizen control varies in each country.

The Anglo group

In the Anglo group, the emphasis since the 1980s has been on the NPM. It would be wrong to characterize NPM as entirely against citizen involvement. In fact, one of the aims of these reforms is to break down existing barriers that have prevented a full sensitivity to consumer and citizen demands. The reader of *Reinventing Government* (Osborne and Gaebler, 1993) can find many examples of entrepreneurial bureaucrats connecting to citizens by reshaping their bureaucracies and pioneering policies and mechanisms for delivering policy. One of the appeals of NPM is that the parts of Europe that have hidebound and slow moving bureaucracies which serve the interests of bureaucrats and elites can innovate to concentrate on delivering services and responding to client needs. The other factor to bear in the mind is that NPM is a many-headed monster – it can mean market mechanisms, top-down measurement of outputs and freedom for entrepreneurial bureaucrats – an odd mixture of individualism, exhortation and Taylorism. But it is unified by seeking to create a new balance in public organizations between control and decentralization by removing hierarchy and replacing it with decentralized units that are guided by targets and precise mechanisms of regulation. Whilst NPM appears to be consumer-friendly, it depends on highly centralized and measured notions of consumer need. In the NPM world, objective assessments of need are preferred whilst bureaucrats ascertain citizens' views by polls, surveys and focus groups.

Surveys should not be dismissed as agents of participation. In fact, as the e-governance debate shows (see below), mechanisms to involve people need to bear in mind that participation is costly in time and people do not always find political activity with its meetings, arguments and organizational activities pleasant. Top-down measures to ascertain citizens' views may be effective. It is also possible to include an aspect of deliberation in polling, what is called deliberative polling, and this leads to more informed choices (McComas and Scherer, 1999). Nevertheless, there is a top-down approach to these management experiments that needs to be countered if participation experiments are going to be anything other than token. In fact, the rigidity of performance assessment may shut out the citizen from forms of participation that require time and adjustment of the aims of public programmes.

The deep hold of NPM interacts with the extensive experiments to involve citizens in the UK and also a move away from New Public Management toward citizen engagement in the Netherlands (Hendriks and Tops, 1999). The rediscovery of the citizen in the aims of public policy-makers is a major shift in public policy focus for the UK in particular and is a reaction against a more market-led form of policy-making. It also follows from a crisis in democracy, particularly local democracy, where there is declining confidence in government, falling turnout in local elections, increasing cynicism about politicians and increasing recourse to alternative forms of political participation. More generally, politicians and bureaucrats in local government started to realize that they had always stressed issues of service quality rather than the democratic rights of the citizen. As a result, local government has lost its connection to its publics.

The British experience

Academics and commentators, such as Stewart and Stoker, started to shift the agenda in central and local governments. Local authorities started to experiment with a variety of mechanisms to involve the public which were either similar to those of representative democracy or based on deliberative ideas. For example, Stirling Assembly is a civic assembly which provides local people with the opportunity to participate in the development of the council's strategies and initiatives, and Kirklees' Talkback is a consultative mechanism that tries to make sure that ethnic minority residents or young people are not under-represented (Stoker and McGarvey, 2000). Citizens' juries, focus groups, citizen panels, consultation exercises and new forms of executive leadership have featured in policy statements and have been adopted by health and local authorities. The Labour government elected in 1997 adopted many of these ideas in its policy document *Modern Local Government: In Touch With the People* (DETR, 1998). The rapidity with which democratic experiments have been seized by central and local policy-makers and also the quick succession of trends is probably a feature of Britain's hyperactive political system where central and local politicians have to produce quick results to show their effectiveness and to win elections. In contrast, the initiatives in Scandinavia, which started in the late 1980s and 1990s, have gradually built up over a long period of time. Whilst it is too early to evaluate the UK ones, there must be some concern that they replicate the top-down approach inherent in NPM and that they exist for legitimation purposes. Authorities lose interest once the fad has passed, as has already happened with citizens' juries. In the UK far too many participation projects are tied to short-run funding programmes that do not give enough time for participating networks to get established and to become self-sustaining. They are too weakly embedded and fail once the initial interest has passed away.

Northern Europe

There have been similar worries in northern Europe, as in the USA, about declining participation and trust in government (Norris, 1999). Sweden, for example, has faced a consistent decline in trust in political institutions since the 1960s (Holmberg, 1999). Such concerns are also present in Norway (Rose and Pederson, 2000). Nevertheless, as Kaase and Newton (1995) note, in comparison to the USA, trust in government has held up. Moreover, many citizen initiatives have been in play for a long time. In Finland, for example, the right to take initiatives – either a petition or broader policy measure – was codified in the 1976 Local Government Act (Sjoblom, 1992). One city, Turku, had 387 initiatives between 1977 and 1979, many of which were responded to positively by the local council. There has been quite an expansion of referendums (Setälä, 1999), especially wherever they are constitutionally provided in Italy and Switzerland. Referendums in these two countries contribute most of the overall increase. Political culture in Switzerland is, to a large extent, influenced by its direct democracy. Compared to purely representative systems, direct democracy leads to a different type of communication among citizens and also between citizens and representatives. The opportunity of deciding for themselves on political issues provides citizens with incentives to collect more information. Also, all German states have instituted legal provisions for binding local referenda (Schröter, 2000). These examples illustrate that the 're-invention' of local democracy through new forms of participation is nothing new. Countries such as Germany invested much energy in participation initiatives in the 1970s, particularly in areas such as planning (Wollman, 2000: 920).

Reformers have sought to increase participation on bodies such as school councils, as in Denmark, for example. Within the Netherlands there are public consultation programmes (*brede maatschappelijke overleg*) which are held by the government to allow citizens to have a say in policy-making. They have been used frequently with infrastructural/environmental projects. All relevant parties (communities, interest groups, local authorities) are involved and they can raise their objections to any plans. Usually this leads to long delays in policy-making.

The Danish experience

In Scandinavia there has been a move to involve users of services in the setting of standards. This has occurred in Sweden and Norway (Kleven et al., 2000: 97), but it is in Denmark during the 1990s that many public services moved away from being controlled by elected local government to local boards made up of representatives of users (Bogason, 1996a, 1996b, 1996c, 2000). The changes are: the introduction of community councils in 1994, neighbourhood bodies appointed by the local council mainly for physical planning, traffic regulation and environment and the governance of schools; the introduction of elected boards of directors for schools from 1990, with general powers of management in schools; the introduction of user boards for day care for children in 1993 which runs the daily affairs of the organizations, controls budgets and determines the eligibility of children; and advisory boards for the services for the care for the elderly composed of users, but where the interest organizations of the elderly play a role. The organizations often end up running the service. Some communes set up general advisory boards for the elderly.

The powers of these bodies vary by type of service as communes have discretion. What communes do is to determine the budgetary limits to the service and leave actual decisions about management, personnel matters and making policy to the boards. The main difference is that the boards of the elderly are advisory whereas the rest make their own decisions. These mechanisms were introduced by central government legislation, but some arrangements are in the discretion of local communes. The main aim was to move away from hierarchical management and to incorporate user choices into service delivery. Derived from successful experiments, the new rhetoric of citizenship participation and the free commune experiments allowed communes the freedom to decide their own policies and administrative arrangements. In the case of community councils, the main voice is local residents; in the schools the board is elected by the parents and includes the school director and representatives of parents and pupils. In the case of the service-orientated boards, the voice was users directly; for the advisory boards it was representative groups. For day care for children, the users of the service – parents – are appointed by local government. The director has a place on the board. For the elderly, it is the residents or interest groups representing them. The general advisory boards are mostly appointed. In the advisory case, this strengthens the representation of interest groups rather than citizens *per se*.

In some cases, representative groups rather than users themselves became the representatives; in other cases some of the user representatives were closely associated with political parties, so limiting the citizen/user perspective. In general, the advisory groups replicated the corporatist decision-making structure of Danish policy-making, whereas the user groups were a new direction and input. In general, the interest groups oppose the decentralization of power to user groups as it loses their established position. There was also a conflict of roles between the new neighbourhood councils, which have a more general remit, and the user boards tied to specific services.

There is a great variation in the influence of the boards. In schools, it is principals who have gained power and influence rather than citizens. Principals have a role on the board and as the person who implements the policy. There are limited opportunities for parental influence because most curricular decisions are within the discretion of the individual teachers. There is more opportunity for user influence on other groups. But even on the boards for the elderly, the professionals can find the users an unwelcome intrusion into their autonomy. There are examples in Denmark of obstruction and the circumvention of user input. In order to make policy, the users have to be assertive and to move the agenda away from narrow bureaucratic concerns.

In all cases, the Danish tradition of negotiation means that relationships between professionals and users are protracted. This also occurs in cases of conflict between the user boards and the communal council, especially where the distribution of resources is concerned. Often the result of such disagreements is the reduction of the powers of the boards. One of the other effects of user representation is that the boards become very parochial and tend to become solely interested in representing the interest of their service. There are implications for citizens who are not users and/or are weak in articulating their interests.

Participation and associational life is strong in Scandinavia. Thus even with a bureaucratic welfare state, such experiments are likely to be successful in Denmark in spite of professional opposition and obstruction. The boards are mainly limited by their formal set up, such as whether they are advisory or make decisions and the extent to which users as opposed to interest groups dominate representation. The extent the special factors in Scandinavia are present elsewhere in Europe will determine the success of these experiments. But that they appear in many northern European countries, such as the UK, shows the cross-national attraction of such mechanisms. These sorts of experiments have replicated over space and time. Indeed, the neighbourhood experiments in Denmark derived from one commune – Herlev.

Citizens' juries

Many countries in Western Europe have experimented with new forms of decision-making – citizens' juries. Juries are small groups of citizens, sometimes randomly selected, who deliberate on public policy options, where the public authority provides support and perhaps a mediator, and experts and officials provide evidence. Such European experiments draw on the long-running US research and advocacy of the Jefferson Center established in 1974. Germany has a long experience of planning cells (Dienel and Renn, 1995), pioneered by Peter Dienel of the Research Institute for Citizen Participation of the University of Wuppertal. Whereas US juries have received much publicity, they have had little impact on public policy; in contrast, they are taken much more seriously in Germany. Government bodies commission the institute to run large juries, with often more than fifty members. Before the jury comes into existence, the public authority makes a prior agreement to take into account its recommendations.

Many participation initiatives are environmental in character, sponsored by DG-XI and stimulated by the Agenda 21 focus on local empowerment. The European Union has been active here. There was the Poverty 3 Programme (based in DG-V), which has sought to integrate the economically and socially less privileged groups in society. Then there are the URBAN and URBAN II initiatives, and the Urban Pilot Projects. Many of these projects try to hand over responsibility for policy to the citizens themselves, such as budgeting and management.

Southern Europe

In the south of Europe, much community politics remains trapped in close local elite networks where powerful local interest groups have captured political parties. As a result there are few successful initiatives in southern Italy, Greece and Portugal. Much power remains with the traditional centralized bureaucracy and citizens tend to distrust authority and are reluctant to participate. In Portugal, even through interest groups have increased in importance, they face a strong bureaucracy (Silva, 2000). The exception is the requirement of consultation and participation in some European Union initiatives and the more dynamic politics in the larger cities. Spain has largely changed in this respect, with its interesting initiatives. Barcelona City Council, for example, introduced a decentralized administration in 1979 to improve services, promote the use of new technology, encourage citizen participation, bring management closer to the citizen and act as an agent of social policy (Amoros, 1996). Over time, the council focused more on the administrative tasks of decentralization, rather than the political objectives. Decentralization assisted the introduction of new technology, leading to a rationalization of staff activities and improved information storage and retrieval. Mechanisms to improve democratic access through the Internet have become increasingly common. European localities have been developing their own initiatives, such as Bologna's city Internet which involves telematics for citizens, businesses, and the third sector. Another European example is 'Citizen's Participation through Internet' organized by the City of Barcelona.

New technology

It is important to be sceptical about the impact of these technologies on participation. This is not just the well-rehearsed argument that many citizens are excluded from such technologies, because new technology can offer certain excluded citizens such as youth opportunities for participation. It is also possible to correct for technological inequality by public provision in libraries and other public spaces of PC terminals and to have educational programmes to match. Rather, it is the lack of imagination of public bureaucrats that is often to blame. Public organizations tend to adopt unimaginative websites with little possibility of citizen interaction. In Belgium, Steyaert (2000) finds that electronic services tend to reduce the citizen to a customer. Civic roles as being a voter and being a contributor to policy-making are reduced to a minimum. Consequently, local government websites are primarily one-way streams to the citizen as customer and decision-makers neglect the interactive possibilities of municipal websites. Some research shows that electronic forms of communication have the benefits of reviving democracy (Klein, 1999), suggesting that online forums may allow associations to be more responsive, more robust and better able to attract more members.

Conclusion

It is possible to view these experiments as the last gasps of a declining system. At the point when local government has lost its relevance and connection to the everyday experiences of citizens, partly inspired by the growing complexity of social and economic life and a lack of a pure local dimension to local politics, local councils grasp at any reform that appears to offer some chance of renewal. As with so many initiatives, local government is a victim of the latest fashions that spread like wildfire from innovators to imitators. And just when the imitators have caught on, so a new set of pioneers advocate a new idea with as great fervour as the first. The instability of ideas and practices merely shows how ungrounded local government has become and signal its eventual demise amid a plethora of invisible self-governing networks, quangos and partnerships, which take a minimal problem-solving function. Meanwhile, most decision-makers in local government, such as its political leaders, continue in their roles and articulate values derived from the structure and norms of representative democracy, as one study found of local authorities in Denmark, Norway and Sweden (Kleven et al., 2000: 112–113).

A more optimistic view regards the rapidity of change of ideas and the proliferation of democratic experiments as evidence of successful adaptation and renewal. In the UK at least, some experts have always been keen to pronounce the end of local democracy, such as those who did so at the end of the period of municipal enterprise in the 1930s (Robson, 1933), but meanwhile, the governing system evolved to be an adjunct of the welfare state. In a similar fashion, local decision-makers are not helpless in the face of international competition, the influence of NPM practices, Europeanization and rapid policy change. They seek to adapt to the new environment, by crafting political strategies and attempting to find new forms of legitimacy for decisions made in loose networks of relationships. This strategy requires trials and errors and a constant searching for solutions that work in both the functional and democratic senses. In such a way the transition from government to governance might prompt a rediscovery of a wider practice of politics that were narrowed by representative democracy. Ironically, privatization and de-institutionalization may have been just the kick that tired local governments needed to reinvent themselves.

9

Conclusions

From local government to local governance

The move from local government to governance implies that traditional institutions have become less important in local politics. Such a breakdown of certain types of formalized and routinized patterns of behaviour and organization follows from the influence of economic competition, the impact of NPM, the fragmentation of organizations and the growing role of the EU. Old patterns of party politics and traditional forms of bureaucracy, which were central features of local governing systems, are more suited to managing the institutions of the traditional welfare state and accessing the central ministries for resources and favourable treatment than for responding to current conditions. New practices and ideas about how to govern mean that such stable configurations of persons and organizations are no longer so viable. The changes mean that local decision-makers adapt to new challenges and institutional frameworks. Because of the competition between sub-national authorities, a process of adaptation is increasingly at work whereby innovators keenly seize the agenda and followers swiftly follow once the idea catches on. Economic development policies and governing in public–private partnerships create long-term networks between organizations which municipalities copy across and within nation-states. In a similar fashion, reformers become tempted by NPM reforms to fragment and de-centre formerly hierarchical public bureaucracies. Central governments create regional authorities to try to manage the complexity, but they too become another part of the multi-layered governing framework.

Stronger leaders also emerge to rise above the machinations of local politics, seeking to distance themselves from traditional party machines and professional bureaucracies. At a higher level of abstraction, reformers are tempted to put into place institutional structures that are better able to make local policies. The institutional reforms of local executive structures detach leaders from their party machines and often split the executive and legislature into more US-style divided institutions. The de-bureaucratization of the local state and the fragmentation of political institutions are the nub of local governance. More diffuse networks, the lack of predictability, complex policy challenges, gridlock and multi-level decision-making characterize the system. Such are the arguments and claims of the previous chapters.

Enough evidence has been summarized to show that what has happened to local politics since the early 1980s resembles governance and is qualitatively different from what went on before. Across Western Europe there have been many changes in institutional structures, attempts at coalition formation, stronger leadership styles, more visible executive structures, new management ideas and more of a focus on European liaison. These changes justify the claim that local politics has been transformed.

Imagine, for example, a large French municipality in the 1960s. There were few tiers of local government with which it had to compete and its tasks were straightforward. Complex coalitions with other local communes would not be a common feature of its daily life. European legislation did not greatly impact on its work. The commune may have been concerned with local planning, but economic development issues would not have been so prominent as they are today. In general, the mayor, especially if it was a large commune, was a powerful local baron and bargained with the central state to gain resources and favours and there was a close relationship with the prefect who was the point of access to the state. Consider the local commune of today. It is in competition with elected departments and regions; it probably participates in a local urban community and other inter-communal organizations; its mayor is the leader of several public–private partnerships; and the authority is a partner in a contractual relationship with the central state. It has a much wider range of functions and its activities cross over with those of other public bodies, especially in new policy sectors. Economic development is an obsession. The commune now considers experiments in privatization and NPM. Its environment is more complex, which puts strains on the holder of the main elected office and releases some of the grip of the power of the old *notables*. Whilst the prefect has returned to power, the office is no longer so powerful. Other parts of the central state, such as the field services and the regional prefecture, have become more important. Even though different stories may be told about other local government systems across Europe, the same general pattern of increased complexity and greater uncertainty has emerged. Whilst there is variation in the extent to which counties have reformed their institutional structures, no municipality can shelter from the demands of municipal and economic competition and the need to respond to the EU.

Having made the argument and reviewed the evidence, the conclusion first considers the caveats and limitations of the government to governance argument and, secondly, examines the comparative experience and its implication for the study of local government systems.

Caveats and limitations

There are several objections that scholars make to the claim that Western Europe has moved from government to governance.

A satisfactory account of local government?

The first is that the account of change does not provide a satisfactory account of the old system of government. The suspicion is that apologists for governance present a stereotype of the old system. They imply that government was only about bureaucracies and political parties, when most accounts of local politics described the context in which local decision-making took place. Moreover, networks and complex interorganizational relations were essential parts of local political systems, as some accounts of local politics show (Friend et al., 1974). The idea that business was never an important actor in local politics belies the well-documented role of the local private sector in France or other private sector firms in southern Europe. In the UK, the home of the professionalized and detached local bureaucracy, local businesses played a key role in developing housing policies in the 1960s. In some councils they formulated policies and played a role in local economic development (Saunders, 1980).

The counter to such attacks is that the concept of government does not imply that networks and institutional proliferation do not constitute a governing system. There have been enough studies of policy networks at national and local levels to show that networks and interrelationships have always played an essential role in oiling the governmental machinery. Rhodes' (1986, 1988) accounts of intergovernmental relations in the 1970s and early 1980s show the complex networks at play between central and local government in the so-called dual British political system in a similar way that Tarrow (1977) found complex networks between mayors and central institutions. Nevertheless, Italian and French local politicians were more effective in obtaining resources and favours from the centre. Similarly, the pattern of intergovernmental relations in Germany is primarily characterized by interlocking networks (Scharpf et al., 1978). The argument is not that flexible and networked patterns of decision-making did not exist, but there has been a step-shift in the pattern of governing away from formalized patterns of government.

The longevity of institutions

The second and similar attack on the idea of governance is that current politics and administration are characterized by institutions and formal processes of government as much as before. Even if there are more agencies and public bodies, they are still constituted by legal rules and routines that determine how the networks operate. Even if there are four levels of elected government when once there were two, institutional processes determine how decision-making works. Much of local government practice may be explained by legal systems that bestow powers and duties on public authorities, and affect the discretion of local councils and the ability of central ministries to determine decisions, which is particularly important in centralized local government systems, such as in England (Davies, 2000). Moreover, accounts of decision-making show the prominence of elected local government rather than fragmented networks (Michel, 1998). Nevertheless, the legal position of many public authorities has changed in recent years. Local government in the UK has moved away from its generally permissive powers to adopting a more restrictive legal framework with much stronger central government powers to intervene (Loughlin, 1986).

Systems of local government finance differ massively (Gibson and Batley, 1992; John and Carter, 1991), which largely follow the north–south pattern, and show the UK and Ireland to be exceptional in the small amount of revenue local governments raise to finance their expenditures. Indeed, the tumultuous history of local government finance in the UK, with the introduction of the hated poll tax in 1989 and 1990 followed by its rapid abolition in 1993, seem to show the exceptional path of UK central–local government relations (Butler et al., 1994). The contrast across Europe between countries is embedded because central and state governments find it hard to reform local government finance systems even when they allocate new functions to local governments. Nevertheless, despite different amounts of revenue raised locally, most systems of local government finance face similar pressures of rising costs of delivery and the tendency for central government to place services upon them. Indeed, one of the common causes of the reform of local government, such as contracting out of services and the introduction of the techniques of NPM, is new demands on public expenditure. Whilst countries that have larger sources of local revenue appear to be cushioned from fiscal austerity, they also have rising costs and growing client groups. Different tax systems are not necessarily a shield against the pressures for change in local government.

Neither is local governance inconsistent with softer forms of institutional processes – routines, standard operating procedures and organizational cultures – highlighted by new institutionalist writers, such as Lowndes (1999). What happens is that external pressures for public sector reform are mediated by the power relationships and values within bureaucracies that vary in each nation-state. One of the characteristics of local governance is the rediscovery of local variation that national institutional arrangements hide, which implies that local cultures and institutional practices count for more than hitherto.

The counter to the argument that governance implies an interaction between institutional processes and non-institutional ones is that the laws, routines and cultures of state traditions constitute such a force that they define the practice of decision-making and the exercise of power. The path dependence of institutions and the power of the state mean that reforms may appear to resemble each other across Europe; yet when they are examined closely, they express the power and legitimacy of the state, the logic of its legal system and ideas about politics. Reforms that appear to show the importance of networks and co-ordination, such as the use of contracts between elements of the state in France, are highly hierarchical and embody the power of the state and its institutions (Mabileau, 1997). However, such an approach is just as reductionist as the naïve convergence or globalization arguments. It would appear that every change must by definition be evidence for the power of the state, when most are changing in their capacity, their tools of government and in their legitimacy. The sensible application of the governance idea recognizes the power of institutions, but at the same time maps out the direction of change.

Re-institutionalization

A third criticism is that Western European politics is moving toward a more institutionalized form of politics rather than the other way round. As conceived by writers on policy networks, political actors relied on personal contacts and avoided the legislative procedures to get business done. One of the effects of the fragmentation of institutions, privatization, contracting out, loss of trust and increase in participation of interest groups is the growth of more formal relationships between different parts of the state and between state and societal institutions. There has been an expansion of the framework of public law, such as the regulation of utilities, the institution of inspectorates and regulation bodies, and an increase in the role of the courts (Loughlin, 1986). The conflicts that emerge between the organizations involved in governance do not imply a smoother form of interrelationship. Rather, it is possible that a more juridified and legalized form of decision-making may be emerging. Governance need not imply co-operation or growth in trust, but require legal institutions to adjudicate the disputes that arise. As Jessop (2000) points out, governance implies both success and failure in the way the relationships emerge and decision-makers solve problems. None the less, it cannot be argued that the institutional structures and relationships that have emerged are the same as the ones that preceded them. When governing a fragmented context, there are institutional solutions to decision-making at the same time as there are informal relationships and networks. As such, the governance account becomes more subtle and acknowledges the changes in institutional practices rather than assumes that institutions have automatically declined.

The imprecision of governance

The fourth criticism is that the concept of governance is so vague, imprecise and infinitely flexible as to apply to all changes to the context of local politics. Provided there has been some reform, it is possible to attach the label to any reorganization, even attempts to make institutions more powerful as a result of the pressures of fragmentation, a change that appears to be the opposite of fragmentation. All that governance becomes is a synonym for the new and so becomes quickly dated. Any major differences can be disposed by the interaction between continuity and innovation. Whilst researchers need to be careful what they label, such an attack is of the blunderbuss type. Critics can let off such guns at almost any target in the social sciences as most concepts suffer from lack of precision and are an attempt to generalize from complex reality rather then reflect its entirety. The answer to such criticisms is to find out whether the set of causes and consequences of governance make sense in a history of reforms and developments in interrelationships. If such changes make sense, then the concept has use. In other words, the success of the concept indicates its utility. Time will be the judge of governance.

Governance as a northern European phenomenon

A fifth criticism, and one that has emerged throughout this book, is that governance is something that applies only to either the UK or to the UK and the Netherlands or to the northern local government systems. The concept is of limited relevance in understanding the evolution of sub-national governing systems across Europe. But much of the evidence of this book shows the development of regimes, institutional fragmentation, privatization, institutional formation, new patterns of leadership and the spread of NPM is cross-European. None the less, critics of the governance idea can argue that the patterns of change in the north and in the south of Western Europe replicate old patterns, and whilst there may be some similarities, they are qualitatively different. Regionalism appears to be a southern phenomenon whereas NPM is concentrated more in the north. This book does not argue that the north–south experience disappears but that the overall picture becomes more complex. The next section explores the comparative dimension to governance to respond to this potential criticism and to draw inferences from experiences across Europe.

The comparative experience of governance

This section summarizes the various elements to governance as they are experienced by the Western European countries the book discusses. The aim is to find out the common patterns and to infer the sources of variation. To this end, Table 9.1 sets out the findings of the chapters for each of the

TABLE 9.1 Comparing the six dimensions of governance

	Regimes	Europeanization	NPM	Regional formation	Executive reform	Democratic renewal
Northern group						
Denmark	Low	Medium	Medium	Low	Low	High
Finland	Low	Medium	Medium	Low	Medium	Medium
Ireland	Low	Medium	Medium	Low	Low	Low
Netherlands	High	Medium	High	Low	Medium	High
Norway	Low	Low/n.a	Medium	Medium	Medium	Medium
Sweden	Medium	Medium	Medium	Low	Low	High
Uk	High	High	High	High	High	High
Southern Group						
Belgium	Low	Low	Low	High	Low	Low
France	Medium	Medium	Medium	High	Low	Low
Greece	Medium	Low	Low	Low	Low	Low
Italy	Medium	Medium	Medium	High	High	Medium
Portugal	Medium	Low	Low	Medium	Low	Low
Spain	High	High	Medium	High	Low	Medium
Hybrids						
Germany	High	High	High	Medium	High	High
Switzerland	Low	Low/n.a	Medium	Low	Low	Low

countries in relation to the six dimensions of governance. The idea is to offer approximate assessments of the degree of change in each country in each dimension of governance. The table uses three indicators, of low, medium and high, though the judgement is qualitative, derived from the secondary literature. This table comes with a strong health warring: the measures are broad brush and are far from absolute; they are merely designed to facilitate a comparison rather than state the outcomes of a research programme.

The table illustrates several themes that the book has discussed. The first is that the UK does appear to be at the end of a continuum of governance, but that the charge of exceptionalism should be rejected since the Netherlands, Germany and Spain are as reforming as the UK on certain dimensions. The second pattern to observe is that the north–south dimension does not appear to be replicated along all the dimensions. Take regimes. Here there is variation in each group, but the southern group's revival of public–private coalitions is consonant with the economic renaissance of cities in countries such as Spain. Similarly, there is variation within each camp in the reaction to Europe, with some countries being highly Europeanized whilst others are not. On the other hand, regional formation appears to fit the north–south pattern. As indicated by both Sharpe (1993) and Wright (1994), regionalism appears to be a response to the problems of functional capacity of southern states, as well as to the mobilization of territorial movements. The exception is the UK, a northern state in its functionally based and service-orientated local government system, which has introduced regional structures since 1997 largely because of territorial mobilization. Executive reform also appears to be concentrated in the north, but then Italy is in the southern country group. This pattern replicates itself with NPM and democratic renewal, as they are prevalent in northern countries with less interest in the south with the important exceptions of parts of Spain and Italy. As with other categories, there is substantial variation within each group.

The results do not confirm a simple north–south dichotomy as predicted in the literature, but reveal similarities along some dimensions, but not according to others. Moreover, there is variation within each group which suggests that countries experience different aspects of change. If there seems to be a cause of variation, it is according to size of country, with smaller countries being less willing to experiment and change, whereas the bigger ones have pushed through reforms. Though small countries have experienced rapid reform, such as the move to a federal state in Belgium and the impact of NPM in the Netherlands, overall these are less wide-ranging changes.

The results neatly counter the criticisms covered in the previous section. The UK does not stand alone to show the Anglo nature of governance. Moreover, the low interest in governance in the Republic of Ireland shows that such practices do not travel well across the Celtic sea. Instead, governance practices have diffused and emerged across mainland Europe. There are no northern and southern groups, except for the impact of NPM and the emergence of regionalism, and even here there is not a uniform experience. What Table 9.1 shows is that most countries show some movement to governance, though only the UK displays all the elements. If it can be accepted that governance does not have necessary conditions, then the Western European pattern shows different paths of development away from traditional local government. Just as there are variations within each country, so there is a contingent and variable development across nation-states. The comparative approach shows how governance takes various forms according to country and locality. There is no uniform pattern. There is a massive variety of political arrangements and practices across and between local political systems in the first place; flexibility, networks and fragmentation compound the variations. Politics has changed. Political systems have adapted to create new forms of political relationships.

References

Aglietta, M. (1979) *A Theory of Capitalist Regulation: The US Experience*. London: New Left Books.

Albæk, E., Rose, L., Strømberg, L. and Ståhlberg, (1991) *Nordic Local Government Developmental Trends and Reform Activities in the Post-War Period*. Helsinki: The Association of Finnish Local Authorities.

Almquist, R. (1999) 'Measuring the threat of competition – services for the elderly in the city of Stockholm', *Local Government Studies*, 25 (1): 1–16.

Amin, A. (ed.) (1994) *Post Fordism: A Reader*. Blackwell: Oxford.

Amoros, M. (1996) 'Decentralisation in Barcelona', *Local Government Studies*, 22 (3): 90–110.

Anderson, B. (1983) *Imagined Communities: Reflections on the Origins and Spread of Nationalism*. London: Verso.

Anderson, J. J. (1990) 'Skeptical reflections on a Europe of regions', *Journal of Public Policy*, 10 (4): 417–447.

Anderson, J. J. (1996) 'Germany and the structural funds: unification leads to bifurcation', in L. Hooghe (ed.) *Cohesion Policy and European Integration*. Oxford: Oxford University Press.

Andrew, C. and Goldsmith, M. (1998) 'From local government to local governance – and beyond', *International Political Science Review*, 19 (2): 101–117.

Ansell, C., Parsons, C. and Darden, K. (1997) 'Dual networks in European regional development policy', *Journal of Common Market Studies*, 35 (3): 347–375.

Archer, M. (1979) *Social Origins of Education Systems*. London: Sage.

Areilza, G. (1998) 'Urban regimes and governance: a cross-national analysis', unpublished paper.

Bache, I. (1998) *The Politics of European Union Regional Policy*. Sheffield: Sheffield Academic Press.

Bache, I. (1999) 'The extended gatekeeper and the implementation of EC regional policy in the UK', *Journal of European Public Policy*, 6 (1): 28–45.

Bache, I., George, S. and Rhodes, R. (1996) 'The European Union, cohesion policy, and sub-national authorities in the United Kingdon', in L. Hooghe (ed.) *Cohesion Policy and European Integration*. Oxford: Oxford University Press.

Bagnasco, A. and Le Galès, P. (1997) 'Les villes comme acteurs et comme societiés locales en Europe', in A. Bagnasco and P. Le Galès (eds) *Villes en Europe*. La Découverte, Paris.

Bailey, S. (1999) *Local Government Economics*. Basingstoke: Macmillan.

Baine, S., Benington, J. and Russell, J. (1992) *Changing Europe: Challenges Facing the Voluntary and Community Sectors in the 1990s*. London: NCVO Publications.

Baldersheim, H. (1986) *Men Har Dei Noko Val? Styrings- Og Leiingsprosessar I Storbykommunane*. Oslo.

Baldersheim, H. (1992) '"Aldermen into ministers": Oslo's experiment with a city cabinet', *Local Government Studies*, 18 (1): 18–30.

Baldersheim, H. (2000) 'Glocalisation: policies and networks of cities and regions in the Nordic countries', paper to XVIII World Congress of the International Political Science Association, Quebec, 1–5 August.

Balme, R. (1995) 'French regionalization and European integration: territorial adaptation and change in a unitary state', in B. Jones and M. Keating (eds) *The European Union and the Regions*. Oxford: Oxford University Press.

Balme, R. (1998) 'The French region as a space for public policy', in P. Le Galès and C. Lequesne (eds) *Regions in Europe*. London: Routledge.

Balme, R. and Jouve, B. (1996) 'Building the regional state: Europe and territorial organisation in France', in L. Hooghe (ed.) *Cohesion Policy and European Integration*. Oxford: Oxford University Press.

Balme, R. and Le Galès, P. (1997) 'Stars and black holes: French regions and cities in the European galaxy', in M. Goldsmith and K. Klausen (eds) *European Integration and Local Government*. Cheltenham: Edward Elgar.

Barzeley, M. and Armajani, B. (1992) *Breaking Through Bureaucracy: A New Vision for Managing in Government*. Berkeley, CA: University of California Press.

Bassett, K. (1996) 'Partnerships, business elites and urban politics: new forms of governance in an English city', *Urban Studies*, 33: 539–555.

Bassett, K. and Harloe, M. (1990) 'Swindon: the rise and decline of a growth coalition', in M. Harloe, C. Pickvance and J. Urry (eds) *Place, Policy and Politics: Do Localities Matter?* London: Unwin Hyman.

Batley, R. (1991) 'Comparisons and lessons', in R. Batley and G. Stoker (eds) *Local Government in Europe*. Basingstoke: Macmillan

Baxter, R. (1972) 'The working class and Labour politics'. *Political Studies*, 20: 97–107.

Baylis, J. and Smith, S. (1997) *The Globalization of World Politics*. Oxford: Oxford University Press.

Benington, J. (1994) *Local Democracy and the European Union*. Commission for Local Democracy Research Report, no. 6. London: CLD Ltd.

Benington, J. and Harvey, J. (1994) 'Spheres or tiers?: the significance of transnational local authority networks', in J. Lovenduski and J. Stanyer (eds) *Contemporary Political Studies*. Belfast: Political Studies Association.

Bennett, R. J. (1989) 'European economy, society, politics and administration: symmetry and disjuncture', in R. J. Bennett (ed.) *Territory and Administration in Europe*. London: Frances Pinter.

Bennett, R. J. (1993) 'European local government systems', in R. J. Bennett (ed.) *Local Government in the New Europe*. London: Belhaven.

Benz, A. (1998) 'German regions in the European Union: from joint policy-making to multi-level governance', in P. Le Galès and C. Lequesne (eds) *Regions in Europe*. London: Routledge.

Benz, A. and Eberlein, B. (1999) 'The Europeanization of regional policies: patterns of multi-level governance', *Journal of European Public Policy*, 6 (2): 329–348.

Benz, A. and Goetz, K. (1996) 'The German public sector: national priorities and the international reform agenda', in A. Benz and K. Goetz (eds) *A New German Public Sector*. Aldershot: Dartmouth.

Berry, J., Portney, K. and Thomson, K. (1993) *The Rebirth of Urban Democracy*. Washington, DC: Brookings.

Biggs, S. and Dunleavy, P. (1995) 'Changing organisational patterns in local government: a bureaushaping analysis', in J. Lovenduski and J. Stanyer (eds) *Contemporary Political Studies*. Belfast: Political Studies Association.

Blair, P. (1991) 'Trends in local autonomy and democracy: reflections from a European perspective', in R. Batley and G. Stoker (eds) *Local Government in Europe*. Basingstoke: Macmillan.

Boeckhout, S., Hulsker, W. and Molle, W. (1996) 'The Netherlands', in H. Heinelt and R. Smith (eds) *Policy Networks and European Structural Funds*. Aldershot: Avebury.

Bogason, P. (1991) 'Danish local government: towards an effective and efficient welfare state', in J. Hesse (ed.) *Local Government and Urban Affairs in International Perspective: Analyses of 20 Western Industrialised Countries*. Baden-Baden: Nomos Verlagsgesellschaft.

Bogason, P. (1996a) 'Local democracy: community power based on institutional change', in B. Greve (ed.) *Comparative Welfare Systems: The Scandinavian Model in a Period of Change*. New York: St Martins Press.

Bogason, P. (1996b) 'The fragmention of local government in Scandinavia', *European Journal of Political Research*, 30: 65–86.

Bogason, P. (1996c) 'Local democracy: community power based on institutional change', in B. Greve (ed.) *Comparative Welfare Systems: The Scandinavian Model in a Period of Change*. New York: St Martins Press.

Bogason, P. (2000) 'Associative values and local governments', in B. Greve (ed.) *What Constitutes a Good Society?* Basingtoke: Macmillan.

Bogdanor, V. (1991) *Local Democracy and the European Community – Challenge and Opportunity*. Belgrave Paper no. 6. Luton: Local Government Management Board.

Boix, C. (1996) 'Searching for competitiveness: the role of the Spanish public sector in the 1980s and 1990s', in J-E. Lane (ed.) *Public Sector Reform*. London: Sage.

Bomberg, E. and Peterson, J. (1996) *Decision-making in the EU: Implications for Central–Local Government Relations*. York: Joseph Rowntree Foundation.

Bonaduce, A. and Magnatti, P. (1996) 'Italy', in H. Heinelt and R. Smith (eds) *Policy Networks and European Structural Funds*. Aldershot: Avebury.

Bongers, P. (1992) *Local Government and 1992*. Harlow: Longman.

Borraz, O. (1994) 'Mayoral leadership in France' in O. Borraz, U. Bullmann, R. Hambleton, E. Page, N. Rao, and K. Young (eds) *Local Leadership and Decision Making*. York: Joseph Rowntree Foundation.

Borraz, O., Bullmann, U., Hambleton, R., Page, E., Rao, N. and Young, K. (eds) (1994) *Local Leadership and Decision Making*. York: Joseph Rowntree Foundation.

Bowman, M. and Hampton, W. (eds) (1983) *Local Democracies*. Melbourne, Longman Cheshire.

Boyer, R. (1990) *The Regulation School: A Critical Introduction*. New York: Columbia University Press.

Boyne, G. (1995) 'Population size and economies of scale in local government', *Policy and Politics*, 23 (3): 213–222.

Bradbury, J. and Mawson, J. (eds) (1998) *British Regionalism and Devolution*. London: Jessica Kingsley.

Bukve, O. (1996) 'Consensus, majority rule and managerialism in local government: Norwegian experiences and prospects', *Local Government Studies*, 22 (1): 147–168.

Bullmann, U. (1996) 'The politics of the third level', *Regional and Federal Studies*, 6 (2): 3–19.

Bullmann, U. and Page, E. (1994) 'Executive leadership in German local government', in O. Borraz, U. Bullmann, R. Hambleton, E. Page, N. Rao, and K. Young (eds) *Local Leadership and Decision Making*. York: Joseph Rowntree Foundation.

Bulpitt, J. (1983) *Territory and Power in the United Kingdom*. Manchester: Manchester University Press.

Burch, M. and Holiday, I. (1993) 'Institutional emergence: the case of the North West of England', *Regional Politics and Policy*, 3: 29–50.

Burgess, M. and Gress, F. (1991) 'German unity and EU: federalism restructured and revitalised', *Regional Politics and Policy*, 1 (3): 242–259.

Burns, J. M. (1979) *Leadership*. New York: Harper and Row.

Butler, D., Adonis, A. and Travers, T. (1994) *Failure in British Government*. Oxford: Oxford University Press.

Calderon, L. and Cabrera, R. (1991) 'The organisation of municipal government in Spain', *Local Government Policy Making*, 18 (2): 56–63.

Cassese, S. and Torchia, L. (1993) 'The meso level in Italy', in L. J. Sharpe (ed.), *Meso Government in Europe*. London: Sage.

Castells, M. (1977) *The Urban Question: Marxist Approach*. London: Edward Arnold.

Castells, M. (1978) *City, Class and Power*. London: Macmillan.

Castells, M. (1994) 'European cities, the informational society, and the global economy', *New Left Review*, 204: 18–32.

Castells, M. and Godard, F. (1974) *Monopolville*. Paris: Mouton.

Castles, F. (ed.) (1982) *The Impact of Parties: Politics and Policies in Democratic Capitalist States*. London: Sage.

Cecchini, P. (1988) *The European Challenge, 1992: The Benefits of a Single European Market*. Aldershot: Wildwood House.

Christiansen, T. (1996) 'Second thoughts on Europe's "Third Level": the EU Committee of the Regions', *Publius: The Journal of Federalism*, 26: 93–116.

Christiansen, L. and Dowding, K. (1994) 'Pluralism or State Autonomy? The Case of Amnesty International (British Section): the Insider/Outsider Group', *Political Studies*, XLII: 15–24.

Christofilopoulou-Kaler, P. (1991) 'Local government reform in Greece', in J. Hesse (ed.) *Local Government and Urban Affairs in International Perspective: Analyses of 20 Western Industrialised Countries*. Baden-Baden: Nomos Verlagsgesellschaft.

Clark, D. (1997) 'Local government in Europe: retrenchment, restructuring and British exceptionalism', *West European Politics*, 20 (3): 134–163.

Clark, T. and Hoffman-Martinot, V. (eds) (1998) *The New Political Culture*. Boulder, CO: Westview.

Clark, T. and Inglehart, R. (1998) 'The New Political Culture: changing dynamics of support for the welfare state and other policies in postindustrial societies', in T. Clark and V. Hoffman-Martinot (eds) *The New Political Culture*. Boulder, CO: Westview.

Clark, T. and Rempel, M. (1997) *Citizen Politics in Post Industrial Societies*. Boulder, CO: Westview Press.

Clark, T., Jeanrenaud, C., Hoffmann-Martinot, V. and Zimmermann, E. (1989), 'Why are (most) swiss leaders invisible?', paper to conference on New Leaders, Parties and Groups in Local Politics, Paris.

Clarke, S. and Gaile, G. (1998) *The Work of Cities*. Minneapolis: University of Minnesota Press.

Clegg, T. (1987) 'Spain', in E. Page and M. Goldsmith (eds) *Central and Local Government Relations*. Beverley Hills, CA: Sage.

Cochrane, A., Peck, J. and Tickell, A. (1996) 'Manchester plays games: exploring the local politics of globalization', *Urban Studies*, 33 (8): 1319–1336.

Coing, H. (1977) *Des patronats locaux et le défi urbain*. Paris: Editions du Centre des Recherches Urbains.

Cole, A. (1997) 'Governing the academies: sub-central secondary education policy making in France', *West European Politics*, 20 (2): 137–156.

Cole, A. and John, P. (2001) *Local Governance in England and France*. London: University College Press/Routledge.

Coleman, W. D. and Grant, W. P. (1998) 'Policy convergence and policy feedback: agricultural finance policies in a globalizing era', *European Journal of Political Research*, 34 (2): 225–247.

Colomer, J. (1998), 'The Spanish "State of the Autonomies": non-institutional federalism', *West European Politics*, 21: 40–52.

Commission for Local Democracy (1995) *Taking Charge: The Rebirth of Local Democracy* London: Municipal Journal.

Committee of Inquiry into the Conduct of Local Authority Business (1986) *Report of the Committee* (Widdicombe Report). Cmnd. 9797 London: HMSO.

Committee on Management in Local Government (1967) *Report of the Committee* (Maud Report). London: HMSO.

Committee of the Regions (1999) *Voter Turnout at Regional and Local Elections in the EU, 1990–1999*. Brussels: CoR.

Conzelmann, T. (1995) 'Networking and the politics of EU regional policy: lessons from North Rhine–Westphalia, Nord-Pas de Calais and North West England', *Regional and Federal Studies*, 5 (2): 134–172.

Cooke, P. and Morgan, K. (1998) *The Associational Economy*. Oxford: Oxford University Press.

Copus, C. (1999) 'The party group: a barrier to democratic renewal', *Local Government Studies*, 25 (4): 76–97.

Council of Europe (1992) *The Structure and Operation of Local and Regional Democracy – Norway*. Strasbourg: Council of Europe Publishing.

Council of Europe (1995) *The Size of Municipalities, Efficiency and Citizen Participation*. Local and Regional Authorities in Europe, no. 56. Strasbourg: Council of Europe.

Council of Europe (1998) *The Structure and Operation of Local and Regional Democracy – Portugal*. Strasbourg: Council of Europe Publishing.

Council of Europe (1999) *The Structure and Operation of Local and Regional Democracy – Netherlands*. Strasbourg: Council of Europe Publishing.

Coyle, C. (1997) 'European integration: a lifeline for Irish local authorities?', in M. Goldsmith and K. Klausen (eds) *European Integration and Local Government*. Cheltenham: Edward Elgar.

Crozier, M. (1964) *The Bureaucratic Phenomenon*. Chicago: University of Chicago Press.

Crozier, M. and Friedberg, E, (1977) *L'Acteur et le système*. Paris: Seuil.

Crozier, M. and Thoenig, J.-C. (1975) 'La régulation des systèmes organisées complexes', *Revue Française de Sociologie*, 16 (1): 3–32.

Cuchillo, M. (1993) 'The autonomous communities as the Spanish meso', in L. J. Sharpe (ed.) *Meso Government in Europe*. London: Sage.

Dangschat, J. and Hamedinger, A. (1999) 'Fit for competition within the networks of co-operation: new modes of regulation of the local state in the global economy – the cases of Hamburg and Vienna', paper to EURA conference, European Cities in Transformation, Paris, 22–23 October.

Da Rosa Pires, A. (1994) 'Local economic policy, the planning system and European integration', paper to IFRESI conference, Lille.

Da Silva e Costa, M., Felizes, J. and Neves, J. (1997) 'European integration and local government: the (ambiguous) Portuguese case', in M. Goldsmith and K. Klausen (eds) *European Integration and Local Government*. Cheltenham: Edward Elgar.

Davies, J. (2000) 'The hollowing-out of local democracy and the "fatal conceit" of governing without government', *British Journal of Politics and International Relations*, 2 (3): 414–428.

Davies, N. (1997) *Europe: A History*. Oxford: Oxford University Press/Pimlico.

Delmartino, F. (1988) 'Regionalisation in Belgium', *European Journal of Political Research*, 16: 381–394.

Delmartino, F. (1991) 'Belgium: in search of the meso level', in L. J. Sharpe (ed.) *The Rise of Meso Government in Europe*. London: Sage.

Dente, B. (1991) 'Italian local services: the difficult road towards privatisation', in R. Batley and G. Stoker (eds) *Local Government in Europe*. Basingstoke: Macmillan.

Dente, B. and Kjellberg, F. (1988) *The Dynamics of Institutional Change: Local Government Reorganization in Western Democracies*. London: Sage.

Denters, B., Heffen, O. and De Jong, H. (1999) 'An American perestroika in Dutch cities? Urban policy in the Netherlands at the end of the millenium', *Public Administration*, 77 (4): 837–853.

Department of the Environment (1991) *The Internal Management of Local Authorities*. London: HMSO.

Department of the Environment, Transport and the Regions (DETR) (1998) *Modern Local Government: In Touch With the People*. DETR Cm. 4014. London: HMSO.

Dienel, P. and Renn, O. (1995) 'Planning cells: a gate to "fractal mediation"', in O. Renn, T. Webler and P. Wiedemann (eds) *Fairness and Competence in Citizen Participation*. Dordrecht: Kluwer.

DiGaetano, A. (1997) 'Urban governing alignments and realignments in comparative perspective. Developmental politics in Boston, Massachusetts and Bristol, England, 1980–1996', *Urban Affairs Review*, 32 (6): 844–870.

DiGaetano, A. (1998) 'Urban governance in comparative perspective', paper presented to the annual conference of the Political Studies Association, Keele.

DiGaetano, A. and Klemanski, J. (1993) 'Urban regimes in comparative perspective', *Urban Affairs Quarterly*, 29 (1): 54–83.

DiGaetano, A. and Klemanski, J. (1999) *Power and City Governance*. Minneapolis: Minnesota University Press.

Donoughue, B. and Jones, G. (1973) *Herbert Morrison, Portrait of a Politician*. London: Weidenfeld and Nicolson.

Dowding, K. (2000) 'Explaining urban regimes', *International Journal of Urban and Regional Research*, 25 (1): 7–19.

Dowding, K, Dunleavy, P., King, D., Margetts, H. and Rydin, Y. (1999) 'Regime politics in London local government', *Urban Affairs Review*, 34 (4): 515–545.

Dowding, K. and John, P. (1990) 'Collective goods and functional allocation in local government'. Unpublished paper.

Downs, W. (1998) *Coalition Government Subnational Style*. Columbus: Ohio State University Press.

Duchacek, I. (1990) 'Perforated sovereignties: towards a typology of new actors in international relations', in H. Michelman and P. Soldatos (eds) *Federalism and International Relations*. Oxford: Clarendon.

Dunford, M. (1998) 'Regions and economic development', in P. Le Galès and C. Lequesne (eds) *Regions in Europe*. London: Routledge.

Dunleavy, P. (1981) *The Politics of Mass Housing in Britain*. Oxford: Oxford University Press.

Dunleavy, P. (1989) 'The UK: paradoxes of an ungrounded statism', in F. Castles (ed.) *The Comparative History of Public Policy*. Cambridge: Polity.

Dyson, K. (1980) *The State Tradition in Western Europe*. Oxford: Robertson.

Elcock, H. (1998) 'German lessons in local government: the opportunities and pitfalls of managing change', *Local Government Studies*, 24 (1): 41–59.

Eldersveld, S. J., Strömberg, L. and Derksen, W. (1995) *Local Elites in West Democracies*. Colorado: Westview.

Elkin, S. (1987) *City and Regime in the American Republic*. Chicago: University of Chicago Press.

Ercole, E. (1997) '"Yes, in theory. And perhaps in the future." European integration and local government in Italy', in M. Goldsmith and K. Klausen (eds) *European Integration and Local Government*. Cheltenham: Edward Elgar.

Ercole, E., Walters, M. and Goldsmith, M. (1997) 'Cities, networks, Euregions, European offices', in M. Goldsmith and K. Klausen (eds) *European Integration and Local Government*. Cheltenham: Edward Elgar.

Farrows, M. and McCarthy, R. (1997) 'Opinion formulation and impact in the Committee of the Regions', *Regional and Federal Studies*, 7 (1): 23–49.

Featherstone, K. and Yannopoulos, G. (1995) 'The European Community and Greece: integration and the challenge to centralism', in B. Jones and M. Keating (eds) *The European Union and the Regions*. Oxford: Oxford University Press.

Fernàndez, C. (1997) 'The privatisation of public services in Spain', in D. Lorrain and G. Stoker (eds) *The Privatization of Urban Services in Europe*. London: Pinter.

Fesler, J. (1965) 'Approaches to the understanding of decentralisation', *Journal of Politics*, 27: 536–566.

Fried, R. C. (1963) *The Italian Prefects: A Study in Administrative Politics*. London: Yale University Press.

Friend, J., Power, J. and Yewlett, C. (1974) *Public Planning: The Inter-corporate Dimension*. London : Tavistock Publications.

Garcia, E. (1998) 'Multidimensional decentralization in Spain: variable geometry decentralization', *International Review of Administrative Sciences*, 64 (4): 663–680.

Garcia, S. (1991) *Urbanisation and the Functions of Cities in the European Community*. Liverpool: Liverpool John Moores University.

Garmise, S. (1995) 'The Europeanization of sub-national networks: stabilization or change', paper for the ESRC series, regional and local response to European integration, Keele, 18 November.

Garraud, P. (1989) *Profession homme politique. La Carrière politique des maires urbains*. Paris: L'Harmattan

Garrett, G. (1998) *Partisan Politics in the Global Economy*. Cambridge: Cambridge University Press.

Gibson, J. and Batley, R. (1992) 'Introduction: trends in financing Europen local governments', *Local Government Studies*, 18 (4): 1–6.

Giordano, B. (2000) 'Italian regionalism or "Padanian" nationalism – the political project of the Lega Nord in Italian politics', *Political Geography*, 19: 445–471.

Goetz, K. (1995) 'National governance and European integration: intergovernmental relations in Germany', *Journal of Common Market Studies*, 33 (1): 91–116.

Goetz, E. and Clarke, S. (eds) (1993) *The New Localism*. London: Sage.

Goldsmith, M. (1991) 'Decision-making and accountability in local government: a comparative review', paper to the Joseph Rowntree Foundation, unpublished.

Goldsmith, M. (1993) 'The Europeanisation of local government', *Urban Studies*, 30 (4/5): 683–699.

Goldsmith, M. (1996) 'Normative theories of local government: a European comparison', in D. King and G. Stoker (eds) *Rethinking Local Democracy*. Basingstoke: Macmillan.

Goldsmith, M. and Klausen, K. K. (eds) (1997) *European Integration and Local Government*. Cheltenham: Edward Elgar.

Goldsmith, M. and Sperling, E. (1997) 'Local governments and the EU: The British experience', in M. Goldsmith and K. Klausen (eds) *European Integration and Local Government*. Cheltenham: Edward Elgar.

Goldstone, J. A. (1998) 'Initial conditions, general laws, path dependence, and explanation in historical sociology', *American Journal of Sociology*, 104 (3): 829–845.

Grant, M. (1992) 'The case for diversity in local government', unpublished paper.

Grémion, P. (1976) *Le Pouvoir périphérique*. Paris: Éditions du Seuil.

Grote, J. (1996) 'Cohesion in Italy: a view on non-economic disparities', in L. Hooghe (ed.) *Cohesion Policy and European Integration*. Oxford: Oxford University Press.

Grunow, D. (1992) 'Constitutional reform in local government in Germany: the case of North-Rhine-Westphalia (NRW)', *Local Government Studies*, 18 (1): 44–58.

Guay, T. (2000) 'Local government and global politics: the implications of Massachusetts' "Burma Law"', *Political Science Quarterly*, 15 (3): 353–376.

Gunlicks, A. (1986) *Local Government in the German Federal System*. Durham, NC: Duke University Press.

Guyomarch, A. (1999) '"Public service", public management and the modernization of French public administration', *Public Administration*, 77 (1): 171–193.

Gyford, J. (1985) *The Politics of Local Socialism*. London: Allen and Unwin.

Haas, E. B. (1958) *The Uniting of Europe: Political, Social and Economic Forces, 1950–57*. London: Stevens and Sons.

Haas, E. B. (1964) 'International integration: the European and universal process', *International Organization*, 15 (3): 366–392.

Hajer, M. A. (1993) 'Rotterdam: re-designing the public domain', in F. Bianchini and M. Parkinson (eds) *Cultural Policy and Urban Regeneration: The West European Experience*. Manchester: Manchester University Press.

Hambleton, R. (1999) 'The design of local political institutions: a cross-national analysis', paper to conference, European Cities in Transformation, Paris, 22–23 October.

Hambleton, R. (2000) 'Modernising political management in local government', *Urban Studies*, 37 (5–6): 931–950.

Hambleton, R. and Bullock, S. (1996) *Revitalising Local Democracy: the Leadership Options*. London: Association of District Councils/Local Government Management Board.

Hambleton, R. and Stewart, M. (2000) *Leadership in Urban Governance: the Mobilisation of Collective Advantage*. Urban Leadership Working Paper 1. Bristol: University of West of England.

Hansen, T. (1993) 'Intermediate-level reforms and the development of the Norwegian welfare state', in L. J. Sharpe (ed.) *The Rise of Meso Government in Europe*. London: Sage.

Harding, A. (1994a) 'Urban regimes and growth machines, UK style?', *Environment and Planning C: Government and Policy*, 9: 356–382.

Harding, A. (1994b) 'Amsterdam and Rotterdam', in A. Harding, J. Dawson, R. Evans and M. Parkinson (eds) *European Cities Towards 2000*. Manchester: Manchester University Press.

Harding, A. (1994c) 'Urban regimes and growth machines: toward a cross-national research agenda', *Urban Affairs Quarterly*, 29 (3): 356–382.

Harding, A. (1995) 'European city regimes?: Inter-urban competition in the new Europe', paper to the ESRC local governance programme conference, Exeter.

Harding, A. (1996) 'Is there a new community power and why should we need one?', *International Journal of Urban and Regional Research*, 20 (4): 637–655.

Harding, A. (1997) 'Urban regimes in a Europe of the cities?', *European Urban and Regional Studies*, 4 (4): 291–314.

Harding, A. (1999) 'Review article: North American urban political economy, urban theory and British research', *British Journal of Political Science*, 29: 673–698.

Harding, A. (2000) *Is There a 'Missing Middle' in English Governance?* London: New Local Government Network.

Harding, A., Dawson, J., Evans, R. and Parkinson, M. (eds) (1994) *European Cities Towards 2000*. Manchester: Manchester University Press.

Hargreaves, J. (2000) *Freedom for Catalonia?* Cambridge: Cambridge University Press.

Harmsen, R. (1999) 'The Europeanisation of national administrations: a comparative study of France and the Netherlands', *Governance*, 12 (1): 81–113.

Hart, T. and Roberts, P. (1995) 'The single European market: implications for local and regional authorities', in S. Hardy, M. Hart, L. Albrechts and A. Katos (eds) *An Enlarged Europe Regions in Competition?* London: Jessica Kingsley.

Harvey, D. (1989) *The Conditions of Post-Modernity*. Oxford: Blackwell.

Harvie, C. (1994) *The Rise of Regional Europe*. London: Routledge.

Haughton, G. and While, A. (1999) 'From corporate city to citizens city? Urban leadership after local entrepreneurialism in the United Kingdom', *Urban Affairs Review*, 35 (1): 3–23.

Haughton, G. and Williams, C. (eds) (1996) *Corporate City*. Aldershot: Avebury.

Hauswirth, I., Herrschel, T. and Newman, P. (2000) 'Incentives and disincentives to city-regional co-operation', paper to Regional Studies Association, Aix-en-Provence, September 2000.

Hayward, J. (1983) *Governing France*. 2nd edn. London: Butlers.

Hayward, J. and Watson, M. (1975) *Politics, Planning and Public Policy*. London: Cambridge University Press.

Hazell, R. (1999) *Constitutional Futures*. Oxford: Oxford University Press.

Hazell, R. (ed.) (2000) *The State and the Nations*. Thorverton: Imprint Academic.

Heath, A., Jowell, R. and Curtice, J. (1991) *Understanding Political Change*. Oxford: Pergamon Press.

Held, G. and Velasco, A. (1996) 'Spain', in H. Heinelt and R. Smith (eds) *Policy Networks and European Structural Funds*. Aldershot: Avebury.

Hendriks, F. and Tops, P. (1999) 'Between democracy and efficiency: trends in local government reform in the Netherlands and Germany', *Public Administration*, 77 (1): 133–153.

Henry, I. P. and ParamioSalcines, J. L. (1999) 'Sport and the analysis of symbolic regimes – a case study of the city of Sheffield', *Urban Affairs Review*, 34 (5): 641–666.

Hesse, J. J. and Sharpe, L. J. (1991) 'Local government in international perspective – some comparative observations', in J. Hesse (ed.) *Local Government and Urban*

Affairs in International Perspective: Analyses of 20 Western Industrialised Countries. Baden-Baden, Nomos Verlagsgesellschaft.

Hine, D. and Kassim, H. (1998) *Beyond the Market: The EU and National Social Policy.* London: Routledge.

Hintze, O. (1975) *The Historical Essays of Otto Hintze.* London: Oxford University Press.

Hirst, P. and Thompson, G. (1999) *Globalisation in Question,* 2nd edn. Cambridge: Polity.

Hix, S. (1999) *The Political System of the EU.* London: Macmillan.

Hocking, C. (1993) *Localising Foreign Policy.* Basingstoke: Macmillan.

Hoffman, S. (1966) 'Obstinate or obsolete? The fate of the nation state and the case of Western Europe', *Daedulus,* 95: 862–915.

Hoffman-Martinot, V. (1996) 'La relance du gouvernement métropolitaine en Europe, le prototype de Stuttgart', *Revue Française d'Administration Publique,* 71: 499–514.

Hoggett, P. (1987) 'A farewell to mass production? Decentralisation as an emergent public and private sector paradigm', in P. Hoggett and R. Hambleton (eds) *Decentralisation and Democracy: Localising Public Services.* Bristol: School for Advanced Urban Studies.

Hogwood, B. (1996) *Mapping the Regions.* York, Joseph Rowntree Foundation.

Holm-Hansen, J. (2000) 'Internationalisation on the local level in Norway', in J. Gidlund and M. Jerneck (eds) (2000) *Local and Regional Governance in Europe.* Cheltenham: Edward Elgar.

Holmberg, S. (1999) 'Down and down we go: political trust in Sweden', in P. Norris (ed.) *Critical Citizens.* Oxford: Oxford University Press.

Holton, R. (1998) *Globalization and the Nation State.* Basingstoke: Macmillan.

Hood, C. (1995) 'Contemporary public management: a new global paradigm', *Public Policy and Administration,* 10 (2): 104–117.

Hooghe, L. (1995a) 'Belgian federalism and the European Community', in B. Jones and M. Keating (eds) *The European Union and the Regions.* Oxford: Oxford University Press.

Hooghe, L. (1995b) 'Subnational mobilisation in the EU', *West European Politics,* 18 (3): 175–198.

Hooghe, L. (1996a) 'Introduction: reconciling EU-wide policy and national diversity', in L. Hooghe (ed.) *Cohesion Policy and European Integration.* Oxford: Oxford University Press.

Hooghe, L. (1996b) 'Building a Europe with the regions: the changing role of the European Commission', in L. Hooghe (ed.) *Cohesion Policy and European Integration.* Oxford: Oxford University Press.

Hughes, J. P. and Sasse, G. (2002) *Elites and Institutions in Regional and Local Governance in Eastern Europe.* ESRC report.

Hull, C. and Rhodes, R. A. W. (1977) *Intergovernmental Relations in the European Community.* Farnborough: Saxon House.

Humes, S. (1991) *Local Governance and National Power.* London: Harvester Wheatsheaf.

Humes, S. and Martin, E. (1961) *The Structure of Local Government Throughout the World.* Martinus Nijhoff: The Hague.

Humes, S. and Martin, E. (1969) *The Structure of Local Government.* International Union of Local Authorities: The Hague.

Inman, R. and Rubinfield, D. (1997) 'The political economy of federalism', in D. Mueller (ed.) *Perspectives on Public Choice.* Cambridge: Cambridge University Press.

Ioakimidis, P. C. (1996) 'EU cohesion policy in Greece: the tension between bureaucratic centralism and regionalism', in L. Hooghe (ed.) *Cohesion Policy and European Integration*. Oxford: Oxford University Press.

Jeffery, C. (1995) 'Whither the Committee of the Regions?', *Regional and Federal Studies*, 5 (2): 247–257.

Jeffery, C. (1996a) 'Farewell to the third level? The German *länder* and the European policy process', *Regional and Federal Studies*, 6 (2): 56–75.

Jeffery, C. (1996b) 'Regional information offices in Brussels and multi-level governance in the EU', *Regional and Federal Studies*, 6 (2): 183–203

Jeffery, C. (1999) *Recasting German Federalism*. London: Pinter.

Jessop, B. (2000) 'Governance failure', in G. Stoker (ed.) *The New Politics of British Local Governance*. Basingstoke: Macmillan.

John, P. (1994a) 'Central–local relations in the, 1980s and, 1990s: towards a policy learning approach', *Local Government Studies*, 20 (3): 412–436.

John, P. (1994b) *The Europeanisation of British Local Government: New Management Strategies*. Luton: Local Government Management Board.

John, P. (1994c) 'The presence and influence of UK local authorities in Brussels', in J. Lovenduski and J. Stanyer (eds) *Contemporary Political Studies*. Belfast: Political Studies Association.

John, P. (1994d) 'UK sub-national offices in Brussels: diversification or regionalisation?', *Regional Studies*, 28 (7): 739–746.

John, P. (1995) *A Base In Brussels: A Good Investment for Local Authorities? Special Report No 2*. London: Local Government Information Bureau.

John, P. (1996a) 'Centralisation, decentralisation and the EU: the dynamics of triadic relationships', *Public Administration*, 74: 293–313.

John, P. (1996b) 'Europeanisation in a centralising state: multi-level governance in the UK', *Regional and Federal Studies*, 6 (2): 131–144.

John, P. (1998a) *Analysing Public Policy*. London: Cassell.

John, P. (1998b) 'Sub-national partnerships and European integration: the difficult case of London and the South-East', in J. Bradbury and J. Mawson (eds) *British Regionalism and Devolution*. London: Jessica Kingsley.

John, P. (1999) 'New Labour and the decentralisation of power', in G. Taylor (ed.) *The Impact of New Labour*. Basingstoke: Macmillan.

John, P. and Carter, C. (1991) 'Local government in Europe and North America', *Policy Studies*, 12 (3): 56–62.

John, P. and Cole, A. (1998) 'Urban regimes and local governance in Britain and France – Policy adaption and coordination in Leeds and Lille', *Urban Affairs Review*, 33 (3): 382–404.

John, P. and Cole, A. (1999) 'Political leadership in the new urban governance: Britain and France compared', *Local Government Studies*, 25 (4): 98–115.

John, P. and McAteer, M. (1998) 'Sub-national institutions and the new European governance: UK local authority lobbying strategies for the IGC', *Regional and Federal Studies*, 8 (3): 104–124.

John, P. and Saiz, M. (1999) 'Local political parties in comparative perspective', in M. Saiz and H. Geser (eds) *Local Parties in Political and Organisational Perspective*. Boulder, CO: Westview.

John, P. and Whitehead, A. (eds) (1997) *Regionalism in England: Current Trends and Future Prospects*, Special issue, *Policy and Politics*, 25 (1): 3–85.

John, P., Dowding, K. and Biggs, S. (1995) 'Residential mobility in London: a micro test of the behavioural assumptions of the Tiebout model', *British Journal of Political Science*, 25: 379–397.

Judd, D. and Parkinson, M. (eds) (1990) *Leadership and Urban Regeneration*. Newbury Park, CA: Sage.

Judge, D., Stoker, G. and Wolman, H. (eds)(1995) *Theories of Urban Politics*. London: Sage.

Kaase, M. and Newton, K. (1995) *Beliefs in Government* Oxford: Oxford University Press.

Kantor, P., Savitch, H. V. and Haddock, S. V. (1997) 'The political economy of urban regimes – a comparative perspective', *Urban Affairs Review*, 32 (3): 348–377.

Kassim, H. and Menon, A. (eds) (1996) *The EU and National Industrial Policy* London: Routledge.

Keating, M. (1995a) 'The politics of economic development. Political change and local development policies in the United States, Britain, and France', *Urban Affairs Quarterly*, 28 (3): 373–396.

Keating, M. (1995b) 'Europeanism and regionalism', in B. Jones and M. Keating (eds) *The European Union and the Regions*. Oxford: Oxford University Press.

Keating, M. (1998) *The New Regionalism in Western Europe*. Cheltenham: Edward Elgar.

Keating, M. (1999) 'What's wrong with asymmetrical government?', in H. Elcock and M. Keating (eds) *Remaking the Union: Devolution and British Politics in the 1990s*. London: Frank Cass.

Kesselman, M. (1972) *Le Consensus ambigu*. Paris: Cujas.

Kickert, W. (ed.) (1997) *Public Management and Administrative Reform in Western Europe*. Cheltenham: Edward Elgar.

King, D. (1984) *Fiscal Tiers: The Economics of Multi-level Government*. London: George Allen and Unwin.

Klausen, K. (1997) 'Danish local government: integrating into the EU?', in M. Goldsmith and K. Klausen (eds) *European Integration and Local Government*. Cheltenham: Edward Elgar.

Kleger, H., Kühne, A. and Rüegg, E. (1995) 'The transformation of urban regimes: learning in and from Berlin-Bradenburg', paper to ECPR Joint Sessions, 'The changing local governance of Europe', Bordeaux.

Klein, H. K. (1999) ''Tocqueville in cyberspace: using the Internet for citizen associations', *Information Society* 15 (4): 213–220.

Kleven, T., Floris, T., Granberg, M., Montin, S., Rieper, O. and Vabo, S. (2000) 'Renewal of local government in Scandinavia: effects for local politicians', *Local Government Studies*, 26 (2): 93–116.

Koch, A. M. and Fuchs, G. (2000) 'Economic globablization and regional penetration: the failure of networks in Baden-Würtemberg', *European Journal of Political Research*, 37 (1): 57–75.

Kunzmann, K. and Lang, M. (1994) 'Frankfurt', in A. Harding, J. Dawson, R. Evans and M. Parkinson (eds) *European Cities Towards 2000*. Manchester: Manchester University Press.

Ladrech, R. (1994) 'Europeanization of domestic politics: the case of France', *Journal of Common Market Studies*, 32 (1): 69–88.

Laffan, B. (1996) 'Ireland: A region without regions – the odd man out?', in L. Hooghe (ed.) *Cohesion Policy and European Integration*. Oxford: Oxford University Press.

Lane, J. E. (ed.) (1997) *Public Sector Reform*. London: Sage.

Leach, S., Stewart, J. and Walsh, K. (1994) *The Changing Organisation and Management of Local Government*. Basingstoke: Macmillan.

Leach, S. and Wilson, D. (2000) *Local Political Leadership*. Bristol: The Policy Press.

Le Bart, C. (1992) *La Rhetorique du maire entrepreneur*. Paris: Vie Locale.

Le Galès, P. (1993) *Politique Urbaine Et Developpement Local*. Paris: l'Harmattan.

Le Galès, P. (1994) 'Regional economic policies: an alternative to French dirigiste policies', special issue, *Regional Politics and Policy*, 4 (3): 72–91.

Le Galès, P. (1995) 'Urban regimes and comparative urban politics', paper to ECPR Joint Sessions workshop, 'Local governance', Bordeaux.

Le Galès, P. (1998a) 'Regulations and governance in European cities', *International Journal of Urban and Regional Research*, 22 (3): 482–506.

Le Galès, P. (1998b) 'Conclusion – government and governance of regions: structural weaknesess and new mobilisation', in P. Le Galès and C. Lequesne (eds) *Regions in Europe*. London: Routledge.

Le Galès, P. (2000) 'Private sector interests and urban governance' in A. Bagnasco and P. Le Galès (eds) *Cities in Contemporary Europe*. Cambridge: Cambridge University Press.

Le Galès, P. and Harding, A. (1998) 'Cities and states in Europe', *West European Politics*, 21 (3): 120–145.

Le Galès, P. and John, P. (1997) 'Is the grass greener on the other side? What went wrong with French regions, and the implications for England', *Policy and Politics*, 25 (1): 51–60.

Le Galès, P. and Lequesne, C. (eds) (1998) *Regions in Europe*. London: Routledge.

Le Galès, P. and Mawson, J., (1995) 'Contracts versus competitive bidding: rationalising urban policy programmes in England and France', *Journal of European Public Policy*, 2 (2): 205–241.

Leemans, A. (1970) *Changing Patterns of Local Government*. The Hague: International Union of Local Authorities.

Leonardi, R. and Nanetti, R. (eds) (1990) *The Regions and European Integration*. London: Pinter.

Leontidou, L. (1995) 'Repolarisation in the Mediterranean: Spanish and Greek cities in neo-liberal Europe', *European Planning Studies*, 3 (2): 155–172.

Levine, M. (1994) 'The transformation of urban politics in France. The roots of growth politics and urban regimes', *Urban Affairs Quarterly*, 29 (3): 383–410.

Levine, M. and Van Weesep, J. (1988) 'The changing nature of Dutch urban planning', *Journal of the American Planning Association*, 54: 315–323.

Lipset, S. and Rokkan, S. (1967) *Party Systems and Voter Alignments*. New York: Free Press.

Logan, J. and Molotch, H. (1987) *Urban Fortunes The Political Economy of Place*. Berkeley, CA: University of California Press.

Lorrain, D. (1987) 'Le grand fossé? Le débat public privé et les services urbains', *Polititiques et Management Public*, 3 (5): 83–102.

Lorrain, D. (1991) 'Public goods and private operators in France', in R. Batley and G. Stoker (eds) *Local Government in Europe*. Basingstoke: Macmillan.

Lorrain, D. (1997) 'France: silent change', in D. Lorrain and G. Stoker (eds) *The Privatization of Urban Services in Europe*. London: Pinter.

Lorrain, D. (2000) 'The construction of urban service models', in A. Bagnasco and P. Le Galès (eds) *Cities in Contemporary Europe*. Cambridge: Cambridge University Press.

Loughlin, J. (1996) 'Representing regions in Europe: the Committee of the Regions', *Regional and Federal Studies*, 6 (2): 147–165.

Loughlin, M. (1986) *Local Government in the Modern State*. London: Sweet and Maxwell.

Lovering, J. (1999) 'Theory led by policy: the inadequacies of the "new regionalism" (illustrated from the case of Wales)', *International Journal of Urban and Regional Research*, 23 (2): 379–397.

Lowndes, V. (1997) 'Change in public service management: new institutions and new managerial regimes', *Local Government Studies*, 23 (2): 42–66.

Lowndes, V. (1999) 'Management change in local government' in G. Stoker (ed.) *The New Management of British Local Governance*. Basingstoke: Macmillan.

Maas, A. (ed.) (1959) *Area and Power*. Glencoe, IL: The Free Press.

McAleavey, P. (1993) 'The politics of European regional development policy: additionality in the Scottish coalfields', *Regional Politics and Policy*, 3 (2): 88–107.

McAleavey, P. and Mitchell, J. (1994) 'Industrial regions and lobbying in the structural funds reform process', *Journal of Common Market Studies*, 32 (2): 237–248.

McCarthy, R. (1997) 'The Committee of the Regions: an advisory body's tortuous path to influence', *Journal of European Public Policy*, 4 (3): 439–454.

McCarthy, J. (1998) 'Reconstruction, regeneration and re-imaging', *Cities*, 15 (5): 337–344.

McCarthy, A. and Burch, M. (1994), 'European regional development strategies: the response of two northern regions', *Local Government Policy Making*, 20: 31–38.

McComas, K. and Scherer, C. (1999) 'Providing balanced risk information in surveys used as citizen participation mechanisms', *Society and Natural Resources*, 12 (2): 107–119.

McGuick, P. (1994) 'Economic restructuring and the realignment of urban planning systems: the case of Dublin', *Urban Studies*, 31 (2): 287–308.

McKay, D. (1996) 'Urban development and civic community: a comparative analysis', *British Journal of Political Science*, 26: 1–24.

Mabileau, A. (1997) 'Les Génies invisibles du local. Faux-semblants et dynamiques de la décentralisation', *Revue Française de Science Politique*, 47 (3–4): 340–376.

Malanczuk, P. (1985) 'European affairs and the "*Länder*" [states] of the Federal Republic of Germany', *Common Market Law Review*, 22: 237–272.

Marks, G. (1992) 'Structural policy in the European Community', in A. Sbragia (ed.) *Euro-Politics*. Washington, DC: The Brookings Institution.

Marks, G. (1993) 'Structural policy and multi-level governance in the EC', in A. Cafruny and G. Rosenthal (eds) *The State of the European Community*, vol 2. *The Maastricht Debates and Beyond*. Boulder, CO: Lynne Reiner.

Marks, G. (1996) 'Exploring and explaining variation in EU Cohesion policy', in L. Hooghe (ed.) *Cohesion Policy and European Integration*. Oxford: Oxford University Press.

Marks, G., Nielson, F., Ray, L. and Salk, J. (1996) 'Competencies, cracks and conflicts: regional mobilisation in the European Union', in G. Marks, F. Scharpf, P. Schmitter and W. Streeck (eds) *Governance in the European Union*. London: Sage.

Martin, S. (1998) 'EU programmes and the evolution of local economic governance in the UK', *European and Urban Regional Studies*, 5 (3): 237–248.

Martin, S. and Pearce, G. (1999) 'Differentiated multi-level governance? The response of British subnational governments to European integration', *Regional and Federal Studies*, 9 (2): 32–52.

Martinez, Cearra A. (1994) 'Revitalization strategies in metropolitan Bilbao', paper to IFRESI conference, Lille.

Martins, M. R. (1995) 'Size of municipalities, efficiency, and citizen participation: a cross-European perspective', *Environment and Planning C: Government and Policy*, 13: 441–458.

Mateo, J. (1991) 'Improving access to administration in Spain', in R. Batley and G. Stoker (eds) *Local Government in Europe*. Basingstoke: Macmillan.

Mawson, J. (1998a) 'The English regional debate. Towards regional governance or government', in J. Bradbury and J. Mawson (eds) *British Regionalism and Devolution*. London: Jessica Kingsley.

Mawson, J. (1998b) 'The rise of the regional agenda to combat increased fragmentation', in P. Le Galès and C. Lequesne (eds) *Regions in Europe*. London: Routledge.

Mawson, J. and Gibney, J. (1985) 'English and Welsh local government in the European Community', in M. Keating and B. Jones (eds) *Regions in the European Community*. Oxford: Clarendon.

Mayntz, R. (1993) 'Governing failures and the problem of governability', in J. Kooiman (ed.) *Modern Governance*. London: Sage.

Mazey, S. (1995) 'Regional lobbying in the new Europe', in M. Rhodes (ed.) *The Regions and the New Europe*. Manchester: Manchester University Press.

Mazey, S. and Richardson, J. (1993) 'Introduction: the transference of power, decision rules, and the rules of the game', in S. Mazey and J. J. Richardson (eds) *Lobbying in the European Community*. Oxford: Oxford University Press.

Meehan, E. (1997) 'The citizen and the region', *Regional and Federal Studies*, 7 (1): 70–76.

Mény, Y. (1983) 'Le maire ici and ailleurs', *Pouvoirs*, 14: 19–28.

Mény, Y. (1986) 'The political dynamics of regionalisation: Italy, France and Spain', in R. Morgan (ed.) *Regionalism in European Politics*. London: Policy Studies Institute.

Mény, Y. and Knapp, A. (1998) *Government and Politics in Western Europe*, 3rd edn. Oxford: Oxford University Press.

Mény, Y., Muller, P. and Quermonne, J-L. (1996) *Adjusting to Europe*. London: Routledge.

Merloni, F. and Vecchio, G. (1987) *Il Processo di Decentramento Amministrativo in Portugallo Quaderni per la Ricerco/4*. Rome: Istituto di Studi Sulle Regioni.

Michel, H. (1998) 'Government or governance? The case of the French local political system', *West European Politics*, 21 (3): 146–169.

Milan, B. (1997) 'Committee of the regions: in at the birth', *Regional and Federal Studies*, 7 (1): 5–10.

Mill, J. S. (1861) *Considerations on Representative Government in Utilitarianism, Liberty, and Representative Government*. London: J. M. Dent.

Mills, L. (1994) 'Economic development, the environment and Europe: areas of innovation in UK local government', *Local Government Policy Making*, 20 (5): 31–38.

Mintzberg, H. (1983) *Structure in Fives*. Englewood Hills, NJ: Prentice Hall.

Mira, A. (1999) 'Portugal: the resistance to change in the state model', *Regional and Federal Studies*, 9 (2): 98–105.

Molina, I. (2000) 'Spain', in H. Kassim, B. Peters and V. Wright (eds) *The National Co-ordination of European Policy: the Domestic Level*. Oxford: Oxford University Press.

Montin, S. (1992) ' Recent trends in the relationship between politics and administration in local government: the case of Sweden', *Local Government Studies*, 25: 31–43.

Montin, S. (1993) *Swedish Local Government in Transition*, Örebo Studies 8. Örebo: University of Örebo Press.

Montin, S. (1995) 'Local governance in Sweden: from marketisation to political co-ordination', paper to workshop 'The changing local governance of Europe', Bordeaux.

Moynihan, D. (1969) *Maximum Feasible Misunderstanding*. New York: Free Press.

Morata, F. and Muñoz, X. (1996) 'Vying for European funds: territorial restructuring in Spain', in L. Hooghe (ed.) *Cohesion Policy and European Integration*. Oxford: Oxford University Press.

Moravcsik, A. (1993) 'Preferences and power in the European Community: a liberal intergovernmental approach', *Journal of Common Market Studies*, 31: 473–524.

Moravcsik, A. (1999) *The Choice for Europe*. London: UCL Press for Cornell.

Mouritzen, P-E. (ed.) (1992) *Managing Cities in Austerity*. London: Sage.

Myrvold, T. (2000) 'Look to Oslo? The work of parliamentarian models of government in local politics', paper to XVIII World Congress of the International Political Science Association, Quebec, 1–5 August.

Nanetti, R. (1999) 'Adding value to city planning: the EU's Urban Programme in Naples', paper presented at the conference on European cities in transformation, annual meeting of the European Urban Research Association, Paris, 22–23 October.

Négrier, E. (1999) 'The changing role of French local government', *West European Politics*, 22 (4): 120–140.

Neustadt, R. (1960) *Presidential Power: the Politics of Leadership*. New York: Wiley.

Newman, P. (1994) 'Urban regime theory and comparative urban politics', paper to IFRESI conference, Lille, March.

Newman, P. (1995) 'The politics of urban redevelopment in London and Paris', *Planning Practice and Research*, 10 (1): 15–23.

Newman, P. and Thornley, A. (1996) *Urban Planning in Europe*. London: Routledge.

Newton, K. (1980) *Balancing the Books*. London: Sage.

Newton, K. (1982) 'Is small really so beautiful? Is big so ugly? Size, effectivenes and democracy in post-war Britain', *Political Studies*, 30 (2): 190–206.

Nielson, F. and Salk, J. (1998) 'The ecology of collective action and regional representation in the European Union', *European Sociological Review*, 14 (3): 231–254.

Norris, P. (1999) 'Introduction: the growth of critical citizens', in P. Norris (ed.) *Critical Citizens*. Oxford: Oxford University Press.

Norton, A. (1978) 'The evidence considered', in G. Jones (ed.) *Political Leadership in Local Authorities*. Birmingham: Institute of Local Government Studies.

Norton, A. (1991) 'Western European local government in comparative perspective', in R. Batley and G. Stoker (eds) *Local Government in Europe*. Basingstoke: Macmillan.

Norton, A. (1993) *International Handbook of Local and Regional Government*. Brookfield, VT: Edward Elgar.

Oates, W. (1972) *Fiscal Federalism*. New York: Harcourt Brace Jovanovich.

Organization for Economic Co-operation and Development (OECD) (1997) *Managing Across Levels of Government*.http://www.oecd.org/puma/malg/malg97/overview.pdf

Osborne, D. and Gaebler, T. (1993) *Reinventing Government*. New York: Plume.

Page, E. (1991) *Localism and Centralism in Europe*. Oxford: Oxford University Press.

Page, E. and Goldsmith, M. (1987) *Central and Local Government Relations.* Beverly Hills, CA: Sage.

Painter, J. (1991) 'Regulation theory and local government', *Local Government Studies*, 17 (6): 23–44.

Painter, J. (1995) 'Regulation theory, post-fordism and urban politics', in D. Judge, G. Stoker and H. Wolman (eds) *Theories of Urban Politics.* London: Sage.

Parkinson, M., Bianchini, F., Dawson, J., Evans, R. and Harding, A. (1992) *Urbanisation and the Functions of Cities in the European Community.* Brussels: European Commission.

Peck, J. and Tickell, A. (1994) 'Searching for a new institutional fix: the after-Fordist crisis and global–local disorder', in A. Amin (ed.) *Post Fordism: A Reader.* Blackwell: Oxford.

Peck, J. and Tickell, A. (1995) 'Business goes local: dissecting the "business agenda" in Manchester', *International Journal of Urban and Regional Research*, 19: 55–78.

Pedroso de Almedia, J. (1991) 'Portugal: overcoming the central–local government dichotomy', in J. Hesse (ed.) *Local Government and Urban Affairs in International Perspective: Analyses of 20 Western Industrialised Countries.* Baden-Baden, Nomos Verlagsgesellschaft.

Pereira, A. (1995) 'Regionalism in Portugal', in B. Jones and M. Keating (eds) *The European Union and the Regions.* Oxford: Oxford University Press.

Perulli, P. (1999) 'Territorial interests and chambers of commerce in Italy', paper to EURA conference, European Cities in Tranformation, Paris, Sepember.

Peters, T. and Waterman, R. (1995) *In Search of Excellence*, rev. edn. London: Harper Collins.

Pickvance, C. and Preteceille, E. (1991) *State Restructuring and Local Power.* London: Pinter.

Pierre, J. (2000) 'Introduction: understanding governance', in J. Pierre (ed.) *Debating Governance.* Oxford: Oxford University Press.

Pierson, P. (2000) 'Increasing returns, path dependence, and the study of politics', *American Political Science Review*, 94 (2): 251–267.

Pollitt, C. (1993) *Managerialism and the Public Services.* Oxford: Blackwell.

Pratchett, L. (ed.) (2000) *Renewing Local Democracy.* London: Frank Cass.

Przeworski, A. and Teune, H. (1982) *The Logic of Comparative Social Inquiry.* Malabar, FL: Krieger Publishing Co.

Putnam, R. (1993) *Making Democracy Work.* Princeton, NJ: Princeton University Press.

Putnam, R., Leonardi, R., Nanetti, R. and Pavoncello, F. (1983) 'Explaining institutional success: the case of Italian regional government', *American Political Science Review*, 77: 55–74.

Radaelli, C. (1997) 'How does Europeanization produce domestic policy change?', *Comparative Political Studies*, 30 (5): 553–575.

Ragin, Charles (1985) *The Comparative Method: Moving Beyond Qualitative and Quantitative Strategies.* Berkeley, CA: University of California Press.

Rao, N. (1994) 'Continuity and change: responses to pressures for institutional reform in Britain', in O. Borraz, U. Bullmann, R. Hambleton, E. Page, N. Rao and K. Young (eds), *Local Leadership and Decision Making.* York: Joseph Rowntree Foundation.

Rasmussen, N. (2000) 'Regime formation in the UK – a qualitative comparative analysis of ten cities', dissertation submitted to the Department of Government, the London School of Economics and Political Science for the MSc in Public Administration and Public Policy.

Reichard, C. (1997) 'Neues Steuerungsmodell: local reform in Germany', in W. Kickert (ed.), *Public Management and Administrative Reform in Western Europe*. Cheltenham: Edward Elgar.

Reidenbach, M. (1997) 'The privatization of urban services in Germany', in D. Lorrain and G. Stoker (eds) *The Privatization of Urban Services in Europe*. London: Pinter.

Rhodes, M., Heywood, P. and Wright, V. (1997) *Developments in West European Politics*. Basingstoke: Macmillan.

Rhodes, R. A. W. (1986) *The National World of Local Government*. London: Unwin Hyman.

Rhodes, R. A. W. (1988) *Beyond Westminster and Whitehall*. London: Unwin Hyman.

Rhodes, R.A.W. (1997) *Understanding Governance: Policy Networks, Governance, Reflexivity and Accountability*. Buckingham: Open University Press.

Rhodes, R. A. W., Bache, I. and George, S. (1996) 'Policy networks and policy-making in the European Union: a critical appraisal', in L. Hooghe (ed.) *Cohesion Policy and European Integration*. Oxford: Oxford University Press.

Robson, W. A. (1933) 'The central domination of local government', *Political Quarterly*, 4.

Rogers, V. (1998) 'Devolution and economic development in France', *Policy and Politics*, 26 (4): 417–437.

Rokkan, S. (1966) 'Votes count but resources decide', in R. A. Dahl (ed.) *Political Oppositions in West Democracies*. New Haven, CT: Yale University Press.

Rolla, G. (1992) 'The relationship between the political and executive structure in Italian local government', *Local Government Studies*, 18 (1): 59–68.

Rose, L. and Pederson (2000) 'The legitimacy of local government. What makes a difference. Evidence from Norway', in K. Hoggart and T. Clark (eds) *Citizen Responsive Government*. Amsterdam: JAI.

Rose, R. (1996) *What is Europe?* New York: Harper Collins.

Rose, R. and Suleiman, E. (1980) *Presidents and Prime Ministers*. Washington, DC: American Enterprise Institute.

de Rynck, S. (1996) 'Europe and cohesion policy-making in the Flemish region', in L. Hooghe (ed.) *Cohesion Policy and European Integration*. Oxford: Oxford University Press.

de Rynck, S. (1997) 'Belgian local government: far away from Brussels', in M. Goldsmith and K. Klausen (eds) *European Integration and Local Government*. Cheltenham: Edward Elgar.

Salisbury, R (1990) 'The paradox of interest groups in Washington – more groups, less clout', in A. King (ed.) *The New American Political System*, 2nd version. Washington, DC: American Enterprise Institute.

Sassen, S. (1991) *The Global City*. Princeton, NJ: Princeton University Press.

Saunders, P. (1980) *Urban Politics: A Sociological Interpretation*. Harmondsworth: Penguin.

Savitch, H. (1988) *Post-Industrial Cities: Politics and Planning in New York, Paris, and London*. Princeton, NJ: Princeton University Press.

Scharpf, F. W (1988) 'The joint-decision trap: lessons from German federalism and European integration', *Public Administration*, 66: 239–278.

Scharpf, F. W., Reissert, B. and Schnabel, F. (1978) 'Policy effectiveness and conflict avoidance in intergovernmental policy formation', in K. Hanf and F. Scharpf (eds) *InterOrganisational Policy Making*. London: Sage.

Schröter, E. (2000) 'A capital in the making: the government and politics of Berlin', paper to XVIII World Congress of the International Political Science Association, Quebec, 1–5 August.

Scott, A. J. (1996) 'Regional motors of the global economy', *Futures*, 28 (5): 391–411.

Scott, A. J. (1998) *Regions and the World Economy*. Oxford: Oxford University Press.

de Seixas, J. (1999) 'The future of governance in the Lisbon city region', unpublished paper.

Sellers, J. (2001) *Governing from Below*. Cambridge: Cambridge University Press.

Setälä, M. (1999) 'Referendums in Western Europe – a wave of direct democracy?' *Scandinavian Political Studies*, 22 (4): 327–340.

Sharpe, L. J. (1970) 'Theories of local government', *Political Studies*, 18 (2): 153–174.

Sharpe, L. (1988) 'The growth and decentralization of the modern democratic-state', *European Journal of Political Research*, 16 (4): 365–380.

Sharpe, L. (1993) 'The European meso: an appraisal', in L. J. Sharpe (ed.) *The Rise of Meso Government in Europe*. London: Sage.

Silva, C. (2000) 'Politicisation, neo-liberalism and new form of local governance in Portugal', in K. Hoggart and T. Clark (eds) *Citizen Responsive Government*. Amsterdam: JAI.

Sjoblom, S. (1992) 'Citizen initiatives and local government', paper to ECPR workshop 'Local government and the citizen', Limerick.

Smith, A. (1995) 'Going beyond the democratic deficit: the EU and rural development in networked societies', *Regional and Federal Studies*, 5 (1): 45–66.

Smith, A. (1998) 'The sub-regional level', in P. Le Galès and C. Lequesne (eds) *Regions in Europe*. London: Routledge.

Smith, B. (1985) *Decentralization: The Territorial Dimension of the State*. London: George Allen and Unwin.

Snape, S. (1995) 'Contracting out local government services in Western Europe: lessons from the Netherlands', *Local Government Studies*, 21 (4): 642–658.

Somma, P. (1999) 'Leadership in Italian cities', paper to the International Seminar on Governing Cities: International Perspectives, Eurovillage, Brussels, 18–19 September.

Stewart, M. (1996) 'Too little, too late: the politics of local complacency', *Journal of Urban Affairs*, 18 (2): 119–137.

Steyaert, J. (2000) 'Local governments online and the role of the resident – Government shop versus electronic community', *Social Science Computer Review*, 18 (1): 3–16.

Stoker, G. (1990) 'Regulation theory, local government and the transition from fordism', in D. King and J. Pierre (eds) *Challenges to Local Government*. London: Sage.

Stoker, G. (1995) 'Regime theory and urban politics', in D. Judge, G. Stoker and H. Wolman (eds) *Theories of Urban Politics*. London: Sage.

Stoker, G. (1996) *The Reform of the Institutions of Representative Local Democracy: Is There a Role for the Mayor–Council Model*. Commission for Local Democracy Report no. 18. London: CLD Ltd.

Stoker, G. (1997a) 'The privatization of urban services in the Unitied Kingdom', in D. Lorrain and G. Stoker (eds) *The Privatisation of Urban Services in Europe*. London: Pinter.

Stoker, G. (1997b) 'Conclusion: privatization, urban government and the citizen', in D. Lorrain and G. Stoker (eds) *The Privatisation of Urban Services in Europe*. London: Pinter.

Stoker, G. (1998) 'Governance as theory: five propositions', *International Social Science Journal*, 50 (1): 17–29.

Stoker, G.(ed.) (1999) *The New Management of British Local Governance*. Basingstoke: Macmillan.

Stoker, G. (2000) 'Introduction', in G. Stoker (ed.) *The New Politics of British Local Governance*. Basingstoke: Macmillan.

Stoker, G. and McGarvey, N. (2000) 'Achieving responsiveness in public services: lessons from the UK', paper for the DfID Citizens' Voice Project, June.

Stoker, G. and Mossberger, K. (1994) 'Urban regime theory in comparative perspective', *Environment and Planning C: Government and Policy*, 12: 195–212.

Stoker, G. and Mossberger, K. (1995) 'The post-fordist local state: the Thatcherite project?', in J. Stewart and G. Stoker (eds) *The Future of Local Government*. Basingstoke: Macmillan.

Stoker, G. and Travers, T. (1998) 'The mayor–council model: lessons from Barcelona'. Paper to Deloitte and Touche.

Stoker, G. and Wolman, H. (1992) 'Drawing lessons from US experience: an elected mayor for British local government', *Public Administration*, 72 (2): 241–267.

Stone, C. (1989) *Regime Politics, Governing Atlanta, 1946–1988*. Lawrence, KS: University Press of Kansas.

Stone, C. (1995) 'Political leadership in urban politics', in D. Judge, G. Stoker and H. Wolman (eds) *Theories of Urban Politics*. London: Sage.

Streek, W. and Schmitter, P. (1991) 'From national corporatism to transnational pluralism: organised interests in the Single European Market', *Politics and Society*, 19 (2): 133–164.

Strom, E. (1996) 'In search of the growth coalition: American urban theories and the redevelopment of Berlin', *Urban Affairs Review*, 31 (4): 455–481.

Tamenes, R. and Clegg, T. (1984) 'Spain: regional autonomy and the democratic transition', in M. Hebbert and H. Machin (eds) *Regionalisation in France, Italy and Spain*. London: ICERD.

Tarrow, S. (1977) *Between Center and Periphery, Grassroots Politicians in Italy and France*. New Haven, CT: Yale University Press.

Terhorst, P. (1999) 'Urban trajectories, property rights and state structures', paper to EURA conference, Paris, 22 and 23 October.

Teune, H. (1995) 'Local governance and democratic political development', *Annals of the American Academy of Political and Social Science*, 540: 11–23.

Thielemann, E. (1999) 'Institutional limits of a "Europe with regions": EC state-aid control meets German federalism', *Journal of European Public Policy*, 6 (3): 399–418.

Tiebout, C. M. (1956) 'A pure theory of local expenditures', *Journal of Political Economy*, 64: 416–424.

Tilly, C. and Blockmans, W. (eds) (1994) *Cities and the Rise of States in Europe AD 1000 to 1800*. Boulder, CO: Westview.

Tomaney, J. and Ward, N. (2000) 'England and the new regionalism', *Regional Studies*, 34 (5): 471–478.

Toonen, T. (1993) 'Dutch provinces and the struggle for the meso', in L. J. Sharpe (ed.) *The Rise of Meso Government in Europe*. London: Sage.

Toonen, T. (1998) 'Provinces versus urban centres: current developments, background and evaluation of regionalisation in the Netherlands', in Le Galès and C. Lequesne (eds) *Regions in Europe*. London: Routledge.

Torpe, L. (1992) 'New forms of citizen participation in Denmark', paper to ECPR Joint Sessions of workshops 'Local government and the citizen', Limerick, Ireland, 30 March.

Travers, T. (1990) 'The threat to the autonomy of local government', in C. Crouch and D. Marquand (eds) *The New Centralism*. Oxford: Blackwell.

Travers, T. and Jones, G. (1997) *The New Government of London*. York: Joseph Rowntree Foundation.

Travers, T., Jones, G. and Burnham, J. (1993) *The Impact of Population Size on Local Authority Costs and Effectiveness*. York: Joseph Rowntree Foundation.

Von Bergmann-Winberg, M. (1997) 'The impact of European integration on regional and local government in Finland, Norway and Sweden', in M. Goldsmith and K. Klausen (eds) *European Integration and Local Government*. Cheltenham: Edward Elgar.

Walsh, K. (1995) *Public Services and Market Mechanisms*. Basingstoke: Macmillan.

Ward, K.(1997) 'Coalitions in urban regeneration: a regime approach', *Environment and Planning A*, 29: 1493–1505.

Wise, C. and Amna, E. (1993) 'New managerialism in Swedish local government', *Scandinavian Political Studies*, 16 (4): 339–358.

Wollmann, H. (1997) 'Institutional variations in local government: observations of developments in Germany', Paper to the international seminar on 'Governing cities: international perspectives', Eurovillage, Brussels, 18–19 September.

Wollmann, H. (2000), 'Local government modernization in Germany: between incrementalism and reform waves', *Public Administration*, 78 (4): 915–936.

Wollmann, H. and Lund, S. (1997) 'European integration and local authorities in Germany: impacts and perceptions', in M. Goldsmith and K. K. Klausen (eds) *European Integration and Local Government*. Cheltenham: Edward Elgar.

Wolters, M. (1997) 'The Netherlands', in M. Goldsmith and K. K. Klausen (eds) *European Integration and Local Government*. Cheltenham: Edward Elgar.

Woodlief, A. (1998) 'The path-dependent city', *Urban Affairs Review*, 33 (3): 405–437.

Worms, J-P.(1966) 'Le préfet et ses notables', *Sociologie de Travail*, 3: 249–275.

Wright, V. (1984) 'Regions and regionalisation in France, Italy and Spain – some concluding remarks', in M. Hebbert and H. Machin (eds) *Regionalisation in France, Italy and Spain*. London: ICERD.

Young, K. (1994), 'Local leadership and decision-making: the British system reconsidered', in O. Borraz, U. Bullmann, R. Hambleton, E. Page, N. Rao and K. Young (eds) *Local Leadership and Decision Making*. York: Joseph Rowntree Foundation.

Index

accountability, 16, 155
advisory boards for the elderly, 162–3
Agricultural Guidance Fund, 68
Anderson, J.J., 74, 80, 83
Andrew, C., 12
Anglo-American local government systems, 32, 159–61, 174
Areilza, G., 57
Assembly of European Regions, 85
asymmetric regionalism, 124–5, 126, 132
Atlanta, 42, 51, 52
Austria, 87

Bains Report, 95
Baldersheim, H., 10
Barcelona, 57, 106, 127, 145, 165
Basque country, 119, 125
Bassett, K., 50
Belgium, 28, 29, 31, 32, 35, 36, 38; Europeanization, 76, 79; executive, 138; national identity, 118; partnership programme, 82; regional government, 129–30, 132; regional representation to EU, 87
Benington, J., 71
Bennett, R.J., 22
Berlin, 55–6
Berne, 104
Bilbao, 57
Birmingham, 49, 53, 144
Blockmans, W., 46
Bristol, 49, 50, 53
Brussels, lobbying from, 86–7
Bulpitt, J., 30
bureaucratic local authorities, 3, 37, 78, 86, 95, 96, 97, 106, 108
businesses, 10, 41, 50–1, 169; economic development policies, 45; and growth coalitions, 48; and politicians, 42, 43, 44, 50–1

cabinets, 137, 141, 146–7, 148, 149
Catalonia, 119, 125

central government, 1–2, 12, 33, 59, 96, 97, 127, 152, 168; changed role, 45–6; and EU policies, 74; and regional development plans, 80, 81, 82, 83; in UK, 124, 125
central-local government relations, 26–7, 30–1, 32–3, 33–4, 65, 126, 127, 152; EU and, 78, 82–3
central initiatives, 15–16
centralization, 65, 78, 79, 81, 127
chambers of commerce, 48, 55, 57, 59
Christiansen, L., 85
cities, 51, 52, 56–9, 174; entrepreneurial, 46–57; in France, 54–5; in Germany, 55–6; revival of, 46–7; in UK, 53–4; *see also* regimes
citizen initiatives, 162
citizens' juries, 161, 164
Clark, T., 20
Clarke, S., 10
class politics, breakdown of, 20
clientelism, 29, 31, 137, 138
Clos, Joan, 145
coalitions, 53, 54, 55–6, 57, 59; US style, 42, 48, 49, 50–1
Cole, A., 50, 53, 143, 14
collective decision-making, 140, 141, 146, 153
Committee of the Regions and Local Authorities, 70–1, 76, 88–9, 117
communes, 28, 29, 31, 32, 96, 97, 113, 137; Danish, 163; French, 96, 168
community councils, 162, 163
Community Initiatives, 69–70
Community Support Frameworks, 80, 83–4
competition, 11, 32, 45, 62, 168; between cities, 10; between regions, 126
Conference of Peripheral Maritime Regions, 88
constitutional reform, 65–6, 91